CONTEMPORARY YOUTH RESEARCH

*We dedicate this book to all the young people
who in countless ways have enriched our lives.*

Contemporary Youth Research
Local Expressions and Global Connections

Edited by

HELENA HELVE
University of Kuopio and University of Helsinki, Finland

GUNILLA HOLM
Western Michigan University, USA

ASHGATE

Published by
Ashgate Publishing Limited
Gower House
Croft Road
Aldershot
Hants GU11 3HR
England

Ashgate Publishing Company
Suite 420
101 Cherry Street
Burlington, VT 05401–4405
USA

Ashgate website: http://www.ashgate.com

British Library Cataloguing in Publication Data
Contemporary youth research : local expressions and global connections
    1. Youth - Social conditions 2. Youth - Research
    I. Helve, Helena II. Holm, Gunilla
    305.2'35

Library of Congress Cataloging-in-Publication Data
Contemporary youth research : local expressions and global connections / edited by Helena Helve and Gunilla Holm.
      p. cm.
    Includes bibliographical references and index
    ISBN 0-7546-4161-9
    1. Youth -- Research. 2. Globalization. I. Helve, Helena II. Holm, Gunilla.

HQ796.C8155 2005
305.234'072--dc22

2005013244

ISBN 0 7546 4161 9

Typeset by Saxon Graphics Ltd, Derby
Printed and bound by Athenaeum Press Ltd, Gateshead, Tyne & Wear

Contents

List of Contributors

Clarence M. Batan, Dalhousie University, Canada

Fazila Bhimji, University of California, USA

Manuela du Bois-Reymond, University of Leiden, The Netherlands

James Côté, University of Western Ontario, Canada

Noemi Ehrenfeld Lenkiewicz, Universidad Autonoma Metropolitana-Izt, Mexico

David Everatt, Strategy & Tactics, South Africa

Paul Farber, Western Michigan University, USA

Carles Feixa Pampols, University of Leida, Spain

Yanko González Cangas, Universidad Austral de Chile, Chile

Liora Gvion, The Kibbutzim College of Education, Israel

Helena Helve, University of Helsinki, Finland

Gunilla Holm, Western Michigan University, USA

Ross Jennings, Strategy & Tactics, South Africa

Siyka Kovacheva, University of Plovdiv, Bulgaria

Carmen Leccardi, University of Milan-Biococca, Italy

Diana Luzzatto, The Academic College of Tel-Aviv-Yaffo, Israel

Sunaina Maira, University of California at Davis, USA

Thomas Ray, Western Michigan University, USA

Sipho Shezi, Sirius Development Foundation, South Africa

Barbara Stauber, Institute for Regional Innovation and Social Research, Germany

Vappu Tyyskä, Ryerson Polytechnic, Canada

Henk Vinken, Tilburg University, The Netherlands

Yen Yen Joyceln Woo, Long Island University, USA

Johanna Wyn, University of Melbourne, Australia

Yang Xiong, Shanghai Academy of Social Sciences, China

Jin Zhikun, Shanghai Academy of Social Sciences, China

Julia A. Zubok, Centre for Sociology of Youth, Russian Academy of Sciences, Russia

List of Contributors

Preface and Acknowledgements

The process of editing this book has taken three years to complete. The idea for the book arose originally at the Research Committee on Sociology of Youth (RC 34) Board's 1998–2002 meeting at which both the editors were present and where they agreed to edit the book together. Helena Helve, as RC34 President 2002–2004, took the main responsibility for the content of the book and commissioned articles for it, many of which were papers presented originally at the RC 34 session on youth research in ISA's World Congress of Sociology held in Brisbane in 2002. The structure of the book and its development was worked out through numerous meetings by the editors held in Helsinki during 2003 and 2004. Gunilla Holm did the major editing of all the chapters, except for chapter two and corresponded over text revisions with the authors. The book was formatted by Helena Helve and her assistant Pia Pietilä and included considerable efforts to ensure that the text was up-to-date with relevant notes and references for each chapter.

We thank all the chapter contributors for their work as well as their patience with this book project. We would also like to thank our colleagues and universities for their support with this project and in particular Pia Pietilä and Stephanie Higdon for their technical editing. Furthermore, we thank the RC 34 board members in working with us on conceptualizing this book and our editor Mary Savigar at Ashgate for her generous support.

Introduction

Gunilla Holm and Helena Helve

Introduction

Although scholars have written about youth and young people for centuries, social science research on youth has focused mainly on young people in the United States and Western Europe. Currently, however, researchers throughout the world are increasingly engaged in topics relevant to youth and research exists on youth populations globally. Although youth research has a long history, until the last 20–30 years there were no strong attempts to make it a distinct field of research. Both theories and methodologies of youth research were indistinguishable from those of its core disciplines such as social psychology, developmental psychology, sociology, ethnology, medicine, criminology, political science, demography and history. Empirically youth research was either a place to gather information for social policy or a place to test theories from other disciplines.

Today we conceptualize youth as a transition into adulthood as well as a key to societal change. Today, large numbers of young people in all parts of the world go from one type of job to another, back and forth between education and working life, often interrupted by periods of travelling or voluntary work – they have many ways of preparing for adult life – they simply have a new way of life. Of course we as youth researchers cannot predict what kind of lifestyle those who are now in their teens will have in twenty or thirty years, but as this book shows there are many ways to reflect on questions concerning the lives and experiences of contemporary youth and young people.

This volume is organized in collaboration with *Research Committee on Youth of the International Sociological Association, RC 34*. The Research Committee on Youth consists of an international, loosely connected community of researchers that communicates by way of diverse professional meetings, the RC34 website and the electronic International Bulletin of Youth Research IBYR. This book is intended to enhance awareness of the global youth research community and thereby to foster and further the exchange of knowledge and ideas related to youth research. The production of the book is also evidence of the global participation of youth researchers, to a large extent members of ISA RC 34.

A second, equally important rationale for this book is to promote a reconceptualisation of youth. Youth researchers spend their lives researching and writing about inequality, exclusion, non-participation, disadvantage and disengagement, in other words treating youth research as research on youth related problems. This is important work that we esteem highly. But as the basis of an orientation to youth, it is rather one-sided. In this book we also highlight young people as a positive force in society, as a resource that is changing the culture as well as societal structures.

The chapters in the book promote the inter-cultural understanding and the cross-fertilization of the theoretical, substantive and methodological perspectives of youth research. This book, written by authors from across the world, is intended as a resource book in a non-traditional sense for students and faculty in youth studies. People who are new to youth studies receive a solid grounding through the exploration of what youth research means as well as some historical exploration of youth research. Since most researchers, policy makers and youth workers tend to be focused exclusively on the local or national situation, the first section of the book gives an overview of what is happening in various parts pf the world. The individual chapters provide more in-depth analysis of specific issues that are of concern and interest across the world. Although the case studies are locally grounded, such as the cultural integration of Indian Americans in the US by Sunaina Maira or Filipino teenagers' use of text messaging by Clarence Batan, the studies have global relevance. A book like this one gives youth workers, researchers, and policy makers a history and context for contemporary issues. Looking at issues in a global, international perspective deepens our understanding as well as provides new ideas for how to approach young people and their issues and interests.

The book is divided into two principal sections, the first providing an international over view and the second centered on current issues. The first section is comprised of a chapter focused on the concept of youth research and a series of chapters exploring the development of and trends in youth research globally. The first chapter by Vappu Tyyskä explores the conceptualisation and theorizing of youth globally. She examines the differences between the southern and the northern hemisphere as well as issues related to the impact of globalization on and the need for human rights for young people. The following six chapters report on regional trends in youth research, including: Europe (by Helena Helve, Carmen Leccardi and Siyka Kovacheva), Australia and New Zealand (by Johanna Wyn), North America (by James Côté), Africa (by David Everatt), China (by Jin Zhikun and Yang Xiong) and Latin America (by Carles Feixa Pampols and Yanko González Cangas). Collectively, these provide an overview of the state of youth research globally. In these overview chapters, several authors emphasize the importance of a youth research community as a stimulus for new ideas and sometimes as a political support group. Some authors focus the discussion more on the issues studied as well as on who is included in youth research. This is the case, for example, in the chapters on Australia and New Zealand and on Latin America. Others, as in the chapter on European youth research, provide more of an historical account of the development of youth research. The importance of the state and state funding in establishing and furthering youth research is evident in several parts of the world but in different ways. In the Nordic countries the state has been instrumental in establishing youth research networks nationally and even across state borders. On the other hand, in the United States there are no formal networks but in important ways federal funding tends to drive the focus of youth research. In the former Eastern and Central European countries the state apparatus controlled both where and what kind of research was conducted. This trend can also be observed in China, although the span of research topics is opening up. In most countries and regions youth research and policies tend to be closely connected to the political and economic situation, a tendency clearly exemplified in South Africa.

The second section, devoted to research on current issues is divided into three topic areas. The first topic area is focused on issues related to education, technology, and work. In particular, the transition from youth to adulthood is explored from several different perspectives. Manuela du Bois-Reymond and Barbara Stauber's comparative study explores the alternative learning trajectories of European youth motivated to develop different strategies and alternative solutions to their transition problems. They emphasize the importance of informal and non-formal learning for young people.

Gunilla Holm and Paul Farber likewise focus on college students' transition to professional jobs as teachers in culturally diverse settings in the US. They argue that academic service-learning is one way for students to learn to appreciate cultural diversity as well as to develop a sense of civic responsibility in a democratic society. University students' self reflections indicate that students very rarely reflect on or are aware of their own privileges as white middle class students or the hardships people living in poverty or facing discrimination due to ethnic or racial heritage. Academic service-learning assisted them in understanding both their own privilege as well as others' hardships.

The difficulties young people face in their transition to adulthood is discussed by David Everatt and Sipho Shezi and Ross Jennings in the context of rural poverty in South Africa. Rural young people are ignored by politicians and with the high unemployment and other social problems facing them, their situation is bleak. For example, in some areas over 50 per cent of the young are unemployed. In addition, HIV pose a substantial threat to the welfare of rural youth. Young people were ignored in the political process in the post-apartheid period and they became disengaged as their very low participation in, for example, elections show. The young themselves view jobs and education as the most important forces that could change their living conditions. Everatt and Shezi describe a model program of youth service for sustainable employment for rural youth as a viable step towards progress for young people living in poverty. They argue for the importance of working with youth and the communities themselves in order for these kinds of programs to succeed.

Likewise, Julia Zubok discusses the vulnerable situation of young people in post-socialist Russia. Her chapter delves into what it means to live in a high risk society with an unstable future. She argues that Russia is a crisis society due to socio-economic, socio-legal and socio-political factors. For example, Zubok examines how the lack of a strong legal system fails to protect the young but also feeds criminalization among the young especially in a society where political power is misused and economic policies encourage increased economic differentiation and thereby social tension. How do young people create a life and an identity in a crisis society.

On the other hand, Clarence Batan examines the role of technology, and in particular cellular phones and text messaging, among already privileged college students in a developing economy, namely the Philippines. Text messaging has become a cultural practice transforming communication forms among peers as well as across generations, while it also serves to differentiate this privileged upper-middle class group from their lower class counterparts. Hence, this chapter shows how technology opens up new avenues and possibilities for the wealthy while it also increases the gap between the poor and the affluent.

Many of the chapters in this section focus on the difficulties and choices young people face in the transition from youth to adulthood. At the easiest level the young face new technology that they need to adjust to and adopt, and that will change their lives in many ways. Most young people have to struggle with personal choices as in the DuBois and Stauber study as well as with how to prepare themselves for a life as professionals as in the Holm and Farber study. However, in addition to these kinds of personal struggles young people living in societal crisis situations face seemingly insurmountable difficulties in finding jobs and getting an education. These studies show how young people are capable of adjusting to new and often difficult circumstances.

The second topic area centers on the societal engagement of youth. Henk Vinken argues against the proclaimed decline in civic virtues and civic engagement among youth. He encourages us to think about new forms of citizenship for young people (especially as they relate to consumption and leisure). This new kind of civic engagement is more dynamic, fluid, and expressed through short-lived commitments and more common in more affluent societies. However, young people's civic engagement will be expressed in different ways in different societies depending on their cultural, institutional and political diversities. Tom Ray also raises questions about citizenship in a democratic society but in a different way. He questions western schooling with regard to its impact on whether young people learn to care for or destroy the environment by continuing current living patterns. He argues that we especially in the US know what the environmental problems are but that we fail to act on them. He further explores the ways of thinking that underlie this problematic way thinking and acting. In his view young people acquire this problematic way of thinking and not acting in school. On the other hand, the new kinds of youth movements rooted in inner-city neighborhoods as described by Fazila Bhimji provide a counterweight to the claim that young people are not engaged in their own communities or not engaged in traditional way. These movements encourage Latina/o high school youth in the US to restructure their own educational experiences in view of the structural inequalities they face. They have formed alliances with politically conscious white students and labor unions in order to challenge policies and initiatives that they consider anti-immigrant and anti-youth. Furthermore, Bhimji discusses how these movements and the direct confrontations with racist policies influence the political identity of young Latinas/os.

The third topic area is focused on how the larger societal culture attempts to shape or shapes the cultural identity of young people in a culturally diverse and global world. All chapters point to the influence of the larger societal structures and culture but also indicate that young people create their futures and identities. Gender but also ethnicity play important roles in the identity of most of the young people discussed in this section. All writers in this section use interviews or participant observation as their data collection methods, which is an indication of the trend towards more qualitative work in youth research. Especially with regard to sensitive issues such as the development of young people's cultural identities, methods are required that allow researchers to go in-depth in order to understand more fully the views of the participants

Yen Yen Joyceln Woo examines how Singapore's attempts to create an ideal citizen who will be able to meet the challenges of an ever more global world. This means being among other things creative, loyal and self-reliant. However, by focusing in-depth on only a handful of students she is able to explore the reasons why the students will not fulfil the expectations for the ideal citizens. The official policy encourages students in many ways to venture outside the familiar boundaries while the realities of the students' lives make it very difficult for them to contest the citizenship requirements. In a traditional society is it difficult to forge alternative life paths and as a consequence the students end up with familiar ways of thinking and behaving despite the official policies. On the other hand, Noemi Ehrenfeld Lenkiewicz shows how the larger culture and societal structure limit the opportunities for young women. She focuses on how teenage girls are limited in what they can do and who they become by poor educational and employment opportunities but who also in turn contribute to further to limiting their opportunities by becoming teenage mothers. Although in this case they manage to raise their own individual status, but not opportunities, to some extent by becoming a mother instead of being a young girl.

Sunaina Maira documents how second generation Indian American young men and women forge their own identities by merging traditional Indian culture and American youth cultures. Many of these young Indian Americans, and especially the women, feel also compelled adjust to the cultural constraints impsed by traditional Indian culture. Interestingly, the young use popular culture, in developing their own cultural identities, to negotiate questions related to ethnic authenticity, racial ambiguity, gender ideology, and class mobility. Likewise, Liora Gvion and Diana Luzzatto's chapter is focused on the ethnic, social class and gender identities of, in this case, Mizrachi Jewish lesbians in Israel. They explore how in the context of the Israeli social stratification system an often somewhat disempowered position as a lesbian can be empowering for the young Mizrachi lesbians who can improve their educational and social standing through their relationships with more established and better educated Ashkenazi lesbians. The in-depth interviews allow authors to give the reader a view of Mizrachi lesbians' perceived opportunities and barriers from their own perspective and of how a lesbian identity may become an asset that provides access to higher education and blurs barriers stemming from ethnic identity.

This edited collection on international youth research contributes to the debate on the globalization of youth and youth research. One important goal of this volume is to provide policy makers, researchers, graduate students and youth workers information about trends and issues concerning contemporary youth globally. Looking at issues from an international perspective deepens our understanding of youth and suggests new ideas for how to work with young people. The chapters in this book are from a wide geographical area as well as from both more and less industrialized and developed regions. Most of the chapters in this book have been written mainly from a sociological perspective. Hence, whether the chapters are theoretical and empirical, the categories of gender, ethnicity, race, and social class are important. These are the dimensions that lead to young people even in the same communities or in different parts of the world to have very different experiences. From the chapters in this book it becomes very clear that it is close to impossible to talk about youth as a monolithic group without qualifying who the young people are.

PART I
OVERVIEW OF YOUTH
RESEARCH GLOBALLY

Chapter 1

Conceptualizing and Theorizing Youth: Global Perspectives

Vappu Tyyskä

Defining Youth

Worldwide, there is a distinct lack of consistency in defining the category 'youth' (Galambos and Kolaric, 1994; Danesi, 1994, p. 6; Tyyskä, 2001), both in everyday usage and government policy. This great variety signifies both the fluidity of age categories and the degree to which they are contested globally.

During the International Year of the Youth, in 1985, the United Nations defined youth as those between 15 and 25 years of age (Brown, 1990). Thus, youth overlaps with the category of 'childhood', which is commonly defined as anyone under the age of eighteen (de Waal, 2002a). In its western usage, the category of youth is elastic. For example, Galambos and Kolaric (1994) distinguish between 'young adolescents' (10–14), 'teens' (15–19), and 'young adults' (20–24). Further, in common Anglo-American usage, the term 'teen' is reserved to those 13–19 years of age. The term 'adolescent', previously used for a wider age category (15–24) is now used interchangeably with 'teens'. And the term 'tweens' was introduced in the 1990s to refer to young people aged 10–12.

Notably, many youth researchers in the southern hemisphere are highly critical of the concept of 'youth' as it is applied in the northern hemisphere, i.e. as a relatively uniform and age-bound category. In many areas of the southern hemisphere, the age boundaries are wider, as those in the younger age groups move toward full adulthood in the locally specific sense of the term (de Waal, 2002a; Wyn and White, 1997; Argenti, 2002; Sharp, 2002; Allatt, 2001). Practices specific to local populations and cultures vary as to what is seen as a proper point of transition from one age group to another (de Waal, 2002a). Thus, youthful categories start as early as age five and stretch till age 35, based on political and economic cultures (Allatt, 2001).

Further, age-specific international comparisons are prevented by the vastly different demographic structures of the northern and the southern hemispheres. Whereas in the northern hemisphere, there is an aging of the population and a lowered birth rate, resulting in a relatively smaller youth population (Galambos and Kolaric, 1994; Sharp, 2002), the southern hemisphere is largely characterized by a disproportionately large population of children and young people, and a smaller proportion of older people (Bakilana and de Waal, 2002; de Waal, 2002).

Increasing numbers of youth researchers try to avoid a homogenizing western bias in defining youth as specific age categories (Allatt, 2001; Rahman, 2001; Wyn and White, 1997). There is a preference to define youth as 'not a particular age range' but as 'a social status' (Marquardt, 1998, p. 7), characterized by a period of life in which a person is either partly or fully dependent on others, usually adults and members of one's family, for material support. Some approach youth in relational terms, with reference to the 'social processes whereby age is socially constructed, institutionalized and controlled in historically and culturally specific ways' (Wyn and White, 1997).

In the industrialized west, there is pressure to extend youth well into the twenties if not beyond, through lengthened education, part-time employment, and the corresponding lengthening of young people's dependence on their parents and/or the state. This western phenomenon of prolongation of youth in its upper years is in contrast with the apparent shortening of childhood and youth in large segments of the southern hemisphere. This is partly due to long-term and persistent cultural influences. In addition, children in many parts of the south are compelled, through the legacy of colonialism, war, and increasing economic globalization, toward an earlier 'maturity', through child labour, shorter education, and increased poverty, with the associated ills of poor health, hunger and starvation, and a life on the streets and the use of children for the purposes of war and of sexual gratification (de Waal, 2002b; Rizzini, Barker and Cassaniga, 2002; Ogwal-Oyee, 2002).

Theories of Youth: The Northern Hemisphere

According to dominant western ideology, youth is the most wonderful, carefree stage of our lives, a time to gradually develop a distinct identity and place in society. This ideal acknowledges the relative wealth of the northern hemisphere. Some theorists focus on the positive aspects of this wealth, and on the role of social institutions in shaping young people. This approach is largely uncritical and conservative, and focuses on the biological and social development of human beings, most frequently expressed in socio-biology, and developmental and life stage theories. These views are popularized, among other things, in imagery of young people enslaved to their tumultuous biological states, and requiring firm regulation, so that they will learn to modify their behaviours and act in accordance with mainstream rules and norms. In contrast, critical theories point out that despite abundance, young people in general and women and minority youth in particular, do not benefit equally from the resources, and their voices are largely unheard.

Conservative Theories: Conformity

Many contemporary conservative theories are rooted in social Darwinism, which flourished from the 19th century onward, premised on the evolutionary theories of Charles Darwin. His theory of biological adaptation and natural selection is extended to society by socio-biologists and structural-functionalists, with specific reference to changes that took place in age strata as industrial capitalism emerged. A new stage of youth presumably developed out of specific biological imperatives of maturation. This developmental stage involves biologically driven disruptive elements, often identified as 'hormonal hurricanes', as young people learn to adapt to their environment. In order for society not to suffer, youth need to be subjected to a number of control mechanisms. These controls are often presented as natural parts of preparation of adult life. The main form of control is education.

As industrial societies require increased education levels to meet the demands of the developing economy, other aspects of life have to be delayed, including marriage and family formation. Functionalists promote the notion that youth is a stage for instilling conformity within the requirements of prevailing economic and social conditions. This conservative script calls for mechanisms of control on youth in order to ensure a smooth functioning of society (e.g. Eisenstadt, in O'Donnell, 1985; Côté and Allahar, 1994; Jones and Wallace, 1992). A central role in the functionalist scheme is played by family members, particularly mothers, who socialize and educate their children toward taking their proper roles in the economy and the family (Parsons, 1956 cited in Jones and Wallace, 1992).

In addition to this primary socialization, secondary socialization is taking place through schools and peers (Parsons, 1961, Parsons, 1973; Coleman, 1961 cited in Jones and Wallace, 1992). In the 1960s and 1970s, scholarly attention in Britain and the United States turned to peer groups and youth subcultures as vessels for transmitting proper work values, social attitudes and behaviours to young people (Jones and Wallace, 1992). Brake (1985) notes that this approach is exemplified by the works of Eisenstadt (1956), Parsons (1942), and Mannheim (1952).

In this functionalist variant of subculture theory related to youth, there is a tendency in the Northern Hemisphere to dwell on the problematic aspects of delinquent youth subcultures, and the problem of how to control this element (Brake, 1985; Blackman, 1995). The destructive actions of youth are seen to reflect 'status frustration' arising from a mismatch between 'cultural goals' and 'institutional means'. Thus, youth subcultures are seen as results of inadequate socialization into their 'proper' position in society (Blackman, 1995). Another variant of conservative sub-culture theories focuses on the biological and bodily changes accompanying puberty. The changes that signify a transition toward adulthood are seen to create a need to bond with others who are in the same stage of development, amidst a heightened awareness of the physiological and cognitive changes young people are going through (Danesi, 1994; Offer and Offer, 1972).

The influence of socio-biology and structural-functionalism is evident in a number of influential life stage or developmental theories of the twentieth century. Most of these focus on the stresses of youth, and the need to bring the naturally destructive inner tendencies of youth under control. The earliest contribution comes from the American youth theorist G. Stanley Hall who, in 1904, proposed that human development from birth to death mirrored the evolutionary path of the human race. Fuelled by Darwinism, Hall developed his recapitulation theory proposing that adolescence was a stage of savagery, a period of 'Sturm und Drang' (storm and stress) (Danesi, 1994; Côté and Allahar, 1994; Jones and Wallace, 1992). The path toward adulthood, and a higher stage of development, is a stormy one, as youth learn to subject their instincts to their environment (Grinder, 1973). Other well-known twentieth century scholars, Sigmund Freud, Erik Erikson, and Jean Piaget developed different variants of stage theories, each stamped with the same notions of internal states that need to be brought under control at different stages of development, in order to achieve a well-developed adult identity (Grinder, 1973; Danesi, 1994).

From the 1980s onward, a different type of stage theory was developed, called life-course perspective. These theorists examine the transitions to adulthood in different spheres of life, including employment and family. Life-course theories see youth as a 'series of processes in transition to adult life, roughly parallel longitudinal processes which take place in different spheres, such as home and the labour market, but which must be understood together because they relate closely to one another' (Jones and Wallace, 1992, p. 13).

With significant changes in the economic structures and associated social behaviours in western societies, the uniformity of youth transitions was called into question. It was evident that the changing nature of the economy, including a shift toward a service economy and widespread unemployment; and significant changes in families, including women's labour force participation, lead toward lessening standardization in the lives of everyone, youth included (Jones and Wallace, 1992).

Related to this approach is the so-called 'individualization thesis' developed by the German sociologist Ulrich Beck (Beck, 1986, cited in Jones and Wallace, 1992). This thesis argues that people's lives are an individual project, for them to achieve in a competitive world. There are increased 'risks' for people at all levels of society, as people are dissociated from the old social structures and create their own pathways. This view is exemplified by studies that examine the ways in which young people develop their own 'trajectories' as they face a world that is different from that of their parents (Jones and Wallace, 1992; Chisholm and Hurrelmann, 1995).

This focus on the atomization of individuals and the need for more social cohesion, while downplaying the analysis of power structures in societies, puts many life course theorists within the structural-functionalist tradition. In general, structural-functionalists promote the idea of common good over narrower group interests that are seen to disrupt the orderly development of societies (O'Donnell, 1985). Little attention is paid either to the problems that youth may face through this stage of the suspension of their rights, or to any active role that young people may play in changing the ground rules. Furthermore, and most importantly, these theories can be criticized for putting pressure on young people to adapt to society rather than changing societies to accommodate them. In fact, there has been extensive criticism of structural-functionalist theories, particularly from the 1960s onward when youth in North America and Europe exhibited widespread discontent with their marginalized status (Jones and Wallace, 1992).

Critical Theories: Age and Stratification

In contrast to conservative theories, critical theorists point to the institutionalized powerlessness of youth. Especially in the last two decades, studies and reports point to the many problems that young people face and are finding difficult to confront and change, due to the rules and boundaries set by adult-led social institutions, including the family, the economy, and the state (Marquardt, 1998; Carrigan, 1998).

The Marxist or political economy approach, when applied to different social positions by age, is a type of age stratification theory. There are several varieties of age stratification theory (Dowd, 1981; O'Rand, 1990), but in the Marxist variant, economic inequalities are linked to age inequalities because of the specific features of the capitalist economy. In order to exploit the work force to the fullest, different age categories of workers are granted different types of work, allowing for the exploitation of the young, as a part of the weakest segment of the working population. At the same time, these age categories provide useful divided groupings of workers whose interests differ. They are prevented from the realization of their common interests by employers' 'divide and conquer' methods. Further elements of control are the ideological forces that are utilized by the capitalist class, including the education system and media. These provide a form of control and ongoing indoctrination of people into the expectations of the economic system (Côté and Allahar, 1994; Mattson, 2003; Strickland, 2002).

Thus, youth have been effectively disenfranchised. Employers and the state have created, over more than a century, a system in which youth are deprived of full access to economic and political rights. They are processed through an education system that creates credentials, while the jobs in the labour market do not require the kind of extensive education that young people are made to believe they need in order to succeed. Rather than having access to economic institutions, youth are exploited as an underpaid working mass, and form a convenient 'target market' for goods that are sold to them as a part of a ready-made package of corporate-driven youth culture. This process has escalated since the 1970s with neo-conservative and neo-liberal state policies in western industrial countries (Coté and Allahar, 1994).

The pros and cons of employment of young workers are constantly debated. The loaded term 'child labour' is surrounded by extreme conceptual ambiguity, partly because of the definitional difficulties of youth and child categories outlined above. Further, problems abound regarding the detrimental versus beneficial effects of employment for young people. The most notable ill effect is the general sense of exploitation the word conveys, and also the potential for a delayed or prevented educational attainment. Among the positive outcomes are those related to personal autonomy, independence, and sense of self worth (Tienda and Wilson, 2002; McKechnie and Hobbs, 2002). Estimated numbers of child labourers range from 73 million to 500 million worldwide. Whereas the prevalence of child labour has previously been established in the southern hemisphere, it is also noted increasingly, that the phenomenon is also an essential part of the industrialized nations of the northern hemisphere where ever increasing numbers of children and youth combine education with part-time wage work (McKechnie and Hobbs, 2002; Tyyskä, 2001).

These phenomena are a part of young people's political disenfranchisement, exemplified by the political apathy of youth, and their harsher treatment as they are policed and incarcerated at younger ages, particularly in North America (Tyyskä, 2001; Giroux, 2003; White, 2002; Jones and Wallace, 1992; Mattson, 2003).

Even if we are to acknowledge the power of the Marxist age stratification theory in explaining the emergence of and the present condition of youth, we are still left with only a partial picture of the many facets in the lives of young people. Adolescence and youth are age strata, but they are also age strata that are differentiated along other dimensions. Increasing numbers of equity theorists who research youth point to the necessity of taking into consideration the social divisions of gender, race, and ethnicity (Chisholm, 1990, in Wyn and White, 1997; Tienda and Wilson, 2002; Ghuman, 1999). It is emphasized that regardless of region, nation, or hemisphere, young women and members of minorities fare far worse than the young men who themselves may not be faring that well overall (Tienda and Wilson, 2002; Heitmeyer, 2002; Back, 1996; Rozie-Battle, 2002). These layers of inequality are manifested in critical variants of theories of peer groups and youth sub-cultures.

Peer groups provide freedom from parents and other authority figures, and provide alternative norms and information about expected behaviours, and a setting for conforming to these expectations about 'a given group's *own* norms, attitudes, speech patterns, and dress codes' (Kendal et al., 1997, p. 145 – emphasis in the original; also see Côté and Allahar, 1994; Elkin and Handel, 1989, in Kendal et al, 1997). At the same time, peer groups are formed based on sociodemographic factors including 'grade level, age, gender, religion, and ethnicity' (Akers et. al, 1998; also see Kelly, 1998; Brake, 1987; Holmes and Silverman, 1992; Danesi, 1994; Strickland, 2002). For example, bonding among minority high school students is partly in reaction to racist attitudes and practices around them (Kelly, 1998; Ghuman, 1999) and young males and females engage in different peer group activities (Holmes and Silverman, 1992; Brake, 1987).

Unlike conservative youth theories, critical approaches to peers and sub-cultures reflect an understanding of youth sub-cultures both as manifestations of youth rebellion and as mirrors of the dominant power relations under capitalism, patriarchy, and racism (Blackman, 1995; Jones and Wallace, 1992; Côté and Allahar, 1994; Tyyskä, 2001; Brake, 1987; Ghuman, 1999; Giroux, 2003). Crucial in this structural neo-Marxist re-interpretation of the youth subculture theory was the work of the Centre for Contemporary Cultural Studies (CCCS) in Britain (Blackman, 1995). Gradually, through their work and the work of others, theorists have developed an understanding of youth subcultures in a richer way, acknowledging youth as active agents. Subcultures are seen as a reaction to oppression, an expression of youthful creativity (Filmer, 1977, cited in Blackman, 1995), and emotionally satisfying and a means toward an identity and a sense of community (Doherty, 1988, cited in Danesi, 1994; Brake, 1987; Kendal et al., 1997). Critical theorists also note that youth sub-cultures can be co-opted with targeting of youth as a consumer group (Strickland, 2002; Brake, 1987; Côté and Allahar, 1994; Tyyskä, 2001). At the same time, youth consumerism has been interpreted as potentially 'subversive' in that pockets of resistance arise in reaction to the corporate marketing strategies (Strickland, 2002).

Post-Colonialism, Globalization and Development

Whereas sociological approaches in the northern hemisphere still retain uncritical mainstream elements, the stark realities of many young people's lives in the industrialized and non-industrialized southern hemisphere have resulted in almost solely critical approaches, combined with political activism.

To begin with, the global applicability of the North-American and European model of youth as a uniform stage of transition from childhood to adulthood has been called into question through research that has found that youth in less complex and non-industrialized societies can make a smoother transition from childhood into adulthood than in industrialized societies (Evans-Pritchard, 1951, and Mead, 1943, cited in Jones and Wallace, 1992; Sharp, 2002). For example, despite great diversity in traditional pre-colonial African societies (and also in large parts of Asia – see

Manderson and Liamputtong, 2002), what united them was the presumption of the subjection of young males and females to the power of male elders. Adulthood for men was determined by their achievement of a level of economic well being to afford a wife or wives, who then gained their adult status through marriage (Argenti, 2002; Rhodes, Mihyar, and El-Rous, 2002).

The orderliness of these transitions was destroyed by colonialism, resulting in 'disrupted age categories' (Argenti, 2002, p. 124), amidst multiple problems in young people's lives, including high mortality and morbidity rates, due to war, poor sanitation, lack of clean water and proper nutrition, and lower school enrolment, particularly for girls (Tienda and Wilson, 2002; De Waal, 2002a). These problems are not simply the results of successive inexplicable 'crises'. Rather, they are the comprehensible results of important social changes that have occurred in Africa over the last few generations, so that the social systems that exist today have been substantially transformed from the local-level kinship-based systems that existed a century ago. The roles of young people have been dramatically and irreversibly changed, and, as often as not, young people are orchestrating these changes themselves (Argenti, 2002, p. 124).

The few benefits in the colonial era accrued mainly to men, through education and jobs in the new bureaucracy. However, the great majority of the population remained outside the colonial system of employment, resulting in widespread discontent and a generation of young males who became defined as the 'youth' to the colonial powers, not by their age alone but by their defiance of colonial rule supported by the older generation of colonized males (Argenti, 2002; De Waal, 2002a). 'Youth' in politics obtained two meanings: (1) men who actively participated in the social movements that lead to the emergence of independent African nations from colonialism; and (2) maleness, as only men can retain a status of 'youth' even if married and with children, but women cannot (De Waal, 2002a).

The problems of marginalization and exclusion continue in post-colonial Africa. With stalled economic development, and high population growth, ever larger numbers of youth are being excluded from the economy while their political input is not called for. As families are uprooted, young people face significant changes in their family structure, resulting in conflicting values and norms. In the atomized and frequently impoverished urban environment, these problems may multiply and result in youth anger, violence, and armed conflict (Rhodes, Mihyar, El-Rous, 2002; Rahwoni, 2002; Everatt, 2001; Argenti, 2002).

The Human Rights Perspective: Rights for Children and Youth

Arising from these grim premises is a research orientation toward issues of child and youth survival, amidst poverty, war, illness, and famine (de Waal, 2002a). There are two major perspectives to this group of problems. One of these is the 'development perspective' arising from the northern hemisphere. This perspective is exemplified by the international monetary policies of the World Bank and International Monetary Fund. These have created paternalistic programs aimed at 'helping the poor' (Ali, 2002, p. 73) in the context of providing international experts who advise about financial policy on the macroeconomic level. Financial aid is tied to technical assistance, which means that most of the money toward 'development' goes to this very slew of international experts. Most projects are premised on developing the private sector, under the guise of creating local self-sufficiency. These 'development programs' are criticized on many grounds, including their short-sightedness, failure to take into consideration local conditions, and the multiple problems faced by African countries (Ali, 2002). Development policies are also based on targeting. Thus, programs may target 'street youth' while ignoring the wider problems of impoverishment that drives increasing numbers of children and youth to the streets (Rizzini, Barker and Cassaniga, 2002).

In the southern hemisphere, the development perspective is widely criticized. Instead, the preferred model is a 'children's rights perspective' that is largely based on African research on the status of children and youth. Rooted in the United Nations' Convention on the Rights of the Child, and the Universal Declaration for the Rights of the Child, the children's rights framework emphasizes the obligation of 'states to realize the rights of children', and a corresponding responsibility to recognize children as a 'global public good', whose well-being benefits the whole global community (de Waal, 2002a; Swart-Kruger and Chawla, 2002; Rahman, 2001). The theoretical focus is on policy-related issues, combining activism and academic approaches. Widespread action took place in the 1990s, starting with the World Summit for Children in 1990, the adoption of the World Declaration on the Survival, Protection and Development of Children in the 1990s, and the Plan of Action for implementing the World Declaration. Heads of State and Government participated from 71 countries, including 17 African nations, plus an added 31 senior officials representing African countries. Shortly after, the Convention on the Rights of the Child (CRC) came into force, ratified by African countries. Only Somalia and USA have still not ratified the CRC. Earlier in 1990, the Organization for African Unity proposed The African Charter on the Rights and Welfare of the Child. This was adopted in December 2000 (Bakilana and de Waal, 2002; Temba and de Waal, 2002). The points of emphasis are: the rights of children and youth to a fulfilment of their potentials, and a global responsibility of adult generations over the younger generations. In addition, the African charter 'stresses the responsibilities of children as social actors who need to uphold and strengthen the social fabric within which their personal rights are embedded' (Swart-Kruger and Chawla, 2002, p. 35).

Conclusions: Globalizing Theories

The main tendency in current sociological theories of youth is an apparent wane in mainstream theorizing and an increase in critical approaches that take to task the negative effects of globalization, capitalism, patriarchy and racism, as interrelated phenomena. With global economic restructuring, associated with demographic shifts in the age structure of populations, governments all around the globe are faced with enormous challenges. In the southern hemisphere, the invasion of the capitalist economy puts pressure on the large child and youth populations. In the northern hemisphere, there is an associated pauperization of youth, as their families' economic well-being deteriorates, and their needs are pitted against those of the increasing population of the elderly (Tienda and Wilson, 2002; Allatt, 2001; Rahman, 2001).

The realities of an increasingly interconnected world with linked problems have resulted in a global attention to the citizenship rights of children and young people (Giroux, 2003; Earls and Carlson, 2002; Helve and Wallace, 2001; Tyyskä, 1998; de Waal and Argenti, 2002; Jones and Wallace, 1992). Globally, young people's lives are marked by structural inequalities that prevent them from attaining full civil, political, and social citizenship rights. Worldwide, governments grapple with their countries' future social, political, and economic development. A key question is: How well prepared can any nation of the world be for the future when, in the present, they perpetuate the disenfranchisement of large child and youth populations?

References

Akers, J., Jones, R. and Coyl, D. (1998), 'Adolescent Friendship Pairs: Similarities in Identity Development, Behaviours, Attitudes, and Intentions', *Journal of Adolescent Research* **13** (2), 175–195.

Ali, Ali Abdel Gadir (2002), 'Africa's Children and Africa's Development: A Duration of Development Framework' in A. De Waal and N. Argenti (eds.), *Young Africa. Realising the Rights of Children and Youth*, Trenton, NJ: Africa World Press, Inc., pp. 55–88.

Allatt, P. (2001), 'Critical Discussion: Globalization and Empowerment', In H. Helve and C. Wallace (eds.), *Youth, Citizenship And Empowerment*, Aldershot, England: Ashgate Publishing Limited, pp. 250–259.

Argenti, N. (2002), 'Youth in Africa: A Major Resource for Change', in A. De Waal and N. Argenti (eds.), *Young Africa. Realising the Rights of Children and Youth*, Trenton, NJ: Africa World Press, Inc., pp. 123–154.

Back, L. (1996), *New Ethnicities and Urban Culture. Racism and Multiculture in Young Lives*, New York: St.Martin's Press.

Bakilana, A. and De Waal, A. (2002), 'Child Survival and Development in Africa in the 21st Century', in A. De Waal and N. Argenti (eds.), *Young Africa. Realising the Rights of Children and Youth*, Trenton, NJ: Africa World Press, Inc., pp. 29–54.

Blackman, S. J. (1995), *Youth: Positions and Oppositions*, Aldershot: Avebury.

Brake, M. (1985), *Comparative Youth Culture. The Sociology of Youth Culture and Youth Subgroups in America, Britain and Canada*, London and New York: Routledge and Kegan Paul.

Bridges-Palmer, J. (2002), 'Providing Education For Young Africans', In A. De Waal and N. Argenti (eds.), *Young Africa. Realising The Rights Of Children And Youth*, Trenton, NJ: Africa World Press, Inc., pp. 89–104.

Brown, C. J. (1990), 'Generation X. Youth in the 1980s were unemployed, underemployed, marginalized and poor', *Perception* **14** (2), 62–65.

Carrigan, D. O. (1998), *Juvenile Delinquency In Canada: A History*, Concord, Ontario: Irwin Publishing.

Chisholm, L. and Hurrelmann, K. (1995), 'Adolescence In Modern Europe. Pluralized Transition Patterns And Their Implications For Personal And Social Risks', *Journal Of Adolescence*, 18, 129–158.

Cohen, P. (1999), *Rethinking the Youth Question. Education, Labour and Cultural Studies*, Durham: Duke University Press.

Côté, J. A. and Allahar, A. (1994), *Generation on Hold: Coming of Age in the Late Twentieth Century*, Toronto: Stoddart.

Danesi, M. (1994), *Cool. The Signs and Meanings of Adolescence*, Toronto: University of Toronto Press.

De Waal, A. (2002a), 'Realising Child Rights in Africa: Children, Young People and Leadership', in A. De Waal and N. Argenti (eds.), *Young Africa. Realising the Rights of Children and Youth*, Trenton, NJ: Africa World Press, Inc., pp. 1–28.

De Waal, A. (2002b), 'Hiv/Aids And Young Africans', In A. De Waal and N. Argenti (eds.), *Young Africa. Realising The Rights Of Children And Youth*, Trenton, NJ: Africa World Press, Inc., pp. 171–192.

De Waal, A. and Argenti, N. (eds.) (2002), *Young Africa. Realising the Rights of Children and Youth*, Trenton, NJ: Africa World Press, Inc.

Dowd, J. J. (1981), 'Age and inequality: a critique of the age stratification model', *Human Development*, 24, pp. 157–171.

Earls, F. and Carlson, M. (2002), 'Adolescents as Collaborators: In Search of Well-Being', in M. Tienda and W. J. Wilson (eds.), *Youth in Cities. A Cross-National Perspective*, Cambridge: Cambridge University Press, pp. 58–86.

Everatt, D. (2001), 'From Urban Warrior to Market Segment? Youth in South Africa 1990–2000', in H. Helve and C. Wallace (eds.), *Youth, Citizenship and Empowerment*, Aldershot, England: Ashgate Publishing Limited, pp. 290–299.

Galambos, N. L. and Kolaric, G. C. (1994), 'Canada', In K. Hurrelman (ed.), *International Handbook of Adolescence*, Westport, Connecticut: Greenwood Press.

Galperin, A. (2002), 'Child Victims of War in Africa', in A. De Waal and N. Argenti (eds.), *Young Africa. Realising the Rights of Children and Youth*, Trenton, NJ: Africa World Press, Inc., pp. 105–122.

Ghuman, P. A. S. (1999), *Asian Adolescents in the West*, Leicester, UK: The British Psychological Society Books.

Giroux, H. A. (2003) *The Abandoned Generation. Democracy Beyond the Culture of Fear*, New York: Palgrave Macmillan.

Grinder, R. E. (1973), *Adolescence*, Toronto: John Wiley and Sons.

Heitmeyer, W. (2002), "Have Cities Ceased to Function as 'Integration Machines' for Young People?", in M. Tienda and W. J. Wilson (eds.), *Youth in Cities. A Cross-National Perspective*, Cambridge: Cambridge University Press, pp. 87–112.

Helve, H. and Wallace, C. (eds.) (2001), *Youth, Citizenship and Empowerment*, Aldershot, England: Ashgate Publishing Limited.

Holmes, J. and Silverman, E. L. (1992), *'We're Here, Listen to Us!' A Survey of Young Women in Canada*, Ottawa: Canadian Advisory Council on the Status of Women.

Howe, N. and Bukowski, W. M. (1996), 'What Are Children And How Do They Become Adults? Childrearing and Socialization', In M. Baker (ed), *Families: Changing Trends In Canada,* Third Edn, Toronto: McGraw-Hill Ryerson Limited, pp. 180–190.

Jones, G. and Wallace, C. (1992), *Youth, Family and Citizenship*, Buckingham: Open University Press.

Kelly, J. (1998), Under the Gaze. Learning to be Black in a White Society, Halifax, NS: Fernwood.

Kendal, D., J. Murray and Linden, R. (1997), *Sociology in Our Times: First Canadian Edition*, Scarborough. ON: International Thomson Publishing.

Manderson, L. and Liamputtong, P. (2002), 'Introduction: Youth and Sexuality in Contemporary Asian Societies', in L. Manderson and P. Liamputtong (eds.), *Coming of Age in South and Southeast Asia. Youth, Courtship and Sexuality*, Richmond, Surrey: Curzon, pp. 1–12.

Marquardt, R. (1998), *Enter at Your Own Risk: Canadian Youth and the Labour Market*, Toronto: Between the Lines.

Mattson, K. (2003), *Engaging Youth. Combatting the Apathy of Young Americans Toward Politics*, New York: The Century Foundation Press.

McKechnie, J. and Hobbs, S. (2002), 'Work by the Young: The Economic Activity of School-Aged Children', in M. Tienda and W. J. Wilson (eds.), *Youth in Cities. A Cross-National Perspective*, Cambridge University Press, pp. 217–245.

O'Donnell, M. (1985), *Age and Generation*, New York: Society Now.

Offer, D. and Offer, J. (1972), 'Developmental Psychology Of Youth', In S.J. Samsie (ed.), *Youth: Problems And Approaches*, Philadelphia: Lea and Febiger, pp. 55–78.

Ogwal-Oyee, Fred (2002), 'Life Skills for Ugandan Youth', in M. Tienda and W. J. Wilson (eds.), *Youth in Cities. A Cross-National Perspective*, Cambridge: Cambridge University Press, pp. 246–268.

O'Rand, A. M. (1990), 'Stratification And The Life Course', *Handbook Of Aging And The Social Sciences*, New York: Academic Press, Inc, pp. 117–128.

Prothrow-Stith, D. (2002), 'Youth Violence Prevention In America: Lessons From 15 Years Of Public Health Prevention Work', In M. Tienda and W. J. Wilson (eds.), *Youth In Cities. A Cross-National Perspective*, Cambridge: Cambridge University Press, pp. 165–190.

Rahman, M. (2001), 'The Globalization of Childhood and Youth: New Actors and Networks in Protecting Street Children and Working Children in the South', in H. Helve and C. Wallace (eds.), *Youth, Citizenship and Empowerment*, Aldershot, England: Ashgate Publishing Limited, pp. 262–275.

Rahwoni, O. (2002), 'Reflections on Youth and Militarism in Contemporary Africa', in A. De Waal and N. Argenti (eds.), *Young Africa. Realising the Rights of Children and Youth*, Trenton, NJ: Africa World Press, Inc., pp. 155–170.

Ramphele, M. (2002), 'Steering by the Stars: Youth in Cities', in M. Tienda and W. J. Wilson (eds.), *Youth in Cities. A Cross-National Perspective*, Cambridge: Cambridge University Press, pp. 21–30.

Rhodes, C. N. Jr., Mihyar, H. A. and Abu El-Rous, G. (2002), 'Social Learning and Community Participation with Children at Risk in Two Marginalized Neigbourhoods in Amman, Jordan', in M. Tienda and W. J. Wilson (eds.), *Youth in Cities. A Cross-National Perspective*, Cambridge: Cambridge University Press, pp. 191–216.

Rizzini, I., Barker, G. and Cassaniga, N. (2002), 'From Street Children to All Children: Improving the Opportunities of Low-Income Urban Children and youth in Brazil', in M. Tienda and W. J. Wilson (eds.), *Youth in Cities. A Cross-National Perspective*, Cambridge: Cambridge University Press, pp. 113–137.

Rozie-Battle, J. L. (ed.) (2002), *African-American Adolescents in the Urban Community. Social Services Policy and Practice Interventions*, New York: Haworth.

Sharp, L. A. (2002), *The Sacrificed Generation. Youth, History, And The Colonized Mind In Madagascar*, Berkeley: University Of California Press.

Strickland, R. (2002), 'Introduction: What Is Left Of Modernity?', In Strickland, Ronald (ed.), *Growing Up Postmodern. Neoliberalism And The War On The Young*, Lanham, Maryland: Rowman and Littlefield Publishers, Inc., pp. 1–14.

Swart-Kruger, J. and Chawla, L. (2002), 'Children Show the Way: Participatory Programs for Children of South African Streets and Squatter Camps', in M. Tienda and W. J. Wilson (eds.), *Youth in Cities. A Cross-National Perspective*, Cambridge: Cambridge University Press, pp. 31–57.

Temba, K. and De Waal, A. (2002), 'Implementing the Convention on the Rights of the Child', in A. De Waal and N. Argenti (eds.), *Young Africa. Realising the Rights of Children and Youth*, Trenton, NJ: Africa World Press, Inc., pp. 207–232.

Tienda, M. and Wilson, W. J. (2002), 'Comparative Perspectives of Urban Youth: Challenges for Normative Development', in M. Tienda and W. J. Wilson (eds.), *Youth in Cities. A Cross-National Perspective*, Cambridge: Cambridge University Press, pp. 3–20.

Tyyskä, V. (1998), 'Changing Family Structure and Children's Welfare: Global Perspectives', in A. Sev'er (ed.), *Frontiers in Women's Studies: Canadian and German Perspectives*, Toronto: Canadian Scholars' Press, pp. 45–58.

Tyyskä, V. (2001), *Long and Winding Road. Adolescents and Youth in Canada Today*, Toronto: Canadian Scholars' Press.

Wyn, J. and White, R. (1997), *Rethinking Youth*, London: Sage.

Chapter 2

Youth Research in Europe

Helena Helve, Carmen Leccardi and Siyka Kovacheva

Interpreting European Youth Research

The enlargement of the *European Union* in May, 2004 means that between the 25 European Union countries there are now 75 million young people between 15 and 25 years old. The White Paper, *A New Impetus for European Youth,* was accepted by the *European Commission* on November 21, 2001. In this White Paper (COM 2001; 681) the Commission suggests a new framework for European cooperation in the youth policy issues implementing an open method of coordination. One of the aims of the White Paper is to improve public awareness of young people's concerns at the European level in the field of youth policy.

Gaining a greater understanding and knowledge of youth requires gathering information through statistical data, surveys and other forms of research, and the interpretation thereof.[1] However the channels of communication and dissemination on youth issues are not developed enough throughout Europe (Chisholm and Kovacheva 2002). At present the *Council of Europe* provides contact information about researchers and institutes via its *Directory of Youth and Sport* and *European Youth Research Network Correspondents.* The purpose for this researchers' network is to reflect on the European Commission's and Council of Europe's current agendas on youth research and youth policy reviews, and to focus on how to implement the European Commission Common Objectives for a 'Better Understanding of Youth'. The aim is for correspondents to disseminate information through national youth research networks, or to spark an interest in developing national networks where they do not exist.

In fact much more effort is still needed to develop an effective infrastructure for European youth research co-operation. One important channel for the development of a youth research agenda for our continent has been the international network of the *International Sociological Association Research Committee on Youth Research* (RC34). European youth research strongly depends on forming and strengthening such research communities. At the same time social developments in Europe are moving in a more global direction, where the internationalization of cultural, economic, and political spheres means a globalization of problems like unemployment and social exclusion. At the same time we are witnessing the rise of small, local nationalistic groups among young people in some European countries.[2] The fact is that Europeanness is a contested concept among young Europeans.[3] There are many images of Europe with multiple local cultures, involving similarities and dissimilarities, and various levels of economic development, unemployment, urbanization, access to the means of mass communication and so forth.

The Eurobarometer surveys are designed regularly monitor the social and political attitudes in EU (European Union) and in EC (European Commission) societies. For example when the European Commission examined the views of 15 to 24-year olds on the functioning of the European Union, the survey asked two main questions: what practical measures can be taken to make young people identify more with Europe; and what are the key issues that the Convention should address? This Eurobarometer flash survey revealed that 15 to 24-year-olds feel that employment, solidarity, mobility and respect for democratic values are crucial for the European project. Survey data about young Europeans is plentiful, in contrast with the scarcity of comparative research concerning young Europeans, though at present there are also several comparative studies on young Europeans being funded by European Commission.[4]

While it is not easy to find a common identity for European youth research – given the gap between different countries in terms of adequate funding in the field, and relatively underdeveloped transnational networks and professional mobility – some cooperation does exist. Since the mid-1980s already, the Council of Europe's *European Youth Centre* (EYC) has been making a significant contribution to building closer links between national youth research communities and between youth researchers and youth policy. After the UN *International Year of Young People* in 1985, the Council of Europe established an *Expert Committee on Youth Research and Documentation* from 1987 to 1989. This committee was interested in getting Central and Eastern European youth researchers to take part in European and International joint youth research conferences, and to become members of the International Sociological Association's (ISA) Research Committee 34 'Sociology of Youth'. Also in the mid-1980s the Nordic countries began to develop a Nordic youth research network through the *Nordic Youth Research Information Symposium* (NYRIS) series (Jonsson 1995; Hübner-Funk, Chisholm, du Bois-Reymond and Sellin 1995). The *Youth and Generation in Europe* Research Network was created at the end of the Budapest *European Sociological Association* (ESA) conference, in 1993. This network uses chiefly two instruments: an e-mail discussion list and the ESA congress.[5]

In the 1990s some networks in the field of youth studies were developed and coordinated by the European Union, the Council of Europe and other international institutions. Themes such as marginalization, social inclusion and exclusion, citizenship and European identity (see e.g. Helve and Wallace 2001) became themes for European discussions. In May, 2000 the European Commission sponsored a meeting in Lisbon to debate future challenges for European youth research and policy. This meeting brought together some 150 researchers and policy experts from across Europe. This shows that we can speak about European youth research. In 2003 the Council of Europe and the European Commission agreed to cooperate in the area of youth research in terms of a two year partnership agreement. This cooperation is linked to the 'White Paper' mentioned above. Briefly, European youth researchers have, since the 1990s, become experts on European youth policies.

This has helped the field of youth research to strengthen its autonomy by legitimating itself as a common field where theory and empirical research could meet. Theoretical discussions in youth research have related to social theory, globalization theory and new theoretical developments (e.g. Habermas, Bourdieu, Giddens, Beck and Bauman). Whereas earlier youth theories by Stanley Hall (and also Erik H. Erikson) from 1950s, 1960s and 1970s focused on working class boys, later youth research has also included girls. This is related to the growing participation of European and especially Nordic women in the labor market in the sixties, which has been followed by an explosion of women's participation in education. Nordic youth researchers have also been active in gender studies (e.g. Aapola 2000; Gordon 1990; Bjerrum, Nielsen and Rudberg 1994; Helve 1997). The first international girl research conference, *Alice in Wonderland,* was organized in Amsterdam in 1992.

There has always been a loosely knit network of Western-European scholars, with strong links to Australia and Canada. They share a similar approach, while still allowing for individual profiles. Western European youth research is strongly connected with the Post-War British sub-culture research tradition of the 1970s, when Stuart Hall and Tony Jefferson published their book, *Resistance through Rituals* (1976) and Paul Willis did his famous study on *Profane Culture* (1978).[6] These researchers were all associated with the *British Centre for Contemporary Cultural Studies* (CCCS) at the University of Birmingham.[7] The CCCS has included many different kinds of school positions: feminist, post-modern, criminologist, constructivist, etc. Some CCCS positions have leaned on older traditions (e.g. Coleman and Eriksson), and newer French Bourdieuan positions also have emerged. Although the Birmingham school never achieved an autonomous position, it has had a high status among European youth researchers, especially in the Nordic countries.

The post-Birmingham developments imply a new split between cultural and social youth studies (cf. Furlong and Cartmel 1997). For example there have been two big research programs funded by the British Economic and Social Research Council (ESRC): the 1985–1991 research program, the *16–19 Initiative,* which included an associated comparative study of the transition from school to work in England and Germany (see Bynner 1987); and the *Youth, Citizenship and Social Change* program.[8] The British Youth Research Group hopes to attract existing British Sociological Association (BSA) members as well as to promote links with other disciplines and agencies involved in youth work and research. A key aim of the group is to organize a number of one-day seminars and workshops which will explore all aspects of the study of young people. The focus on cultural studies has been mostly on cultural production and innovation, whereas the focus of social science youth studies has been on social reproduction, not least on social inequalities (cf. Fornäs 1995).

As the largest and oldest Youth Research Institute in Europe, the German Youth Institute *Das Deutsche Jugendinstitut (DJI),* established in 1963, has played an important role in bringing youth onto the European Agenda. The first female president of RC34 Sibylle Hübner-Funk came from this institute. It has actively participated in many research projects on the European level, including the multi-national report to the European Commission: *Study on the State of Young People and Youth Policy in Europe* (2001), coordinated by IARD at Milano, Italy. The institute contributed significantly to the Commission's White Paper on youth and youth policy.

The European Group for Integrated Social Research (EGRIS) is an East-West European research network (based in Germany). In its more than 10 years of activities it has led several EU research projects such as: 'Misleading Trajectories: Evaluation of the Unintended Effects of Labour Market Integration Policies for Young Adults in Europe' and 'Families and Transitions in Europe'. It acts as a forum for a Europe-wide discussion on social integration and social policy.

In the 1980s youth research in Europe was mostly located in cultural studies, media studies and gender studies. However at the same time Nordic youth studies kept a broader inter-disciplinary profile, which was seen in the first Nordic Youth Research Symposium (NYRIS 1) in Oslo, in January, 1987 (see also Gudmundsson 2000). The Oslo symposium was the cornerstone for building up an interdisciplinary Nordic youth studies community. The 7th Nordic Youth Research Information Symposium, *Breaking and Making Borders*, which took place in Helsinki in the year 2000, was a Europe-wide conference. In NYRIS 7 more attention was given to gender as a specific focus throughout the program. In Nordic countries the youth cultural studies school has been especially strong in Sweden (see e.g., Fornäs 1994), and the theoretical concerns have been focused more on identity or culture than on general gender theory (see also Jonsson, Helve and Wichström 2003).

Formal Structures of Youth Research: A Nordic Model

Now we try to characterize the formal structures of youth research in Europe, especially in the Nordic countries, where the infrastructure of the youth research is extensively developed. compared to the fact that youth research is still a relatively new research field. Researchers are dispersed through several academic disciplines and institutes. In the Nordic countries the first Nordic Youth Research Symposium, in 1987, was the start of NYRI, the Nordic Youth Research Information and Nordic Youth Research Institute. NYRI is,the general organization for a range of networking activities and information systems for youth researchers in the Nordic countries: Denmark (including the Faroe Islands and Greenland), Finland, Iceland, Norway and Sweden. The coordination of NYRI activities is financed by the *Nordic Council of Ministers* through a *Nordic Youth Research Coordinator*, and by the national youth ministries through an Advisory Group (AG). This research organization and strategy has developed connections between youth administrators, youth organizations, national youth councils and youth researchers on specific topics in need of more research-based information. NYRI has also had connections with the Council of Europe[9] and EU youth research. About 1700 researchers and users of research based information have been linked through NYRI networks. The development of this cooperation started in 1985, and the present framework was established in 1992.[10]

A research project on living conditions of young people in the Nordic periphery began in 2001. This study has investigated young people living in remote regions of Finland, Iceland, the Faroe Islands, Denmark, Greenland, Norway and Sweden, using methods of secondary analysis. The research project focused on societal, individual and cultural factors that influence the development of young people into adults in the periphery. The project also analyzed processes of integration and marginalization among young people in the periphery.[11] A Nordic-Baltic PhD level doctoral school network of 36 youth researchers and 23 universities with workshops and summer school courses began in 2000. The Youth Research Network invites junior researchers into effective and regular cooperation with Nordic and Baltic Universities and research institutions. In the year 2003 Russia as well became involved in the network. This Youth Research Network is interdisciplinary. There are posts available for young researchers, for example, from the fields of cultural, social, psychological and educational studies. The costs of participating in the workshops and summer schools are paid by *NorFa*, the *Nordic Academy for Advanced Study Network*.[12]

NYRIS symposiums and the publication of the Nordic Journal of Youth Research, YOUNG,[13] have been interrelated, each supporting the other and being influenced by Nordic networks of youth research. YOUNG has become (together with the international *Journal of Youth Studies*) one of the major academic journals in the youth studies arena.[14] YOUNG has initiated dialogue between disciplines concerned with youth such as sociology, political science, pedagogy, psychology, anthropology, ethnology, cultural geography, economics, criminology, law, history, media studies, gender studies, medicine, psychiatry, literature, musicology, film, theatre, linguistics and cultural studies.

In the Nordic countries, as well as in other countries of Europe and other parts of the world, many new things are happening in the field of youth research, youth work and youth policy: In Finland the *Youth Research Society,* established in 1987, has around 200 members. Early in 1999 the Society in turn founded a new research group called *Nuorisotutkimusverkosto (The Youth Research Network),* involving over 20 researchers and projects, financed mainly by the state. The network was based on the *Youth Research 2000* program, which began in 1994. The Finnish Scientific Journal of Youth Research, *Nuorisotutkimus,* had its 20th anniversary in 2003.

The Icelandic Centre for Social Research and Analysis (ICSRA), *Rannsóknir og Greining,* is an independent non-profit organization. The Centre analyzes the social well-being of youth in Iceland, and works closely with various governmental and non-governmental organizations to provide funding and logistic support for research regarding adolescent problems and problem behavior.

The Danish Youth Research Centre in Roskilde, *CeFu,* organized the eighth NYRIS Symposium, *Youth Voice and Noise,* in the year 2003. The Danish Youth Council and Roskilde University have cooperated to develop the Centre as a new structure. The Centre is closely associated with members coming from different central institutions, organizations and enterprises in Denmark, which thus play a part in ensuring that research is in contact with environments that work with young people on a daily basis.

In Norway a new Youth Research Journal, *Ungdomsforskning,* started in 2001, published by *NOVA*.[15] The youth research group at NOVA is multi-disciplinary, comprising mostly sociologists, anthropologists and psychologists. Empirical research on adolescents is based on local and regional qualitative and quantitative studies, as well as national surveys. Its main research topics are youth culture and leisure activities, school adjustment, transitions from school to employment, alcohol and drug use, delinquency and conduct problems, inter-generational relations and issues concerning ethnicity and a multi-cultural society.

In Sweden the Swedish Council for Labour and Social Science Research, *Forskningsrådet för arbetsliv och socialvetenskap,* has evaluated Swedish youth research (*Youth Research in Sweden, 1995–2001. An Evaluation Report*; Jonsson, Helve and Wichström 2003). According to their evaluation there is a fundamental division in the field of youth research: The first section is associated with the Birmingham school Cultural Studies, which often focuses on how young people are socially constructed as youth, how they shape their identity and what lifestyles they choose. The other tradition includes studies in academic disciplines ranging from social medicine/epidemiology and psychology to social work, education, the humanities and sociology.

At the Nordic level, youth research has been active with the *Unga i Norden* (Nordic Youth) research program. The different networks have integrated platforms for knowledge-based decision making. This multidisciplinary research program has been developed in cooperation with researchers, administrators and politicians. For example the *Barents Youth Research Network* and *Arctic Youth Research Network* are new networks founded through cooperation between the Nordic countries. The key themes of these programs have been the living conditions of young people, the transition from childhood to adulthood and Nordic identity and youth culture (cf. Bjurtström, 1997). These topics embrace comparative research, evaluation research and both quantitative and qualitative research.

Modernizing Youth. Youth Research in Italy

In the following chapter we focus on issues that have been at the forefront for young people and youth research for the past fifty years in Europe. Our case is taken from Italian youth research but it fits in many ways also to the youth and youth research in other European countries specially in Southern Europe. We will see how the modernizing path that transformed Italy in a few decades from an agricultural country to a post-industrial one also thoroughly changed youth profiles. The studies briefly taken into consideration here highlight the nature of these changes and their main characteristics.

The Birth of Youth: The Fifties and Sixties

The few studies done in Italy in the early 1950s (Grasso 1954; Dursi 1958) give us a fairly dull picture of youth. Young people seemed to be in a defensive position, subjected to intense forms of social control, intent mainly on introspection and uninterested in the social and political situation. This changed, however, beginning in the last years of the 1950s with the arrival of the 'economic boom' – the period of rapid and intense economic growth, continuing into the early 1960s, that radically transformed the Italian social landscape (Ginsborg, 1989). The flight from rural areas,[16] especially by younger people, was a tool for asserting their right to an existence different from that of the older generations.

Together with the spread of consumer goods – material and symbolic emblems of economic development – this period also revealed the first forms of youth culture in the proper sense. In fact, young people used consumer goods to trace their own generational profile distinct from that of adults: from scooters to record albums, from clothing to pictures of stars, consumer goods and their symbols became an effective tool of emancipation from the world of adults. As documented by studies of the time (cf. Cristofori, 2002) – no matter whether conducted in cities like Milan (Diena, 1960) or Genoa (L. Cavalli, 1959) or in provincial Tuscany (Carbonaro and Lumachi, 1962) or Veneto (Allum and Diamanti, 1986) – it was primarily by means of consumer goods that young people, workers and students, were able to construct spaces of freedom and independence unknown to earlier youth generations.

New consumption possibilities also appeared to be of great importance in decoding the messages carried by the 'gangs' of juveniles who menacingly populated urban areas in the early sixties (Piccone Stella, 1993). Through various kinds of transgression, first and foremost in acts of gratuitous delinquency, groups of young people – male and mainly of working-class origin – attempted to translate into daily practice the hedonism being touted by mass culture. This is the picture emerging from a number of studies on the phenomenon of Italian *teddy boys* (Bertolini, 1964) conducted mainly by psychologists, pedagogues and criminologists. At that time, in fact, Italian sociology was only minimally concerned with this phenomenon.

Instead, sociologists in those years were asking themselves about the new generational identity of so-called 'normal youth'. Research done at the time in Milan (Baglioni, 1962), for example, identified among young people (as Schelsky had done in Germany some years earlier) a *gray* generation, the so-called generation of the three M's: *m*oglie (wife), *m*acchina (car) *m*estiere (job), an image that research by Alfassio Grimaldi and Bertoni (1964) would later confirm: a generation without flights of fancy and with little interest in politics, desirous only of playing adult roles as soon as possible.

In the mid-sixties a new profile of the youth world began to take shape, parallel to an increase in secondary school attendance and the spread of great optimism about the future. Meanwhile, in the years preceding 1968 the beat culture began to flourish. According to a study done in Milan in 1967 (Ardigò et al., 1968), the young people in the beat movement were mainly middle and lower-middle class, anti-authority, anti-consumption and fighting against the constituted order that the adult generation embodied. Often midway between dissent and consumption, at least in its mass expressions,[17] the beat generation spread a message of liberation from dominant cultural schemes and searched for more authentic relations. In fact, it paved the way for the long youth movement era, which in Italy lasted until the end of the 1970s.

From the 'Movement Era' to the 'Era of Uncertainty'

Anti-authoritarianism and the redefinition of the borders between public and private; the primacy of politics and the centrality of daily life as an arena in which to challenge power; a rejection of book-learning in favor of a closer relation between theory and practice; new forms of communication – these were key points of the 1968 movement. They were not analyzed in sociological research, but rather by the movement's young leaders (Bobbio and Viale, 1968; Viale, 1978). Sociological studies in this period instead focused on the change in values that involved the entire world of youth, not just the activist minority. A good illustration of this trend can be found in the results of a survey done in 1969 by Doxa on behalf of Shell (Inchiesta Shell, 1970). What emerged, among other things, was the conviction – shared by almost all the young people interviewed – of being involved in an authentic conflict with the adult world. Another survey, conducted by the ISVET a year later (Scarpati, 1973) painted a picture of youth in terms of an increasing marginalization. Young people suffered from this due to mechanisms of social exclusion, both at school and in the working world, where youth unemployment was on the rise. These processes went side by side with youth's rejection of the traditional channels of political participation, such as party affiliations.

Thinking in a marginal key was very popular in research on youth throughout the seventies. Aside from the specific research areas – whether young people's relations with the productive sphere (Annunziata and Moscati, 1978) or the transformation of, and crisis in, the traditional socialization apparatus (Bassi and Pilati,1978) – most of the analysis of a sociological, political or cultural nature in those years tended to propose a similar interpretive scheme, with a conjunction of two aspects at its base. On the one hand there was the social and productive marginality of a major part of the youth world – the so-called 'non-guaranteed people': students not attending classes, student-workers doing the many little jobs that do not offer identity, unemployed young people in the suburbs (De Masi, 1978) – and on the other, the emergence of a new subjectivity. From this interweaving sprang the movement of 1977 and the social and political body that constituted its reference point: the 'youth proletariat'. A contemporary of neo-feminism, the 1977 movement borrowed from it the informal, small-group organizational structure and many of the keywords centered on beginning by oneself to understand the world, and the right to be different (Sorlini, 1977).

The youth world emerged from this period – exceptional in the intensity of its forms of protest and cultural innovation – with a profile very different from that of the previous decade. In a seminal study of those years Alessandro Cavalli proposed considering the transformation in terms of a shift in the youthful stage of life from 'process' to 'condition': while in the first case young people appear to be 'in transit' towards adulthood and their eyes are on the future, in the second youth is characterized as 'awaiting an unpredictable outcome' (Cavalli, 1980, p. 524) and is trapped within the confines of the present.

Meanwhile, in the late 1970s and early 1980s – the end of the 'movement era' – a portrait of youthful action in terms of a defensive individualism, inwardly oriented and indifferent to social problems, an expression of a 'culture of narcissism' (c.f. Featherstone, 1991) was making headway. But a study of students in Turin in the late eighties (Ricolfi and Sciolla, 1980) refuted these interpretations. Young people did not manifest forms of egocentric individualism or a retreat from the social. Instead, they were expressing new concepts of politics (for example, 'be yourself' was considered political); they gave great importance to relationships and criticized social conformism. Higher levels of education, interwoven with the by now vast diffusion of media networks, constituted the ideal *humus* for expanding this view. While the most radical political content was being toned down, a closer and closer connection was being forged between a 'culture of the quotidian', attention to the 'personal' and greater reflexivity, and was destined to get stronger and more consolidated in subsequent decades.

In the 1980s a great deal of research was devoted to youth and its cultural expressions (including studies by Guala 1983; Scanagatta 1984; Caioli et al. 1986; Ricolfi, Scamuzzi and Sciolla 1988). A backward glance reveals – although through different routes and methods – some common accents: the new youth culture's privileged relations with pragmatism and the growth of a 'subjectivity culture' (Cesareo 1984). For example, in a well-known study, Garelli (1984) utilizes the term 'daily-life generation' to characterize the youth world of these years, distanced from ideologies and attentive to the sphere of sociality and the expression of personal needs.

Another important study in the 1980s (Cavalli 1985; cf. Leccardi 1990) put into focus the transformations that in the meantime had occurred in the methods and forms of young people's biographical construction and identity definition. There were two particularly innovative dimensions to this study, of a qualitative nature. First there was the choice of the theme of time (treated in the dimensions of historical, biographical and quotidian time) as a tool with which to analyze the condition of youth as a whole; secondly, the use of time to call attention to the break in connections between routes of identity definition and mechanisms of inter-generational transmission.

Beginning in the late 1980s, the relationship between transformations in the experience of time, changes in routes of identity and the construction of modes of relating to the public sphere negotiated mainly by small groups (Diamanti, 1999) became the background for numerous studies of the condition of youth in Italy. Worth mentioning among these are the studies sponsored by the IARD research institute. Founded in 1961, this institute (now well known throughout Europe) sponsors theoretical studies and empirical surveys in the field of youth and education, with approaches that integrate the viewpoints of the different social sciences. Since starting in 1983 and at four-year intervals, the IARD has been surveying Italian youth (Cavalli et al. 1984; Cavalli and de Lillo 1988; 1993; Buzzi, Cavalli and de Lillo 1997; 2002). Through the years this has created an authentic observatory on youth, which analyzes 'either with periodic, nationwide surveys or with specific studies, the direction, pace and intensity of changes involving the attitudes, orientations, expectations and behavior of young people' (Cavalli and de Lillo, 1988, p. 9).

Among other things, IARD research has drawn a realistic picture of the transformations occurring in the past decades in young people's transition to adulthood. Following European trends, this transition has not only been extended in temporal terms but it has become more and more fragmented. In particular, in Italy as in other Mediterranean countries, this process has come to coincide with a prolonged stay in the family of origin, the so-called '*famiglia lunga*' ('long family'): at the end of the nineties, half of Italian men and a third of Italian women were still, at age 29, living with their parents.

Overall, the IARD surveys underscore how the present youthful stage of life is dominated by growing uncertainty, along with great distrust of social institutions. The values that count are increasingly the ones tied to the private sphere (family, love, friendship). Consumer culture is central to identity while decisions are experienced as revocable. The temporal horizon in which one lives tends to contract, and the present becomes the preferred point of reference for action. (Leccardi, 1999.)

Political Aspects of Youth Research in Eastern and Central Europe

Finally we examine some political aspects of European youth research in Eastern and Central Europe. It was the proletariat, the 'leading working class,' that the early Communist regimes proclaimed as the beneficiary of their victory in the mid 20th century (see for example Sztachelski 1950, cited in Sokolowska and Richard 1990, p. 79). The 'proletarian dictatorship' was meant to solve all social problems of the bourgeois society and the ruling parties took its realization seriously, carrying out a forced nationalization of the finance sector, industry and land in most countries, Poland being a notable exception from the latter. When the regimes somewhat softened in the late 1950s, the party nomenclature needed a new ideological construct to demonstrate the shift in their strategy. It was then that youth was discovered as the group with the most significant role in this developed stage of the Communist construction. Young people were seen as being less burdened with the values and practices of the capitalist past than the older generations, and hence more prone to build and live in the classless Communist society.

The establishment of youth studies as a legitimate academic discipline in East Central Europe and the setting up of its research agenda in the 1960s and 1970s came with the rising political concerns and amounting economic difficulties in the Soviet camp. First in the German Democratic Republic in 1966, then in the Soviet Union, Bulgaria, Romania and elsewhere youth research institutes were founded, or research centres were established at the Academies of Sciences and major universities. This strategy followed ideological considerations – youth was perceived as the most optimistic and hence the least dangerous group to be studied empirically. In countries where youth protest movements were mounting, as in Slovenia, the communist state did not develop institutional structures for youth research (Ule and Rener, 1998). Despite the ideological underpinning, the studies, which youth institutes carried out, were among the best examples of empirical research in the eastern part of the continent during the communist regimes while most other fields of sociology were abstractly theoretical and under the strong influence of the official Marxist ideology.

The first phase of youth research in the state socialist countries also gave rise to important conceptual reflections. It started with discussions of class and age as stratifying factors and how to specify youth as a social group, given the biological and developmental components (Mitev, 1969). The work of Russian sociologist Igor Kon (1967) provided an elaborate concept of socialisation, linking the development of the personality to the specific social relations and institutions. The Romanian researcher Fred Mahler (1983) developed the idea of juventisation to reflect the innovation that young people introduce into society and envisioned the development of youth research into the science of juventology (see Mahler, 1983).

In the 1980s youth studies faced new social challenges – the economic limitations of the centrally planned economy becoming more obvious, attempts were made to free space for private initiative. Young people were still the main beneficiaries of the state social policy and were expected to contribute to the intensification and technological innovation of the economy. The amounting problems and discontent among youth were interpreted as a mismatch between their growing aspirations and the 'still' limited job opportunities. Youth researchers have gathered much empirical information about the varying expectations and experiences of young people and started conceptualising youth as comprised of different subgroups: students, workers, peasants. The Bulgarian and Russian researchers theorised about the self-realisation of the personality (See for an overview of the concept Kharchenko, 1999) while the Baltic sociologists advanced the concept of self-determination. The latter focused on the choices young people make during their transitions through life – from one educational stage to another, from education to work, from parents' family to creating their own, etc. Using this paradigm, sociologists insisted on looking closer at young people's own beliefs and values, which were largely neglected up to then (cf. Saarniit 1998, pp. 43–66).

During this second stage (1980s), youth research was already well institutionalised and abundantly subsidised in most Warsaw Pact countries. The communist regimes fostered international co-operation in the youth field in the attempt to advertise the growing successes of the state youth policy. East-West communication flourished despite the obvious barriers – the different political and cultural contexts, different themes and theoretical perspectives, even different methodologies (up to then youth studies in the eastern half were almost wholly identified with large-scale quantitative surveys while small-scale qualitative studies dominated in many research traditions in the West). Good examples were the projects dedicated to the International Youth Year in 1985. The first two presidents of RC34 came from South-East Europe – the Romanian Ovidiu Badina and the Bulgarian Petar-Emil Mitev. International conferences and seminars were organised on a regular base in Primorsko, Costinesti, Leipzig, Moscow, Bratislava. While German youth researchers from the institutes in Munich and Leipzig were not allowed officially to communicate with each other, Munich, Sofia and Bucharest had a 'cultural contract' to hold regular alternating conferences year by year. The only World Congress of Sociology held in Eastern Europe was organised in 1970 in Varna, Bulgaria.

The period of the 1980s was also a time of tightening of state control over youth research. When researchers turned to topics that were inconsistent with the tale of the successful youth policy and loyal youth, such as the deviant behaviour of the 'non-formals' (youth dissident groups), funding was withdrawn. Individual researchers and whole institutes were punished and banned from participation in international research projects or in conferences and seminars abroad. In Romania for example, Chaushesku's regime was particularly oppressive towards the widely known youth researchers Fred Mahler and Ovidiu Badina.

The social transformation in the region after the fall of the Berlin Wall in 1989 affected youth studies in many ways. Although young people played a prominent role in the 'gentle' revolutions in the Soviet Block countries, they lost their privileged position which they enjoyed in the ideology and social policy of the communist regimes. A process of deconstruction of youth took place, similar to the one in advanced market societies: such as the prolongation of the youth phase and the loss of the clear cut age boundaries, the increasing differentiation and individualisation of young people (Wallace and Kovatcheva, 1998). The dominant liberal ideology in most CEE countries stressed the social role of individualism and implied that if only all individuals, independently of their age, were left free from the party and state control, their entrepreneuring activity would alleviate all social problems. Young people were perceived as no longer needing privileges from a patronising state, what they needed were equal chances in life. The disappearance of the former mass official youth organisations is another significant factor for the deconstruction of youth under post-communism. Numerous new youth associations have a too thin spread to make a difference in public discourse and policy considerations.

In this third phase youth research infrastructure suffered a major blow – some institutes were closed as the one in Bulgaria, while others found themselves deprived of the abundant state financing as the Romanian Institute. The old research institutions had to look for new sources of funding, and many, as the Russian Youth Institute in Moscow, discovered them in teaching courses in prestigious subjects such as psychology or business studies or producing opinion polls and market research.

Individual researchers also left youth studies in large numbers to go to the more profitable spheres of private businesses, politics, or advertising. As young people themselves, some youth researchers ventured upon the road of emigration abroad, as far away as the United States and Australia. Those who persisted in the youth field in CEE countries had to rediscover small-scale studies since the sources for financing large nation-wide surveys had disappeared.

The late 1990s were a period of overcoming the initial crisis in society and in youth research. Addressing the increasing individualisation and differentiation among young people, the focus of the social construction of youth was placed on the specific problems of specific groups among youth: the young homeless, the young unemployed, the young drug addicts etc. Youth started to be seen as posing problems to society and not as active resource persons. This resulted in a proliferation of agencies and state departments dealing with youth: education, health, labour, police and army, each of them with differing definitions and diverging approaches to finding solutions.

A process of institutional pluralism took place in the field of youth studies with many new centres coming into being which was not possible when there had been only one recognised state institute in each country. The new university departments teaching social sciences and the numerous marketing and polling companies also started producing youth research. The Centre for Social Psychology/Youth Studies in Slovenia can be cited as an illustration of this trend, developing into a well established and internationally recognised institution for youth research. With the generational change youth research experienced a conceptual opening up for new themes and ideas, new approaches and methodologies. Instead of expecting a 'juventisation' (cf. Mahler, 1983) of society, youth researchers revealed problems in the social integration of youth (Chuprov and Zubok, 1998) and focused on their social exclusion. A most remarkable feature of the fourth stage of youth research in CEE is the methodological pluralism. National and international surveys were matched with case-study approaches, life history and focus group interviewing.

Economic pressures account for a lot of this change. The new centres found themselves competing for scarce sources of funding. These came either directly from foreign funding agencies such as the programmes of the European Commission and the Council of Europe, national governments such as the German, Austrian, Dutch, private foundations such as Ford, MacArthur, the Open Society, or local voluntary organisations, which had the resources and skills to use research data. Again, in most cases this meant NGOs with foreign affiliations. This situation had two important consequences. The national research agenda was largely formed by the visions and perceptions of outside bodies with the risk of missing problems specific to the conditions of youth in the region. Second, there was a lot of interest in comparative studies, in Western concepts and methodologies. The East-West collaboration gave birth to innovative studies (See for example Roberts and Machacek, 1997; Bynner and Koklygina, 1995; Pilkington et al, 2002), on which basis many informal networks developed. These contacts succeeded largely due (or thanks) to the personal devotion of researchers on both sides, strong enough to overcome travel difficulties, loss of mail, collapse of banks, road blockades, etc.

The 21st century started with renewed co-operation between youth researchers and policy makers in many countries in the region and on the European arena, as shown in the Council of Europe process of review of the national youth policies in Estonia,

Rumania and Lithuania. Youth is studied as an active agent in European integration (Baranovic, 2002) and youth participation has become a new topic for research (Kovacheva, 2000). The European and global concerns are matched with research into local problems, such as ethnic tolerance among young people in the multicultural societies in the Balkans (Mitev and Riordan, 2004) or the relations between generations in the transforming Russian society (Semenova, 2002).

The development of youth studies in Eastern and Central Europe has been strongly influenced by the social upheavals in the region in the 20th century. Under state socialism they were under strong pressure to demonstrate the successes of the centralized social policy of the one-party regime. Nevertheless, they managed to reveal some true problems of young people and to create innovative concepts for their interpretation. In the post-Communist era youth research is in a process of reconstruction, experiencing a pluralization of scientific paradigms and institutional structures. Within individual countries youth research lost the security of abundant state support in the same way that young people yielded their privileged position in ideology and welfare. What youth studies gained was in the wider arena of European cooperation. The keywords for European youth research are: building a European infrastructure for youth research networks and forgetting pseudo-East/West borders in a 'New Europe'. For this reason, currently, European youth research cooperation is a reality and it has better perspectives than in the 20th century.

Concluding Notes

In this article our focus has mainly been on the geographical and cultural regions of Europe. The discussion of European youth research cannot be illustrated only with analyses of geographically opposed regions of Europe: Northern versus Southern Europe/Eastern versus Western Europe. The fact of the matter is that the New Europe is a historical, political, cultural, artistic, technological and military entity. This should mean that the role of the EU and its institutions, and old and new ideologies in Europe, contribute to a cultural environment in which we have to define new strategies for European youth research cooperation. Since the end of the Cold War, the unification of Germany, the collapse of Communist regimes, and the violent disintegration of former Yugoslavia there is a growing realization that youth research in Europe still partly suffers from the lack of a European infrastructure, insufficient funding, lack of an environment to stimulate research and exploit results, and the fragmented nature of activities and the distribution of resources.

Notes

1 Source: Cover letter of the European Commission questionnaire on 'Greater Understanding for Youth', 1993.
2 Eurobarometer Flash Survey, carried out between May 27 and June 16, 2002, with a representative sample of 7558 young people.
3 The complex relation between young people and Europe is revealed by their attitudes towards the idea of a European identity. See, Chisholm, du Bois-Reymond and Coffield 1995; Lagrée 2000; and Leccardi 2001.

4 Cf. *Rural Young People in Changing Europe. A Comparative Study of Living Conditions of Rural Young People in Estonia, Finland, Germany, Italy and Sweden*, Helve (ed.) 2000.
5 More than 200 European youth sociologists are registered as member of this e-mail forum.
6 In the 1990s subcultures came out in new forms as fan and consumer cultures (Featherstone 1991), and common cultures (Willis 1990).
7 Willis and Jeffersson had been postgraduate students at the Centre and Hall was its director.
8 Directed by Liza Catan. The project ended in 2003. This programme involves 17 different pieces of research, ranging from social exclusion to citizenship.
9 On the occasion of the 5th Conference of European Ministers Responsible for Youth in Bucharest, April 27–29, 1998, the Council of Europe Youth Directorate published an information document entitled *25 Years of Youth Policy in the Council of Europe: Taking Stock and Looking Ahead*. It points out that the years 1964 – 1969 were the actual stimulus for the creation of European youth policy, when the conflict between young people and society and its values had plainly manifested itself. For that reason the Parliamentary Assembly of the Council of Europe decided in May, 1968 to regularly discuss the situation of youth in Europe and recommended that the European Youth Centre and the European Youth Foundation be established.
10 See the NYRI website: www.alli.fi/nyri/index.htm.
11 Helve, H. (ed.) 2003: Ung i utkant. Aktuell forskning om glesbygdsungdomar i Norden.
12 NorFA is a network of Nordic PhD-level doctoral schools with working connections to youth policy and youth work in the Nordic countries, sponsored by the Nordic Scientific Academy.
13 YOUNG was originally printed in Sweden. The abstracts and articles have also been published in NYRI. The editorial board has been Nordic. Following negotiations with Sage publications, since 2003 the Journal 'Young' has been published by Sage.
14 See more http: //www.alli.fi/nyri/young/index.htm
15 NOVA – Norwegian Social Research – is a national research institute. The board of directors is appointed by the Ministry of Education and Research. The National Assembly, Stortinget, provides the basic funding. The aim of the institute is to develop knowledge and understanding of social conditions and processes of change. It focuses on issues of life-course events, level of living conditions and aspects of life-quality as well as on programs and services provided by the welfare system.
16 After the Second World War, about half the working population was employed in the primary sector.
17 The reference is to the music which, through the Beatles and Rolling Stones, spread across Europe, to youth-oriented magazines, styles of clothing and looks.

References

Alfassio Grimaldi, U. and Bertoni, I. (1964), *I giovani degli anni Sessanta* (Youth in the Sixties), Bari: Laterza.
Allum, P. and Diamanti, I. (1986), *50'/80', vent'anni* (50'/80', Twenty Years), Roma: Edizioni Lavoro.
Annunziata, L. and Moscati, R. (1978), *Lavorare stanca. Movimento giovanile, lavoro, non lavoro* (Work is Tiring. Youth Movement, Work, Non-work), Roma: Savelli.
Ardigò, A. et al. (1968), *Protesta e partecipazione della giovent— in Europa* (Youth Protest and Participation in Europe), Milano: Centro Studi Lombardo.
Baglioni, G. (1962), *I giovani della società industriale* (Youth in Industrial Society), Milano: Vita e Pensiero.

Baranovic, B. (2002), 'National relation of Croatian youth in the period of transition', in: Blanka Tivadar and Polona Mrvar. *Flying over or Falling through the Cracks? Young People in the Risk Society*, Ljubljana: Office for Youth of the Republic of Slovenia.

Bassi, P. and Pilati, A. (1978), *I giovani e la crisi degli anni Settanta* (Youth and the Seventies Crisis), Roma: Editori Riuniti.

Beck, U. (1986/1992), *Risikogesellschaft: Auf dem Weg in eine andere Moderne* (Risk Society: Towards a New Modernity), Frankfurt am Main: Suhrkamp.

Bertolini, P. (1964), *Delinquenza e disadattamento giovanile. Esperienze rieducative* (Juvenile Delinquency and Maladjustment. Re-educational Experiences), Bari: Laterza.

Bjerrum Nielsen, H. and Rudberg, M. (1994), *Psychological Gender and Modernity*, Oslo: Universitetsforlaget.

Bjurtström, E. (1997), *Högt och lågt. Smak och stil i ungdomskulturen* (High and Low. Taste and Style in Youth Culture), Umeå: Borea.

Bobbio, L. and Viale, G. (1968), 'La strategia del movimento'(Movement Strategy), *Problemi del Socialismo*, 28–29: 12–27.

Bourdieu, P. (1992/1996), *The Rules of Art. Genesis and Structure of the Literary Field*, Cambridge: Polity Press.

Buzzi, C., Cavalli, A. and de Lillo, A. (eds.) (1997), *Giovani verso il Duemila* (Youth Towards Two Thousand), Bologna: Il Mulino.

Buzzi, C., Cavalli, A. and de Lillo, A. (eds.) (2002), *Giovani del nuovo secolo* (Youth in the New Century), Bologna: Il Mulino.

Bynner, J. (1987) 'Coping with Transition: ESRC's new 16–19 Initiative', *Youth and Policy*, 22, 25–28.

Bynner, J. and Kokljagina, L. (1995), 'Transition to Employment in Great Britain, Russia and Estonia: towards a Comparative Analysis of Longitudinal Data on Young People's Labour Market Entry', in CYRCE (ed.) *The Puzzle of Integration. European Yearbook on Youth Policy and Research*, 1, Berlin: Walter de Gruyter.

Carbonaro, A. and Lumachi, F. (1962), *Giovani in provincia* (Young Peoples in the Provinces), Firenze: La Nuova Italia.

Cavalli, L. (1959), *La giovent— del quartiere operaio* (Youth in Working-Class Areas), Genova: Pagano.

Cavalli, A. (1980), 'La giovent—: condizione o processo?' (Youth: Condition or Process?), *Rassegna Italiana di Sociologia*, 4: 519–542.

Cavalli, A. (ed.) (1985), *Il tempo dei giovani* (Youth's Time), Bologna: Il Mulino.

Cavalli, A. et al. (1984), *Giovani oggi* (Youth Today), Bologna: Il Mulino.

Cavalli, A. and de Lillo, A. (eds.) (1993), *Giovani anni 90* (Youth in the 90's), Bologna: Il Mulino.

Cavalli, A. and de Lillo A. (1988), *Giovani anni 80* (Youth in the 80's), Bologna: Il Mulino.

Caioli, L. et al. (1986), *Bande: un modo di dire* (Gangs: An Expression), Milano: Unicopli.

Cesareo, V. (1984), *Percorsi e esperienze nella scuola* (Scholastic Routes and Experiences), in: Cavalli, A. et al., *Giovani oggi* (Youth Today), 21–49. Bologna: Il Mulino.

Chisholm, L. (1995), 'European Youth Research: Tour de Force or Turmbau zu Babel?', in: Chisholm, P. Buchner, H-H. Kruger, M. du Bois-Reymond (eds.) *Growing Up in Europe. Contemporary Horizons in Childhood and Youth Studies*, Berlin: Walter de Gruyter.

Chisholm, L., du Bois-Reymond, M. and Coffield, F. (1995), '"What Does Europe Mean to Me?" Dimensions of Distance and Disillusion amongst European Students' in CYRCE (ed.) *The Puzzle of Integration. European Yearbook on Youth Policy and Research*, 1, Berlin: Walter de Gruyter

Chisholm, L. and Kovacheva, S. (2002), *Exploring the European Youth Mosaic. The Social Situation of Young People in Europe*. Strasbourg: Council of Europe Publishing.

Cristofori, C. (2002), 'La costruzione sociale della *prima generazione* di giovani in Italia. Il contributo della ricerca empirica' (The Social Construction of the First Youth Generation in Italy. The Contribution of Empirical Research), in F. Crespi (ed.), *Le rappresentazioni sociali dei giovani in Italia* (Social Representations of Young People in Italy), 77–110, Roma: Carocci.

Chuprov, V. and Zubok, J. (2000), 'Integration versus Exclusion: Youth and the Labour Market in Russia', *International Social Science Journal*, June, Vol. LII, No. 2, pp. 171–182.

De Masi, D. (1978), 'Sui fatti di primavera' (About the Facts of Spring), in D. de Masi and A. Signorelli (eds.), *La questione giovanile* (The Youth Question), 102–112, Milano: Angeli.

Diamanti, I. (ed.) (1999), *La generazione invisibile* (The Invisible Generation), Milano: Il Sole – 24 Ore.

Diena, L. (1960), *Gli uomini e le masse* (Men and the Masses), Torino: Einaudi.

Dubski, V. (1995), 'On the Young Generation's Situation in the Transformation of Czech Society', in: L. Chisholm, P. Buchner, H-H. Kruger, M. du Bois-Reymond (eds.) *Growing Up in Europe. Contemporary Horizons in Childhood and Youth Studies.* Berlin: Walter de Gruyter.

Dursi, M. (1958), *Giovani soli* (Young People Alone), Bologna: Il Mulino.

Featherstone, M. (1991), *Consumer Culture & Postmodernism*, London: Sage Publications.

Fornäs, J. (1995), *Cultural Theory & Late Modernity*, London: Sage.

Furlong A. and Cartmel, F. (1997), *Young People and Social Change: Individualization and Risk in Late Modernity*, Buckingham: Open University Press.

Garelli, F. (1984), *La generazione della vita quotidiana* (The Daily-Life Generation), Bologna: il Mulino.

Ginsborg, P. (1989), *Storia d'Italia dal dopoguerra a oggi* (A History of Italy from Post-War to Today), Torino: Einaudi.

Gordon, T. (1990), *Feminist Mothers.* Basingstoke: Macmillan.

Grasso, P.G. (1954), *Gioventù di metà secolo* (Mid-Century Youth), Roma: AVE.

Guala, C. (ed.) (1983), *Tra i giovani* (Among Young People), Roma: Editori Riuniti.

Gudmundsson, G. (2000) 'Youth Research at Crossroads: Sociological and Interdisciplinary Youth Research in the Nordic Countries', *Journal of Youth Studies* 3: 2, pp. 127–145.

Harris, A., Aapola, S. and Gonick, M. (2000), 'Doing it Differently?: Young Women Managing Heterosexuality in Australia, Finland and Canada', *Journal of Youth Studies,* 2 (4), pp. 373–388.

Helve, H. (ed. and co-authored) (2003), *Ung i utkant. Aktuell forskning om glesbygdsungdomar i Norden* (Youth in the Margins. Current Research on Periphery Young People in the Nordic countries), TemaNord 2003: 519, Copenhagen: Nordic Council of Ministers.

Helve, H (ed.) (2000), *Rural Young People in Changing Europe. A Comparative Study of Living Conditions of Rural Young People in Estonia, Finland, Germany, Italy and Sweden.* Finnish Youth Research Society in co-operation with Directorate General XXII of the European Comission. Helsinki: Hakapaino Oy.

Helve, H. (1997), Attitudes, value systems and gender: A comparative longitudinal study of attitudes and values of young people. In *Invitation to dialogue: Beyond Gender (In) equality.* Institute of Philosophy and Sociology, Latvian Academy of Sciences, Riga, pp. 110–124.

Helve, H. and Wallace, C. (eds.) (2001), *Youth, Citizenship and Empowerment,* England: Ashgate Publishing Ltd.

Hübner-Funk, S., Chisholm, L., du Bois-Reymond, M. and Sellin B. (1995), Editorial. in *The Puzzle of Integration. European Yearbook of Youth Policy and Research Vol.1/1995.* CYRCE, Berlin: Walter de Gruyter and CO.

Inchiesta Shell (1970), *Questi, i giovani* (These, the Young), Genova: Shell Italiana.

Jonsson, B. (1995), Nordic Youth Research Information (NYRI). In *The Puzzle of Intergration. European Yearbook of Youth Policy and Research Vol.1/1995.* CYRCE, Berlin: Walter de Gruyter and CO, pp. 305–311.

Jonsson, J., Helve, H. and Wichström, L. (2003), *Youth Research in Sweden, 1995–2001. An Evaluation Report.* The Swedish Council for Working Life and Social Research. Stocholm.

Kharchenko, I. (1999), 'Zhiznenie plani i orientazii uchaschejsja molodezi' (Life Plans and Claims of Learning Youth), in: T. Zaslavskaja and Z. Kalugina (eds.) *Sozialnaja traektorija reformiruemoj Rossii. (Social Trajectory of Russia's Reformation)*, Novosibirsk: Science.

Kon, I. (1967), *Soziologija lichnosti (Sociology of the Personality)*, Moscow: Politizdat.

Kovacheva, S. (2000), *Keys to Youth Participation in Eastern Europe*, Strasbourg: Council of Europe.

Lagrée, J. C. (2000), *Young People and Europe. Attitudes towards Europe and European Identity*, Research Report, Paris: IRESCO-ULISS.

Leccardi, C. (2001), 'Identità europea?' (European Identità?), in: A. Besussi and L. Leonini (eds.), *L'Europa tra società e politica* (Europe in the Midst of Society and Politics), pp. 105–116, Milano: Guerini.

Leccardi, C. (1999), 'Time, Youth and the Future', *Young Nordic Journal of Youth Research,* 7 (1): 3–18.

Leccardi, C. (1990), 'Die Zeit der Jungendlichen: Was heisst maennlich und weiblich in der Zeiterfahrung?', in: M. du Bois-Reymond and M. Oechsle (eds.), *Neue Jugenbiographie? Zum Strukturwandel der Judendphase*, 95–114, Opladen: Leske+Budrich.

Machacek, L. and Roberts, K. (eds.) (1997), *Youth Unemployment and Self-employment in East-Central Europe*, Bratislava: SAS.

Mahler, F. (1983), *Introduciere in juventologie*, (English summary in IBYR Newsletter No. 1, 1984), Bucaresti.

Mitev, P-E. (1969), *Sozialnijat progres I mladezta* (Social Progress and Youth), Sofia: People's Youth Press.

Mitev, P.-E. and Riordan, J. (2004), *Towards Non-violence and Dialogue Culture in South East Europe.* Sofia: East-West.

Nozzoli, G. and Paoletti, P.M. (1966), *La Zanzara. Cronaca e documenti di uno scandalo* (La Zanzara. Chronacle and Documents of a Scandal), Milano: Feltrinelli.

Piccone Stella, S. (1993), *La prima generazione* (The First Generation), Milano: Angeli.

Pilkington, H., Omel'chenko, E., Flynn, M., Bliudina, U. and Starkova, E. (2002), *Looking West? Cultural Globalization and Russian Youth Cultures.* University Park, PA: The Pennsylvania State University Press.

Ricolfi, L. and Sciolla, L. (1980), *Senza padri né maestri* (Without Fathers or Teachers), Bari: De Donato.

Ricolfi, L., Scamuzzi, S. and Sciolla, L. (1988), *Essere giovani a Torino* (Being Young in Turin), Torino: Rosenberg and Sellier.

Roberts, K., Fagan, C., Tolen, J., Machacek, L., Kovatcheva, S., Jung, B., Kurzynowski, A., Szumblicz, T. and Foti, K. (2000) 'The New East's New Businesses: Heart of the Labour Market Problem and/or Part of the Solution?', *Journal for East European Management Studies*, 5, No. 1, pp. 64–76.

Saarniit, J. (1998), Value change and value marginality of a generation: Ethnic differences in communist and post-communist Estonia. In H. Helve (ed), *Unification and Marginalisation of Young People. Youth Research 2000 Programme. The Finnish Youth Research Society.* Helsinki: Hakapaino, pp. 43–66.

Sak, P. (1997), 'Drugs and Values: Generation Aspects', paper presented at the European Sociological Association Conference 20th Century Europe: Inclusions/Exclusions, Colchester, UK, 27–30 August 1997.

Santambrogio, A. (2002), *Le rappresentazioni sociali dei giovani in Italia: alcune ipotesi interpretative* (Social Representations of Young People In Italy: Some Interpretative Hypotheses), in F. Crespi (ed.) *Le rappresentazioni dei giovani in Italia* (Representations of Young People in Italy), 15–39. Roma: Carocci.

Scanagatta, S. (1984), *Giovani e progetto sommerso* (Young People and Hidden Plans), Bologna: Patron.

Scarpati, R. (ed.) (1973), *La condizione giovanile in Italia* (The Condition of Youth in Italy), Milano: Angeli.

Semenova, V. (1999), 'Gipoteza o vozmoznom konflikte molodeznih kogort na rinke truda v blizajshie godi' (The Hypothesis of the Possible Conflict between Youth Cohorts in the Labour Market in Recent Years), in Z. Golenkova (ed.) *Sozialnoe razsloenie I sozialnaja mobilnost* (Social Stratification and Social Mobility), Moscow: Nauka.

Sokolowska, M. and Richard, A. (1990), 'Alternatives in the Health Area: Poland in Comparative Perspective', in: B. Deacon and J. Szalai (eds.) *Social Policy in the New Eastern Europe*, Aldershot: Avebury.

Sorlini, C. (1977), *Centri sociali autogestiti e circoli proletari giovanili di Milano* (Self-run Social Centers and Proletarian Youth Circles in Milan), Milano: Feltrinelli.

Stafseng, O. (1994), *Associated Youth in Europe. Selected Reports on Czechnia, Germany, Slovakia and Norway*, Oslo: UNGforsk.

Stefanov, M. (1983a), 'Studentskata mladez v Bulgaria I svetovnijat mir' (Academic Youth in Bulgaria and the World Peace), *Express Information*, 4, Sofia.

Stefanov, M. (1983b), *Studentite – zhizneni planove i realisatzija* (The Students – Their Life Plans and Realisation), Sofia: People's Youth Press.

Sviridon, R. (1994), 'Youth Work in Russia and Great Britain Compared', *Youth and Policy*, 44, pp. 70–109.

Titarenko, L. and Rotman, D., 'Social Portrait of Youth in a Transitional Society: The Case of Belarus', paper presented at the XIVth World Congress of Sociology, Montreal, Canada, 25 July–1 August 1998.

Tomic-Koludrovic, I. and Leburic, A., 'Lifestyle of Survival Strategy? Croation Youth in the Late 1990s', paper presented at the conference Young People in a Risk Society, Ljubjana, Slovenia, 30 November- 2 December 2000.

Topalova, V. (2000), 'Europe and European Identity Concepts of Young Bulgarians', in P.-E. Mitev (ed.) *Balkan Youth and Perception of the Other*, Sofia: LIK.

Toth, O. (1995), 'Political-Moral Attitudes amongst Young People in Post-Communist Hungary', in: L. Chisholm, P. Buchner, H-H. Kruger, and M. du Bois-Reymond (eds.) *Growing Up in Europe. Contemporary Horizons in Childhood and Youth Studies*, Berlin: Walter de Gruyter.

Ule, M. and Rener, T. (eds.) (1998), *Youth in Slovenia. New Perspectives from the Nineties*, Ljubljana: Ministry of Education and Sport, Youth Department.

Ule, M., Rener, T., Ceplak, M. and Tivadar, B. (2000), *Socialna ranlivost mladih.* (Social Vulnerability of Youth), Ljubljana: Ministry of Education and Sport, Youth Department.

Viale, G. (1978), *Il Sessantotto: Tra rivoluzione e restaurazione* (Sixty-Eight: Midst Revolution and Restoration), Milano: Mazzotta.

Willis, P. (1978), *Profane Culture*, London: Routledge and Kegan Paul.

Chapter 3

Youth Research in Africa

David Everatt

Youth Research in South Africa

Youth research in South Africa has been very closely linked to practical work amongst youth on the ground. In the early 1990s, in the immediate aftermath of the end of apartheid, a great deal of research took place. Virtually all of that work, however, was in support of moves to organize young people, and to develop policy positions on key issues such as education, job creation, welfare services and so on.

In the mid-1990s, after the ANC came into power, there was a considerable lull in both youth research and work amongst youth. The National Youth Development Forum, formed by youth structures across the country, collapsed amidst funding scandals, which further dampened attempts to generate interest in a sector. The launch of the National Youth Commission saw a considerable amount of policy-formulation work being done, but applied research into youth slowed almost to a standstill.

At the same time, attitudes towards youth began to lose some of the gains made. In the early 1990s, great headway was made in attacking notions of 'lost generation' which were created by reactionary academics and popularised by the media in the 1980s. 'Youth' had become synonymous with urban black male youth involved in political protest. As the research work of the early 1990s began to paint a more nuanced picture of young people, and one placed in a developmental rather than a political context, so the stereotypes began to fall away.

However, by the mid-1990s, in the absence of any concrete avenues for youth in the form of youth brigades or community service, coupled with a near-absence of applied research, old stereotypes have returned. It is again common to hear people talking or writing about the lost generation, and youth are once again being blamed for the situation they find themselves in.

That situation is indeed a worrying one. Rates of HIV infection are extremely high amongst young South Africans. Unemployment stands in excess of 60 per cent. Teenage pregnancies force at least a fifth of young women out of school prematurely. The situation seems set to remain bleak as South Africa enters a recession.

At the same time, however, there are some very positive signs on the horizon. Firstly, on the practical front, a great deal of work is being done to organize youth brigades which will deliver basic infrastructural needs to poverty-struck areas, while rewarding youth in the form of both a stipend and educational access. These initiatives take a number of forms, including youth brigades mentioned at the Presidential Job Summit, Reconstruction Workforce camps proposed by the Department of Public Works, and a National Community Service Initiative spearheaded by the National Youth Commission. These initiatives seem set to create paid labour for hundreds of thousands of young people, and in many instances to reward that labour with access to education, psychological counselling, self-expression fora, and so on.

Once again, as organisation amongst youth increases, so research has begun to increase. On the one hand, there are a growing number of researchers undertaking masters or doctoral theses on youth-related topics. There are also an increasing number of courses in youth work being offered at tertiary institutions, many designed and taught by Australian academic David Maunders. Youth and adolescents seem set to form the core of a new school at the University of the Witwatersrand in Johannesburg.

On the other hand, out of universities, applied research into youth is also on the increase. The National Youth Commission has commissioned a second baseline study of youth in South Africa, and all the initiatives cited above have generated smaller or larger scale work into ways of enrolling young people into public works schemes, trying to attune those schemes to the different needs of youth, and – critically – trying to educate policy formulators and government officials of the need to treat youth on their own terms and not merely as younger and more difficult adults.

We have yet to see whether any of these initiatives bear fruit on the scale and in the manner designed. However, it is clear that we are seeing something of an about-turn: negative stereotypes are coming under pressure, organisation amongst youth is increasing, and real practical opportunities are about to be made available on a large scale. The challenges now for researchers in both applied and more theoretical planes is to ensure that they ride the crest of the wave, and then maintain interest in youth once the attention of politicians moves away to other equally needy groups in society.

Chapter 4

Trends in Youth Studies in (English-Speaking) North America

James Côté

Youth Studies in Canada and the United States is a rather inchoate enterprise with few networks within which to exchange ideas. For example, the American Sociology Association does not have a Youth Studies or Sociology of Youth section. Instead, it has a Child & Youth section which focuses on 'infancy to the legal majority' (http://www.asanet.org/sections/children.html; accessed Aug. 5, 2003). The journal *Youth and Society* stands as the only North American journal with 'youth' as its ostensible focus, but it now targets studies (of interest to American society) on teen pregnancy, gangs, AIDS education, adolescent substance abuse, and sexual harassment, with special interest in gay and lesbian youth, and youth and resistance. However, this journal does not carry a critical mass of researchers from a Society focused on youth issues. The Canadian Society of Sociology and Anthropology has nothing close to a Youth Studies section, and its journal the *Canadian Review of Sociology and Anthropology* rarely publishes anything of interest to youth researchers.

At the same time, Sociological Abstracts lists some 5000 articles published in (mainly American) English-language journals associated with 'the sociology of youth.' However, the concept of 'youth' itself is rarely the direct object of study in these articles as something to be explained or something that explains; rather, young people are more often studied in association with 'problems' – delinquency, risk behaviours, and education failure. More generally, there are no Library of Congress categories for 'Sociology of Youth' or 'Youth Studies,' but there are for topics like 'Youth Substance Abuse' and 'Youth Suicide.'

The reasons for this situation are varied. In the US, research tends to follow funding opportunities and funding tends to policy oriented, where a 'problem-to-be-rectified' is identified by individual researchers or government institutes and in turn massive funding initiatives are undertaken by government agencies (e.g., National Institute of Health or National Institute of Mental Health) or private foundations (e.g., William T. Grant Foundation). Moreover, there is no national youth policy in the US or a recognition of youth as an age category in need of special policies (in contrast to the elderly, for whom massive reforms have been undertaken in the last 30 years). Hence, we find the focus on specific 'youth problems' identified above, rather than on the overall situation confronting young people as an interest group or a disadvantaged group with special needs. This has tended to result in a 'psychologizing' of youth circumstances, where reactions to difficulties are seen to have individual rather than structural causes, drawing psychologists to the burgeoning field of 'adolescence' (more below).

In Canada, much university-research funding is also policy-oriented (as dictated by the Social Sciences and Humanities Research Council of Canada), but most major studies are undertaken by Statistics Canada and Health Canada (which limit their methodologies to survey research), although university youth researchers are sometimes consulted. There are only two sociology journals in Canada (which favour mainstream topics and methodologies), so English-speaking Canadian sociologists generally follow American trends and publish in American journals.

The situation in Canada and the US stands in contrast to the situation in others like the UK, Australia, and the Nordic nations, where there are national youth policies and nationally funded youth councils and ministries. It appears that national priorities, collective anxieties, and funding opportunities tend to drive research activities more that vice versa. It might also be the case that North American youth researchers are simply not as active in influencing policy and government priorities as in the above-mentioned countries. With few exceptions found in several small university Centres and programmes, youth researchers tend to work in isolation, often studying youth as one of several research interests. Without societies like the Nordic Youth Research Information Symposium in Europe, there seems not to be a driving force that organizes research activities to influence social change.

If we were to expand the definition of 'youth studies' to include 'adolescent psychology,' we would find a much more vibrant and organized field. The Society for Research on Adolescence, based in the US but with an international membership, boasts some 1100 active members with biennial conferences attended by more than this number. This society is dominated by psychologists, however, with only a couple of dozen members who identify themselves as sociologists. The topic areas covered at SRA conferences are mainly those of interest to academic and applied psychologists.

The choice of the concept of 'adolescence' as the rallying point tends to be a disciplinary marker, with sociologists preferring the more general term 'youth,' and frowning on the reification associated with essentializing this age period. Psychologists find the term 'youth' vague, however, partly because of its common usage, which includes children as in the above ASA usage. A recent move has been to suggest that what was generally referred to as late adolescence and post-adolescence as 'emerging adulthood' (Arnett, 2001), but this too could constitute an inappropriate reification if it is indiscriminately applied.

At the same time, it is not always clear what sociologists mean by 'youth,' with some seeing it as a 'post-adolescent' phenomenon (e.g., Gauthier and Pacom, 2001), and others including the entire period between childhood and adulthood. Indeed, one of the most serious issues in the field is determining just what constitutes 'youth,' and how researchers should approach its study (e.g., as youth advocates who identify with young people, or as concerned adults who feel they should guide young people). One American journal circumvented the definitional problem from its beginning by taking the name *Journal of Youth and Adolescence*, but its primary allegiance is with psychiatry and the biological sciences.

The most recent shifts in research focus include those found in youth studies in other parts of the world, encompassing issues associated with gender and sexuality, race and ethnicity, and various forms of marginalization. Methodologically, qualitative techniques have become more popular, along with studies that combine qualitative and quantitative approaches. Postmodernism has also had some impact as a driving force behind many of the studies promoting the above new areas of research focus, supplanting other critical perspectives such as critical-materialism and Marxism (indeed, there is a continuing tension between postmodernist and Marxist approaches, with each seeing the other as 'conservative' in key respects that prevent advances in the field). At the same time, more mainstream functionalist-policy theoretical approaches prevail (especially encouraged by funding policies, as above), and quantitative-statistical approaches continue to grow in sophistication, with techniques like structural equation modelling becoming common place.

The future of youth studies in (English-speaking) North America should be one of continual growth, especially as the transition to adulthood continues to grow in duration, and as researchers and theorists find each other. Perhaps local organizations and Centres will be the catalyst for this, but it is also possible that inspiration will be taken from youth researchers elsewhere. In particular, the International Sociological Association, Sociology of Youth Research Committee (34), which currently has only a few North American members, might be able to make inroads into this growing field if the appropriate networks are established around issues of common interest.

References

Arnett, J. (2001), *Adolescence and emerging adulthood: A cultural approach,* Upper Saddle River, NJ: Prentice Hall.
Gauthier, M. and Pacom, D. (eds.) (2001), *Spotlight on ... Canadian Youth Research*, Les editions de l'IRQC, 2001.

Chapter 5

The Socio-Cultural Construction of Youth in Latin America: Achievements and Failures

Carles Feixa Pampols and Yanko González Cangas

One of the conclusions of the conference 'The child and the young in Latin America' (*'A criança e o jovem na America Latina'*), held in Marilia (Brasil) in November 2001, organized by ISA, was the need to reconceptualise childhood and youth from a Latin American perspective (geographically, academically and culturally), tackling new ways of envisaging and experiencing both of those vital ages according to what the change of millennium is bringing along (Feixa, 2002). Most of the social science literature about the history of childhood and youth has been produced according to the western reality, which has brought an ethnocentric nuance to the concepts. From Ariès' (1973) classical work, who collected his data from the Medieval and modern France, to the more recent anthology edited by Levi and Schmitt (1996), and other relevant works of childhood and youth social history (Gillis 1981; Kett 1978, Postman 1990; Mitterauer 1986; Griffin 1993), the theories about the historical invention of childhood and youth have been almost exclusively based upon western sources (to be more precise, central European and Anglo-Saxon sources).

Context for a Debate: An Historical and Trans-Cultural Perspective

In the Latin American context, the beginnings of attention toward youth are traced back to the first decades of the twentieth century (González 2002a, 2002b). A period that could be labelled as being 'essay-like', 'speculative' or 'creative' according to the nature of the authors and the works they produced. Most of the so-called 'Latin American nationalist' intellectuals and their emancipating, prescriptive or edifying essays about youth can be found in this period. Some of the main authors are J.E. Rodó, with *Ariel* (1900) devoted to 'the young people of America', J. Ingenieros with *El hombre mediocre* (1913), J. Vasconcelos with his manifold essays and letters (1924), J. C. Mariátegui with his 'La Reforma Universitaria' included in *Siete ensayos de interpretación de la realidad peruana* (1928), or V. Huidobro with his articles and letters (1925a, 1925b). These are works and authors that used words to spread the renown of youth. This process was interrupted by the arrival and legitimacy of positivism in social sciences, especially in psychology.

Since the 1930s A. Ponce appears as an emblematic 'social scientist' with his works *Sicología de la adolescencia* (1938) and *Ambición y angustia de los adolescentes* (1939). His works converge with most of the research being carried out in the USA and Europe at the beginning of the century in this discipline (the most remarkable influence on Ponce is the work by S.G. Hall and the works about infant and youth psychology by Piaget and Spranger). The theoretical approaches adopted by various researchers from the 50s and 60s, within the period of the modernization are imbued of a stigmatising North-American structural-functionalism or of an instrumental sociological Marxism. The functionalism was striving to normalise 'dysfunctional or diverted young people' (derived from industrialising and rural-urban migration processes); while the Marxism was focused on class awareness, intervention and promotion of youth movements (basically student ones). It can be argued that later Latin American scientific studies about youth cover a wide range of disciplines, from psychological to sociological perspectives. The first – based on E. Erikson's (1959, 1971) work – try to explain individual phenomena within the process of 'construction' and search of the self-identity and physiological changes. Sociological perspectives are influenced by the structural-functionalist tradition, mostly by T. Parsons and R. Merton's works, who had a big presence in Latin America during the 50s and who identified youth in terms of 'problem'. It became relatively mechanical for them to apply concepts such as 'deviant' or 'dysfunctional' to a group of young people whom adult society were concerned about: young immigrants, young offenders, young alcoholic, revolutionaries, 'hippies' or 'rebels'. Nevertheless, all contributions put forward enough concepts as to understand the period of youth as a form of socialisation and preparation for the adultness.

With the advent of the social and 'emancipating' movements in the 1960s and 1970s, studies about youth started to become broader and more institutionalised. It is basically sociology that, under the auspices of the Latin American Institute of Economic and Social Planning (ILPES) depending on CEPAL (Economic Commission For Latin América) 'officially' took on the subject of youth studies. The first scientific studies were carried out by Echevarría (1967), Mattelart (1970), Solari (1971), and Gurrieri, Torres-Rivas et al. (1971). Most of these studies were focused on youth integration processes and social development, and trying to add Latin American youth to modernising projects. A big emphasis was also detected in the political and ideological searches of youth, especially with students. Studies about university reform, and continental and world political processes from the perspective of university youth absorbed most of the attention of these social researchers. After the first comprehensive studies carried out by Solari (1967, 1971), Michelena and Sonntag (1970), and Dooner (1974), among others, regional studies followed later. But it is clear that this kind of research has been developing until today.

Until the International Year of Youth was proclaimed by the UN in 1985, the generational dimension had been ignored. Subjects of socio-cultural studies about indigenous, rural and urban communities had been envisaged as Indians, farmers, colonial farmers, men, women, bourgeois, workers, but not as children and even less as young people. The traditional explanation to these socio-historical omissions unveils the non-existence of the categories of childhood and youth in Latin American societies beyond among some social (elites and middle classes) and territorial (urban areas) minorities. This fact is based upon the general belief that the vast majority of Latin Americans belonging to subaltern classes and cultures have a very early entry to adult life in labour and sexual terms. This could explain that, unlike in Europe, child and youth studies are not separate fields of study in Latin America. With the emergence of urban popular youth movements in the second half of the 80s and the increase of studies for the mentioned International Year of Youth, these important socio-historical omissions and theoretical shortcomings are being slowly restored (Agurto, Canales, *et al.*, 1985; Margulis, 1996; Padilla, 1998; Cubides, Laverde and Valderrama, 1998; Reguillo, 2001). But some invisible actors -rural and indigenous youth, for example – that emerged due to the accelerated modernisation and cultural hybridization, still need to be systematically researched. Moreover, the historical and cultural construction of youth it has not been yet elucidated as an axial subject of research.

Although young people as social actors and identity subjects started to appear in Latin America in the beginning of the twentieth century, this was evident specially with the 1918 University Reform of Cordoba (Argentina), the intellectual production of the 'Latin American nationalists' and the candidature of the poet Vicente Huidobro for president in Chile supported by the Youth Convention *(Convención de la Juventud)*, it is also true that these expressions were a partial identity prototype, compared to the cultural diversity of the region. This prototype, illustrated by upper and middle class young males, lasted for nearly the whole twentieth century. This prototype hid (even for social researchers) cultural differences present within the Latin American national states, especially with regard to original peoples and rural societies. These groups represent a large unexplored field with regard to the diverse symbolic and material responses in the construction of youth. Although in this short space it is impossible to fill in the gaps mentioned, we will focus on a re-conceptualisation of youth in a diachronic and transcultural view. We are offering two ethnographic studies from Mexico (Feixa, 1998b) and Chile (González, 2003) as examples of the re-conceptualisation that needs to take place.

Youth in Indigenous Mexico

The 'deep Mexico' of indigenous societies (as defined by Guillermo Bonfil) presents a rich ethnographic source to begin this reconceptualisation:

> One of the features that more often strikes researchers about indigenous life is the good and respectful treatment that parents give to their children. They rarely use physical violence in the upbringing. The children's participation in family conversation is not inhibited. There is a wide margin of tolerance for premarital sexual experiences and, in certain groups homosexual relations during adolescence are tolerated … The married man is considered to be an adult, regardless of his age.
>
> (Bonfil, 1990, p. 61.)

Pacheco (1997, pp. 100–101) wrote: 'The stage of youth hardly exists in indigenous communities. From being a child, directly dependent on the family, one becomes an adult, responsible for one's own family or for one's parents' family.' Certainly, in many of the indigenous languages there is not a word that defines the youth period, or institutions, or spatial rites for this age group. When there is a denomination, it is usually synonymous of marital status (singleness) and has different names according to the sex. As a matter of fact, minors (children and young people) have tended to be invisible for anthropologic research, which has rather envisaged adult male:

> To talk about the indigenous has always implied talking about the rulers or *chamanes*, prayers or healers, artisans or *milperos*, butlers or *macehuales*. The indigenous subject of ethnological literature has nearly always been the adult male ... But to talk about the indigenous people has meant to talk very little about the Indian children; adolescent and young people, the ones that make up the future population, have not been involved either, in cultural or in economic terms. The fact that they might also have concerns about the progressive and constant worsening of their expectations of socioeconomic improvement has not been taken into consideration.
>
> (Acevedo, 1986, pp. 7–8.)

Among the Zapotecs – an indigenous community descendent from an ancient prehispanic civilization settled in the Oaxaca valley in the south of Mexico- age groups are related to the promotion through the '*sistema de cargos*' (positions system). This system is based on the organization of the Catholic Parish: every age group has a particular function in the religious and social life of the community. According to some historians (Carrasco, 1979), this system was superimposed on the old prehispanic educative institutions, like the *Telpochcalli* (the 'house of the young') of the *Aztecs*, but without its military role, social hierarchies and connections to the indigenous cosmogonies. In the words of an old Zapotec:

> At the age of ten I worked as a labourer on the ranch. You start serving from childhood, at ten. The '*mayor de vara*' (community principal) goes from home to home: 'I'm coming to tell you that your boy has to participate in collecting one third of the firewood for the coming festival'. After that we have to clean the temple ... then we must serve as assistants when we reach the age of 16 by guarding the city palace and public buildings and inside the village we make rounds, as if we were the old night watch ... Then we become butlers and we can organize the patron festival.
>
> (Don Román, quoted in Feixa, 1998b, p. 105.)

Nowadays, the situation has changed for various reasons. First, the symbols of the global youth culture reach the more isolated zones of Mexico (some kids are *paisarockers,* a kind of hybrid between peasant and rocker). Second, more than 50 per cent of the community boys migrate to the United States (the *gabacho*). When they come back (interested in visiting the family during the summer local festival or in choosing a girl for marriage) they bring along with them some cultural elements learned on the other side of Rio Grande. In the words of Ric, a 27 year-old Zapotec who lives in Los Angeles:

> Emigration has had in influence on society. It started like it did in the 75, when young people and the rich emigrated. Once the first young people got a job, the rest wanted to leave too. In 1982 and 1983 the emigration was massive. Every August festival many young people left, as a relative came and took two or three cousins away with them, then they came again at Christmas and took a couple more away. The social effect has been big. Cultural and sports activities had started to grow in this village and then they started to fade again. For instance, little groups used to gather in the corners, friends and such. You don't see this any more, they're all gone. There used to be great respect for elderly people too: they used

to shake hands. They don't do this any more. They see an adult: '-*Orale!*' Good manners, traditional greetings, are disappearing because of the influence of television. Many of these things started to come from outside, and also from people coming from the USA.

(Ric, quoted in Feixa, 1998, p. 106.)

The case of the *Huicholes* is also of significant because it illustrates the double-sideness of the indigenous youth living between two worlds (Pacheco, 1997). Located in West Sierra Madre (States of Nayarit and Jalisco), this ethnic group is composed of about 30 thousand people deeply living their alterity. They descend from the *chichimecas* who lived in North West Mexico since the pre-Hispanic time. During the first five years of life, *Huichole* children celebrate the *Tatei Nayeri*, a feast in honour of the fruits of the earth, where children are presented to gods. By celebrating five feasts, the *nonutzi* (child) has more possibilities to survive and becomes an *uko* or *muchachito* (boy). From this time on, young people join the daily work assigned to each gender: girls learn the house tasks together with the rest of the women of the family and boys learn the tasks of the field with the men. The group singers or *marakame* (adults with magic-religious power), decide the young men's occupation and predetermine them for certain jobs: musician, hunter, healer or farmer. Since the prediction has a divine origin, they can't escape it or if they try they are subject to illnesses and misfortune.

Girls are considered women from the age of eight, and are reserved for a marriage arranged by parents. Sometimes an old singer can ask for them in marriage, which is an honour for the parents. Young women have no individuality, which is exemplified by the fact that they can be exchanged: when an engaged woman decides to defy her parents and choose another man and run away, her place is occupied by a sister. If the marriage is accepted, it happens when the girl is about fifteen, and then an engagement ceremony takes place, which requires the future groom to carry firewood to her house for five days and on the sixth day they close the agreement by smoking a cigar (tobacco is a sign of sexual maturity among men). Nowadays, *Huichole* communities are in transition. In communities near urban areas, young people are questioning their role. When they reach adolescence, a way to show disagreement is to run away from their parents' home. The 'double side of young people's daily life' is thus expressed: they are caught between tradition and the wider society: 'The *Huicholes'* passing through the Earth is related to what goes on in the five courses of their cosmogony. A young *huichole* has the cultural heritage of the specific community he or she belongs to, and reproduces the specific *huichole* culture. To be young means to be in the process of developing one's identity' (Pacheco, 1997, pp. 111–2.)

Youth in Rural Chile

In the wide range of societies based on agriculture consisting of farming and forest activities, subordinated to wider nation-state structures and urban areas, young people usually experience a period of social dependency, which means an early entry into the labour system and a subordinated status as a young person within the family unit. Given the domestic nature of the units of production and consumption, everything is structured according to the material and moral reproduction in the family. The patriarchal domination of the family's women and young people is expressed by the systems of heritage and sexual control. Paradoxically, young people, who constitute a fundamental labour strength, have no prestige or power. As compensation, they occupy a central place in the community amusement sector and they very often participate in many aspects of the festive life (patron saint's celebrations) or leisure activities (sports groups). The preliminary results of our research based on generation life stories since the first decades of the twentieth century on until nowadays, at the small coastal rural community of *Chaihuín* (Region of Los Lagos, Chile) show abundant evidence of a youth identity in transformation, reaching from youth based on the life cycle, through a generational identity, to the beginning stage of a youth culture.

The late 1990s is coloured by high migration, and the arrival of electricity, mass media, roads, means of transportation and tourism. Edgardo, one of the 'biologically' youngest actors interviewed (17 years of age) thinks over these transformations in the context of his conversion to the 'metal' youth style:

> I don't behave like a peasant, but I feel I am from here. Now you can like Metallica and be a rural man, it's not such a change. When I grew up here we were not as uncivilised as when my parents grew up. For example, they didn't have a radio and couldn't listen to music. They knew nothing about groups. They heard about an artist, and they didn't care, they knew nothing about him. They never listened to music until their twenties, when they had a *victrola* (manual phonograph).
>
> (González, 2003, p. 596.)

Edgardo talks about 'youth groups' in the community, made up by 'a few [young] boys' whom he identifies as '*Cumbiancheros*' (who like 'cumbia sound' music), '*Hiphoperos*', '*Metaleros*' and 'normal'. He also describes their aesthetic taste, social practices and *locus* of youth expression, like the recently open pool business, *Taca-tacas* (table football) and table tennis, where the young people meet at weekends. But he also states the struggle within his family between his adscription to metal culture – considered to be demoniac by his evangelical (Protestant) mother – and his transit back to the group of 'normal'. Heriberto's biographical testimony is quite different. His short youth takes place at the beginning of the 1980s, at the beginning of the community's structural transformation, when he left the community for two months for a neighbour village to take a diving course. He then had the opportunity to participate in a different youth culture, going to bars and discos:

> I think that I only lived youth when I took the course on seafood diving in the village ... I went with a few friends to the *Loloteca*, to listen to music, sing and dance. It was pure youth there, pure *cabros* ... On the first day we left the place feeling dizzy, because it was dark inside, and there were those lights going up and down and turning round. Then we came back to *Chaihuín*, nearly poisoned with alcohol from so much *carretear* (partying) ... then I joined my lady, and from then on all snag [work].
>
> (González, 2003, p. 479.)

The community's material and symbolic constrictions on the young disappear with the changing relationship between the country and the city. This is a significant example of the first *delocalized* youth identity experiences. Antecedents can be found from the 1930s to the 1970s with the abundant enrolments of young men in the army and of young women in urban domestic service. But in later decades (1980s and 1990s) these kinds of experiences have become radicalised with the neo-liberalisation of agriculture. The modernisation of transportation and communications as well as the expansion of the educational system, gave new generations access to secondary or vocational education, technical training, or labour outside the community on ships or in international factories. Most of the experiences are periodical and *delocalised*; young people come back to the community of origin and have an impact on it. This repercussion can be seen through the emergence of an imagined youth in the community. On the opposite, nearly sixty years before Edgardo had his *metal* experience, Pascual (born in the 20') knew that his transit to family emancipation and, therefore, to the end of his condition of '*cabro*' (boy-young man) had very well defined biological boundaries set by the *Chaihuín* community:

> According to the rules, a man had to be 25 to be able to get married, as he had to be a mature man who knew how to do all the things in a home ... He could not be any younger, because at the age of 18 or 20 he was still considered a child, even if he was mature, since he worked in the fields or with cattle from the age of 10 or 12.
>
> (González, 2003, p. 384.)

Singleness characterised their 'young childhood', while marriage became crucial in order to change men's socio-cultural status, something that the young men longed for. For 25 years the children/young men were dominated by their fathers despite doing hard labour. However, the award for this dependency and dominations meant in most cases that the men were given land and material to build a house.

Discussion

These stories are only male stories and it would take a much deeper contextualisation to understand them as a whole. It is relevant though, that these testimonies come from a rather 'classical' rural community from the point of view of its structural definition: relatively isolated, main occupations being agriculture and artisan fishing (with a peasant economy), little availability of services, limited population, etc. But they are imbued in a fast process of cultural hybridisation that has produced eclectic responses, as far as youth identity is concerned. Developing a youth identity happens under strong tensions between the urban symbolic goods and the rural structural contractions, like in our second case, with an early start of wage earning labour (fishing and farming jobs) and the temporary leaving for a job or training, still taking place today. Thus, the testimonies clearly exemplify the harsh transformations of youth identity *locus* and the cultural and material resources to live it. But, at least from a biographical point of view, the traces of their youth identities can be seen both on a subjective level and on a societal level.

Modernising transformations appear to be very significant in the construction of rural youth as social actors, both in the city, in rural spaces and their relationships. The mercantilist turn or 'modernisation' of agriculture (Gómez and Echenique, 1988), the consolidation of agro-industry and business and, most of all, the top down proletarian tendency and the weakening of wide subordinated agricultural sectors (peasants and fishermen with self-subsistence economies), all those factors have provoked a process of increased visibility for researchers and planners, and, simultaneously, young people express themselves more intensely in the context of capitalist agriculture than in peasant economies or self subsistence economies. This is demonstrated by the organisation of production and commercialisation cooperatives, micro-companies and other organisations lead and composed by young people that claim their condition as such: in the case of Chile, the '*Servicio Rural Joven*' ('Young Rural Service') of INDAP or at a Latin American level, the manifold associations affiliated to the Latin American network of Rural Youth RELAJUR). But 'rural-urban' frictions start to unveil not only the young people who are organized in the rural context, but also the subordinated and more marginalized ones. It also unveils those whose youth has only arrived, without material places to live it, unemployed or sub-occupied, and without any lands or capital. (Rama, 1986, p. 114.)

References

Acevedo, C. (1986), *Estudios sobre el ciclo vital*, México: INAH.
Agurto, I., Canales, M. *et al.* (1985), *Razones y Subversiones,* Santiago: ECO/FOLICO/ SEPADE.
Ariès, P. (1973), *L'enfant et la vie familiale sous l'ancien régime*, Paris: Seuil.
Bonfil, G. (1990), *México profundo*, México: Grijalbo.
Cubides, H. J., Laverde, M. C. and Valderrama, C. E. (eds.), (1998), '*Viviendo a toda'. Jóvenes, territorios culturales y nuevas sensibilidades*, Santafé de Bogotá: Fundación Universidad Central.
Carrasco, P. (1979), 'La jerarquía cívicorreligiosa en las comunidades de Mesoamérica'. In J. R. Llobera (ed.), *Antropología Política*, Barcelona: Anagrama, pp. 323–340.
Dooner, P. (1974), *Los Movimientos Universitarios*. Santiago: Corporación de Promoción Universitaria, CPU.
Erikson, E. (1959), *Identity, and the life cycle,* New York: International University Press.
Erikson, E. (1971), *Identidad, Juventud y Crisis*, Buenos Aires: Paidós. [*Identity: Youth, and Crisis*, New York, 1968].
Feixa, C. (1988), *La tribu juvenil. Una aproximación transcultural a la juventud*, Torino: L'Occhiello.
Feixa, C. (1998a), *De jóvenes, bandas y tribus*, Barcelona: Ariel.
Feixa, C. (1998b), *El reloj de Arena: Culturas juveniles en México*, México: Causa Joven.
Feixa, C. (2002), 'La construcción social de la infancia y la juventud en América Latina', Reijal (Red de Estudios sobre Infancia y Juventud de America Latina), Universidade Estadual de Sao Paulo (Brasil). Retrieved from www.marilia.unesp.br/seminario/ reijal.html.
Gillis, J. R. (1981), *Youth and History. Tradition and Change in European Age Relations, 1770-present*, New York: Academic Press.
Gómez, S. and Echeñique, J. (1988), *La agricultura Chilena. Las dos caras de la modernización*, Santiago: FLACSO.
González, Y. (2002a), ''Que los Viejos se Vayan a Sus Casas'. Juventud y Vanguardias en Chile y América Latina', in C. Feixa, C. Costa and J. Saura, (eds.), *Movimientos Juveniles. De la globalización a la antiglobalización*, Barcelona: Ariel, pp. 59–91.
González, Y. (2002b), *Privilegio y Omisión: Identidades Juveniles en Chile. (De las vanguardias a las juventudes rurales)*. Unpublished Master thesis, Barcelona: Universitat Autònoma de Barcelona.

González, Y. (2004), 'Edgardo, ex metalero rural'; 'Heriberto: mi juventud duró un mes y medio' y 'Don Pascual y la ley de los veinticinco', relatos de vida. Unpublished PhD thesis, Barcelona: Universitat Autònoma de Barcelona.

Griffin, C. (1993), *Representations of Youth. The study of Youth and Adolescence in Britain and America*, London: Polity.

Gurrieri, A.and Torres-Rivas, E. et. al. (1971), *Estudios sobre la juventud marginal latinoamericana*, México: Siglo Veintiuno Editores/Editorial Universitaria.

Huidobro, V. (1925a), 'Balance Patriótico'. Diario *Acción*, 6 de agosto, pp. 1–2.

Huidobro, V. (1925b), 'Carta de Vicente Huidobro'. Revista *Espiga*, N§ 3. (Avaliable on www.uchile.cl/cultura/huidobro).

Kett, J. F. (1977), *Rites of Passage. Adolescence in America, 1790 to the present*, New York: Basic Books.

Levi, G. and Schmitt, J-C. (eds.) (1996), *Historia de los jóvenes*, Madrid: Taurus.

Margulis, M. (ed.) (1997), *La juventud es más que una palabra*, Buenos Aires: Biblos.

Mariátegui, J. C. (1988), *Siete ensayos de interpretación de la realidad Peruana*, Barcelona: Crítica-Grijalbo. [original 1928, Lima: Biblioteca Amauta].

Mattelart, M. (1970), *Juventud Chilena, Rebeldía y Conformismo*, Santiago: Universitaria.

Medina, G. (1967), *La Juventud Latinoamericana como Campo de Investigación Social*, México: Siglo XXI.

Mitterauer, M. (1986), *I giovani in Europa dal Medioevo a oggi*, Roma-Bari: Laterza.

Musgrove, F. (1964), *Youth and the Social Order*, London: Routledge and Kegan Paul.

Pacheco, L. (1997), 'La doble cotidianeidad de los Huicholes jóvenes'. *Jóvenes 4*, 100–112.

Padilla, J. (ed.) (1998), *La construcción de lo Juvenil*, México: Causa Joven.

Ponce, A. (1960), *Psicología de la Adolescencia*. México: Unión Editorial Tipográfica Hipanoamericana.

Ponce, A. (1939), *Ambición y angustia de los adolescentes,* Buenos Aires: Talleres Gráficos L. J. Rosso.

Postman, N. (1990), *The End of Childhood*. New York: Basic.

Rama, G. (1986), 'La juventud y el Futuro', *Revista de estudios sobre Juventud 20*, 109–122.

Reguillo, R. (2001), *Emergencia de culturas juveniles*, Buenos Aires: Norma.

Rodó, J. E. (1961), *Ariel*, México: Espasa-Calpe Mexicana.

Silva, M. H. and Sonntag, R. H. (1971), *Universidad, dependencia y revolución*. México: Siglo XXI.

Solari A. (1967), *Los Movimientos Estudiantiles Universitarios en América Latina,* Caracas: Monte òbvila.

Solari A. (1971), *Algunas Reflexiones Sobre la Juventud Latinoamericana,* Santiago: CEPAL/ILPES.

Vasconcelos, J. (1925), *La Raza Cósmica*, Barcelona: S/r.

Chapter 6

Contemporary Trends in Youth and Juvenile Studies in China

Jin Zhikun and Yang Xiong

The study of Chinese youth and juveniles emerged in the 1980s as a modern discipline. The Cultural Revolution between 1966 and 1976 brought great changes to the whole society, making the problems experienced by youth and juveniles more salient. After the Cultural Revolution, the whole society showed concern for the problems experienced by youth and juveniles, so relevant studies were undertaken and institutions established quickly. Since 1980, the Social Sciences research departments and the Communist Youth League system in China founded in succession more than 20 institutions engaged in studying youth and juveniles. For example, the Communist Youth League system established the Chinese Centre of the Study of Youth and Juveniles as its core, and the Social Sciences Academy system established central and local institutes for the study of youth and juveniles, including the Institute of Youth and Juvenile Studies of the Chinese Academy of Social Sciences and the Institute of Youth and Juvenile Studies of the Shanghai Academy of Social Sciences, as its representatives. From these efforts, a number of academic periodicals are now published, such as the *Youth Study* (edited by the Section of the Study of Youth and Juveniles, Sociology Institute, Chinese Academy of Social Sciences), *Contemporary Youth Study* (edited by the Institute of the Study of Youth and Juveniles, Shanghai Academy of Social Sciences), *Chinese Youth Study* (edited by the Chinese Centre of the Study of Youth and Juveniles) and the *Southern Youth Study* (edited by the Guangdong Institute of the Study of Youth and Juveniles).

The study of contemporary youth and juveniles in China attaches importance to application and countermeasure topics. With the end of the Cultural Revolution, the research focused on employment problems, marriage, values, social ideas, delinquency, and the problem of moral education with regard to youth and juveniles. Researchers developed a series of countermeasure studies in these areas. Entering the 1990s, due to the great changes in the Chinese society, the whole society shifted from a planned economy system to a market economy system, from a traditional society to a modern society. Accordingly, the study of youth and juveniles became more holistic and in-depth. The research orientation not only started from actual issues, but paid greater attention to the macroscopic and integrated development of the Chinese society, studying youth and juveniles from how they meet the demand of social development from the angle of overall human development. The issues the study of youth and juveniles dealt with in the past twenty years include both the issues specific to different ages in the whole course of the emergence and development of youth groups and the issues of the youth groups with different identities. At present, the foci of the study of Chinese youth and juveniles are the issues related to the development of youth and juveniles in the modernization process, such as the study of raising the quality of youth and juveniles, tapping human resources among youth and juveniles, and so on.

Moreover, the study of youth culture and young people's ways of thinking has special significance. China's reforms and open policy create conditions for the exchange between Eastern and Western cultures, and also pose questions of how to absorb the ideological, cultural and scientific modes of thinking in the world while carrying forward the traditions of the national culture, and of how to produce China's own new cultural and rational modes of thinking. In addition, the sphere of research interests includes various new issues in the society, such as problem of disadvantaged groups of youth and juveniles spawned by imbalanced social development. Targeted on the salient problems of youth and juveniles, scholars analyse, study and explore their causes and evaluate their developmental trends and practical significance. This provides the governmental departments concerned with sources for making relevant youth and juvenile policy, and promote actively the development of youth and juvenile work in China.

But as the study of youth and juveniles started later than in other parts of the world, a lot of work in disciplinary construction and topic application is left to be done. To meet the need of teaching, the academics compiled in the 1990's a batch of theoretical writings such as *Youth Studies, Modern Youth Studies, Youth Sociology,* and *Youth Psychology.* But these writings, as a whole, make merely a periodic disentanglement, far from being ideal when judged for theoretical profoundness. And, the specialties and courses offered in institutions of higher learning are rather limited. Obviously, how to further open up original theories in the study of youth and juveniles and probe into the basic theories in the study of youth and juveniles on the basis of applied studies is still a research task requiring further effort by scholars studying Chinese youth. Chinese youth scholars are working on further developing theories based on applied research as well as vice versa.

In regard to the research methods, the study of youth and juveniles, as a new discipline, adopts not only the traditional empirical study applying many sociological investigatory patterns, but also the research methods specific to other disciplines such as psychology, education, ethics, jurisprudence, cultural anthropology and cerebral science, thereby enriching the results of the overall study of youth and juveniles.

Since the establishment of the Sociology of Youth Research Committee of the International Sociological Association in 1992, China has embraced international exchange in youth study and international comparative study. Since 1993 China has held six international academic seminars in Shanghai and other cities. The international exchange of ideas and experiences has been helpful in developing the field of youth research in China.

Chapter 7

Youth Research in Australia and New Zealand

Johanna Wyn

Youth research in Australia and New Zealand is influenced by the distinctive environment in which it is undertaken. Australia is a large, sparsely populated continent and a population of approximately 19 million people, who live in cities and regional towns, largely concentrated on the coastal fringe. New Zealand consists of two main islands, and has a relatively small population of approximately 4 million people. While they are both migrant societies that have Indigenous populations, the different historical origins and subsequent social and economic development between the two countries means that today there are both historic and contemporary differences that impact on young people's lives. Yet young people in Australia and New Zealand do share some common circumstances. They have grown up in English-speaking countries in the Pacific that were colonized during the 1800s. Young people born in the early 1970s in Australia and New Zealand are shaping their lives in the context of significant changes to many aspects of life that the preceding generation took for granted. In Australia,

> They would have come to the end of their compulsory years of schooling in the mid-1980s at a time when the youth labour market was in a state of collapse. Thus would have stayed on at school as a member of the *first* generation in which the *majority* actually completed their secondary schooling. At the age of 17 or 18 they would have been confronted with a shift in public attitudes about education. By the 1980s, there was an expectation that young people needed further education and training to escape continuing high and long-term unemployment rates for young adults with only a high school qualification. Even university graduates with jobs would be experiencing employment uncertainty about their long-term career prospects in a more 'flexible' restructured workforce. By the time they were completing these further studies and juggling a part-time job at the same time, they and their younger siblings would be faced with the prospect of paying increasing university fees. Of necessity they are actively and positively developing their own responses to these circumstances.
>
> (Dwyer and Wyn, 2001, pp. 77–78.)

Hence, one of the dominant themes of youth research in this region is the goal of understanding the effects of social change on young people's lives. This involves examining shifts in the way that individuals relate to social institutions, especially family, labour markets, and education. Understanding social change has also resulted in a rethinking of the way in which traditional social divisions of class, gender, race, ethnicity and location are conceptualised. In this respect, the issues and trends that youth researchers in this part of the world focus on are similar to those in other developed countries. For example, over the last quarter of a century there has been a focus on the effects of the loss of a full-time labour market for young people and the striking increase in part-time jobs for young people. The shift towards a human capital approach to education and the production of educationally credentialled, 'high skill' workers has also been a strong theme. Hence, youth research has focused on the processes of transition, from school to work and into adulthood, as they are experienced by young people from rural and urban locations, by young women and young men and by young Indigenous people.

At the same time, research has been conducted into associated problem areas related to relationships, health and juvenile justice. These include research into homelessness, drug taking, crime and delinquency. While a focus on youth problems is also evident, youth researchers have largely resisted the temptation to frame research from a 'youth at risk' perspective. Indeed, one of the themes that emerges within youth research in Australia and New Zealand is a consistent body of work seeking to reveal the diversity that exists within the 'mainstream' and to question the assumptions underlying the concept of 'youth at risk' and the 'rediscovery' of youth problems (Kelly, 2001).

The resistance to defining youth as a problem group is especially apparent in research on young Indigenous people and particularly research conducted by Indigenous researchers. The relationship between the government of the country and the first nations people who occupied the land before the arrival of Europeans, (Maori in New Zealand and Aboriginal and Torres Strait Islander people in Australia), has some crucial differences between Australian and New Zealand. The New Zealand government recognises the rights of the Maori people to their land and culture through the Treaty of Waitangi. The Australian government has yet to recognise the land rights of its Indigenous people. It has no treaty with them and few mechanisms to bring about the reconciliation between its Indigenous and immigrant peoples. This difference inevitably has an impact on the lives of young Indigenous people, and on the way in which research on their lives is conducted.

New Zealand research on youth is characterised by the emergence of integrated, national research programs on Maori and Pakeha (non-Maori) youth. The work of the International Research Institute for Maori and Indigenous Education at the University of Auckland, for example, has played a leading role in establishing a tradition of research on the lives of young New Zealanders (Smith et. al, 2002). Their research program *Youth First*, a national study of youth in five provincial towns across the country, focused on obtaining the diversity of young people's views and experiences of growing up. The study was informed by five 'starting points':

- Economic restructuring, state sector reform and more specifically educational reforms have had a dramatic impact on young people's lives.
- Discourses of youth at risk have led to an over emphasis on singular 'issues' that obscure deeper questions about youth as citizens.
- Youth at risk approaches were deeply racialized and links that were being drawn for example between Maori culture and rising suicide rates amongst Maori youth were dangerously self-fulfilling, under theorized and most likely wrong.

- The voices of youth were a missing and silenced component of policies and practices that were being promoted for their 'best interests' and their 'futures'.
- Youth have insightful views and analyses of how society, have solutions to offer and would be willing to voice those if invited (Smith et. al. 2000: 170).

Drawing on these assumptions, the *Youth First* research program has generated insights into what it means to be a young New Zealander at this point in time. The research emphasises the importance of listening to young people and of developing methodologies that enable this to happen. They found that young New Zealanders from very different backgrounds felt that they were not able to participate as citizens in the public domain and that there were high levels of anxiety about their futures. One of the most important findings of the study is the wide diversity of experiences, identities and pathways towards adulthood. They found that young people have 'multiple identities' and are actively engaged in shaping futures in which some of the traditional dichotomies (such as rural/urban) have less salience and others have a shifting meaning (such as Maori/Pakeha).

In Australia, research on young Indigenous people has tended to be framed by agendas that take up the more urgent issue of health for the future of Indigenous Australians (Anderson, 2001; Hammill, 2002). However, research on Australian Indigenous youth conducted by Aboriginal researchers (for example, Palmer and Collard, 1993; Palmer, 1999), has generated important insights into the experiences of Aboriginal youth. Importantly, much of this research provides a challenge to traditional understandings inherited through developmental psychology, of growing up as a process of increasing 'independence'. Instead, young Indigenous Australians must progressively learn more about the complex and rich connections they have with their people and environment. Growing up means learning about their 'interdependence' within a complex matrix of kin and environmental relationships and responsibilities – rather than becoming 'independent'. Aboriginal researchers have tended to be critical of the way in which youth research has categorised Aboriginal youth as problems to society and as victims of change. Palmer has pointed out that research that problematises Aboriginal youth contributes to discourses that construct young Aboriginal people as powerless victims that push their own, more positive priorities to the side. However, referring to Western Australian Aboriginal youth who are called Nyungars, he reflects that

> While discourses on Aboriginal youth subcultures can and do get used to transform governance in ways that do further violence to young Nyungars, the same kinds of discourse can be and are also used by Nyungars in strategic ways to wield power and influence the rule of government, putting tremendous pressure on governments to increase resources and other support (1999, pp. 117–118).

There are many examples of youth research that is positioned to engage with current policy concerns and contribute to policy debates. Several examples of this type of youth research are referred to in this article. Youth researchers identify out-moded assumptions in youth and education policy, systematic mis-matches between youth policy and young people's lives, the failure of governments and institutions to involve youth as participants, and the enduring effects of class, gender and race on young people's outcomes from education.

In the field of youth research more generally, one of the recurring themes over the last decade has been the dissatisfaction felt by many youth researchers with traditional approaches to youth research. In *Rethinking Youth* for example, Wyn and White (1997) have argued that the concepts of youth and of adulthood only have meaning within their local and historical context. They challenge many of the assumptions about youth as a period of life that have been inherited from developmental psychology about the process of growing up and about the nature of 'youth'. In particular, they argue that youth is a 'relational' concept that draws its meaning from the ways in which both 'childhood' and 'adulthood' are conceptualised. *Youth, Education and Risk* (Dwyer and Wyn, 2001) builds on these ideas, drawing on the *Life-Patterns* project of the Australian Youth Research Centre, which analysed the experiences of a cohort of young people for ten years (from the ages of 17 to 27). This study provides evidence that youth is not experienced as a linear progression towards adulthood. Like researchers in many other countries, the *Life-Patterns* study found that young people were not 'growing up' in exactly the same way that the previous generation had. The research challenges the view that these young people's patterns of living and changed priorities are simply evidence of delayed entry into adulthood or faulty transitions. *Youth, Education and Risk* instead presents the argument that the perspectives and choices of these young people should be understood as the effects of social change (and not simply generational change). In subsequent work, the authors argue that rather than 'prolonged transitions' through youth, we are seeing a pattern for early entry into a 'new adulthood':

> Different research traditions have made helpful contributions to our understanding of how much has changed in the transition from youth to adulthood. Nevertheless, after reviewing the range of competing theories about the disruptions of youth transitions, we are convinced that it is time to move on from preoccupations with 'faulty' transitions to an investigation of what young people are able to tell us about their own informed adult choices. We need to concentrate much more on what we can learn from our respondents about:
>
> - the choices they have made for themselves in coming to terms with the adult world; and
> - what shape they envisage their adult lives are likely to take in the future

(Dwyer et. al. 2003.)

These questions have also been taken up in New Zealand where youth researchers have found that there is a mis-match between the assumptions about linear transitions and pathways through education and training and into employment and the actual experiences of young people. Higgins (2002), for example, argues that young New Zealanders are managing their own transition processes in the face of uncertainty in the labour markets, resulting in complex, multifaceted transition processes. She concludes that the development of effective education and training policies in New Zealand will be enhanced by understanding the experiences of transition by New Zealand youth.

Across the wide field of youth research in Australia and New Zealand, the focus on understanding the effects of social change has produced important research on the shaping of new identities and the re-shaping of older social relations. In Australia, Julie McLeod and Lyn Yates have produced important insights into the shaping of new class identities. Based on longitudinal research in different school settings with young people that started when they were aged 12 and followed them through to the age of 18, their research confronts the analytic difficulties faced in representing the effects of social class relations amongst young people in Australia in the 1990s. As they comment:

> For the *12 to 18 Project*, a project concerned with identity, biography, educational and social inequalities, any one of these discussions suggests "class" to be an issue which may be highly salient but which is also problematic. The issue of whether class is a relevant category of representation and analysis enters into consideration of the following:
>
> - How do we represent the meanings, constructions, values, imperatives that each individual subject is working with?
> - How do we understand their engagements with schooling and the schooling/biography effects over time?
> - How do we describe, (analytically) the processes and patterns of inequality, exclusion, power, social formation embedded in these young people's understandings and experiences, and how, similarly, do we think about possibilities of change?
>
> (Yates, 2000, pp. 151–152.)

Yates points out that while the large-scale statistical studies of students' outcomes from education show that socio-economic background is a significant determining factor (Teese, 2000), these broad patterns highlight the extremes (for example, disadvantaged schools or elite schools) and ignore the schools in the middle. Here, Yates argues, the *12 to 18 Project* has revealed complex patterns of meanings, identities, trajectories and outcomes for which 'class' was by no means the whole of the story. She concludes that drawing on 'class' analysis that highlights the psychology, emotions and family dynamics of class experience can obscure generational differences in the ways that personal biographies are shaped.

Other researchers are also engaging with the theme of social change. White's edited collection on youth subcultures (1999) contains a rich collection of studies about the diversity of affiliations, experiences, identities and youth spaces in Australian society. This collection of studies explicitly challenges the usefulness of the idea of a 'mainstream' of youth within Australian society. For example, Wierenga (1999) demonstrates how young people in an isolated and economically depressed rural town in Tasmania follow diverse and unexpected trajectories. She argues for the importance of 'imagined trajectories' and presents an analysis of the role of significant people in young people's lives in shaping workable 'imagined trajectories' which guide the decisions they make.

Changing subjectivities and identities is emerging as an important theme. In a forthcoming book, Harris (2004), has re-visited the issue of girlhood, providing an understanding of the new workings of old divisions and the way in which young women's lives are shaped by contemporary circumstances that provide both constraints, opportunities and new subjectivities. MacDonald has also focussed on the implications of the current context of young people's lives. Based on a study of 150 young people in Melbourne, he concludes that it is necessary to move away from older understandings of class and to explore how they construct subjectivities and identities through 'fields of relationship between actors' (1999, p. 203).

In both countries, youth research has a distinctive quality because of the ready engagement by researchers with knowledge generated in other countries. Youth researchers are receptive to and expect to be informed about contemporary thinking and empirical research about youth that from very different intellectual and political milieu and geographical locations. This broad engagement encourages a critical approach to established theoretical and methodological frameworks. In previous work, I have noted that while many studies of youth and adolescence recognise the widespread upheavals affecting all aspects of the lives of young people, many researchers continue to interpret the lives of young people with reference to the orthodoxies and norms of the past. In different countries and locations established theoretical traditions have usefully informed analysis of young people's transitions in an industrial era. It is also evident that:

> Unfortunately, along with the established success of particular frameworks of research there has also been a considerable degree of academic closure which has prevented inroads being made into the prevailing modes of thinking. Measuring new research against the established literature and the authoritative traditions of a particular nation or a particular discipline has the effect of reducing divergent evidence to what is at best a subtext or else a contextual issue that leaves the accepted wisdom intact. This certainly helps to explain why many of the studies we have examined on the same youth issues but published in different journals or different countries refer almost exclusively to a closed corpus of source material.
>
> (Dwyer and Wyn, 2001: 201–202.)

Choice of methodology makes a significant difference to the capacity of research to move beyond taken for granted theoretical thought and to open up debate. The recurring theme of youth participation in research – of researching about and also *with* young people – has resulted in a body of work that places traditional sociological theory under scrutiny and in many cases finds it wanting. Longitudinal research and research based in local communities has made important contributions to our understandings of how young people are shaping their lives and relationships. Statistical analysis of large populations is matched with in-depth case-study and ethnographic research, facilitating an awareness of how concepts such as 'family' or 'career' can come to have very different meanings for new generations. While class relations continue to be relevant, youth researchers are seeking to understand their effects, drawing selectively on Marx, Bourdieu and Giddens, but also moving beyond, in the attempt to understand the way in which 'choice biographies' are being played out (Beck and Beck-Gernsheim, 2002). Feminism remains relevant, but here too, older approaches appear to be limited in understanding the complex and changing subjectivities and identities of young men and women. While young people's lives are lived in a 'global' context, their countries' distinctive history of colonialism and its geographic location forms a distinctive backdrop. Youth researchers are taking up different positions in regard to these theoretical and methodological issues. Their work is crucial for the development of effective youth policies that enhance the well-being of all Australian and New Zealand youth. Youth research is also an important mechanism for bringing young people's voice into hearing range, for the development of understanding about how our society is changing and for the recognition of young people's citizenship.

References

Anderson, I. (2001), 'Aboriginal health, society and modeling in social epidemiology', in R. Eckersley, J. Dixon and B. Douglas (eds.), *The Social Origins of Health and Wellbeing*, Cambridge: Cambridge University Press.

Beck, U. and Beck-Gernsheim, E. (2002), *Individualization*, London: Sage.

Dwyer, P., Smith, G., Tyler, D. and Wyn, J. (2003), *Life-Patterns, Career Outcomes and Adult Choices*, Research Report 23, Melbourne: Australian Youth Research Centre.

Hammill, J. (2002), 'Aboriginal children and the future', in M. Prior (ed.), *Investing In Our Children, Developing a Research Agenda*, Canberra: Academy of the Social Sciences in Australia.

Harris, A. (2004), *Future Girl*, New York: Routledge.

Higgins, J. (2002), 'Young people and transition policies in New Zealand', *Social Policy Journal of New Zealand*, 18, 2–16.

Kelly, P. (2001), 'Youth at risk: processes of individualisation and responsibilisation in the risk society', *Discourse*, **22** (2), 23–34.

MacDonald, K. (1999), *Struggles for Subjectivity. Identity, Action and Youth Experience*, Cambridge: Cambridge University Press.

Palmer, D. and Collard, L. (1993) 'Aboriginal young people and youth subcultures', in R. White (ed.), *Youth Subcultures: Theory, History and the Australian Experience*, Hobart: National Clearinghouse for Youth Studies.

Palmer, D. (1999), 'Talking about the problems of young Nyungars', in R. White (ed.), *Australian Youth Subcultures, On the Margins and in the Mainstream*, Hobart: Australian Clearinghouse for Youth Studies.

Smith, T. L., Smith, G. H., Boler, M., Kempton, M., Ormond, A., Chueh, H. and Waetford, R. (2002), '"Do you guys hate Aucklanders too?" Youth: voicing differences from the rural heartland', *Journal of Rural Studies*, 18, 179–178.

Teese, R. (2000), *Academic Success and Social Power*, Melbourne: Melbourne University Press.

White, R. (ed.) (1999), *Australian Youth Subcultures, On the Margins and In the Mainstream*, Hobart: Australian Clearinghouse for Youth Studies.

Wierenga, A. (1999), 'Imagined trajectories. Local culture and social identity', in R. White (ed.), *Australian Youth Subcultures, On the Margins and In the Mainstream*, Hobart: Australian Clearinghouse for Youth Studies.

Wyn, J. and White, R. (1997), *Rethinking Youth*, London: Sage.

Yates, L. (2000), 'Representing "class" in qualitative research', in J. McLeod and K. Malone (eds.), *Researching Youth*, Hobart: Australian Clearinghouse for Youth Studies.

PART II
CURRENT TRENDS IN YOUTH RESEARCH

PART II
CURRENT TRENDS IN
YOUTH RESEARCH

Topic Area 1:
Education, Technology and Work

Chapter 8

Biographical Turning Points in Young People's Transitions to Work Across Europe

Manuela du Bois-Reymond and Barbara Stauber

Introduction

Within life-course research, the transition of young people to adulthood is regarded as a crucial period. Young people need to make far-reaching choices in a complex of interrelated areas of life in a relatively short time. This period has always been stressful, in a positive as well as negative way, it is even more so today because of processes of de-standardisation and individualisation. The change from industrial to post-industrial and post-traditional societies are reflected on a subjective level, where young people have to cope with uncertainties and contingencies, especially during their transition period. They have to cope with simultaneous, often contradictory shifts between dependency and independence as a result of prolonged, ambiguous and switching trajectories, which make them feel and (self-)define them as young and adult at the same time, depending on the present situation. This is what we have called the *yoyoisation* in post-traditional life-courses: linear transitions change into reversible and fragmented yoyo transitions with uncertain perspectives and outcomes (see Stauber and Walther 2002).

It is evident that the transitions and trajectories of young people in Europe depend, besides subjective patterns, on different national and cultural traditions, educational institutions, social security systems, labour markets and gender regimes – what we have named transition regimes (see Esping-Anderson 1990; Gallie and Paugham, 2000). But beyond all differences there are some overarching trends which affect the lives of all young people in contemporary Europe. They concern the rapidly increasing importance of education and *informal learning processes* to prepare the young generation for a life in knowledge societies. Therefore their *learning biographies* gain a previously underestimated relevance.

Despite the fact that youth stands high on the national and European research and on the political agenda there is yet scarce *comparative* knowledge about the variations in the transitions and trajectories of young people in the respective countries nor about the way systemic and subjective developments interfere. In EGRIS – a European network of youth researchers[1] – we want to know more about these interrelations in a comparative perspective. In our current project[2] we start from the hypothesis that *motivation to learn and engage in one's own life project* is as important a resource but is threatened through contradictions between individual needs and imperatives of the labour market. We assume that the more young people have the opportunity to participate in their learning and working environments, the more they maintain (or re-achieve) motivation.

In order to research these contradictions, we did not only investigate into the biographies of young people who have lost their motivation to learn, but also into those who, with or without promotion by favourable circumstances, are able to shape alternative transition and learning biographies – e.g. young entrepreneurs, young people with artistic prospects, or young people who combine formal and informal types of learning. We were interested in their strategies and solutions to transition problems that are encountered by all young people. Could their learning environments and learning strategies possibly give us ideas for a better institutional support of less favoured young people? We will report preliminary results of our study with the focus on the *turning points* in the *motivational careers* of these young people. With that notion we take up a well introduced concept in life-course research (Clausen, 1995; Wethington, 2002) and relate it to the learning experiences of young people. We will show the impact of participatory youth measures through which young people can make experiences which facilitate turning points in their motivational careers. We finish our contribution by pointing to the desirability of a further development of European-based youth policies.

Different Processes of Learning – Ideal-Typical Constructions

In order to explore learning processes, we distinguished two contrasting groups of young people:

- Those who have disengaged from the formal transition system and are often forced to yoyo-transitions; we call them *disengaged young people;*
- Those who have been successful in a broad and personally satisfying way by developing individual learning pathways; we call them *biographical trendsetters.*

The young people labeled as disengaged mostly had low resources and few opportunities. However, inter-country comparison showed that this group was highly heterogeneous, including young people from middle class families with post-compulsory qualifications. Biographical trendsetters generally had better starting conditions. Many of them would have been able to choose a secure and high status academic career, but instead preferred a risky and demanding way of finding out their preferences. Usually they were highly motivated in learning, above all in non-formal and informal contexts. In comparison, they had better access to formal qualifications, financial and psycho-social family support and social networks. In case their individualized learning and working careers would flop, they could always switch back to a more standard transition.

Both groups share the same distrust in formal institutions but they cope with it in different ways. Biographical trendsetters are very critical about formal education, training schemes and employment services. They prefer informal learning contexts and networks, they have a kind of strategic feeling for the value of such resources and how to combine formal and informal qualifications and support systems. In contrast, disengaged young people are less able to compensate for the lack of (enough) formal education.

While a rather comprehensive body of work refers to young people with low resources, there is hardly any empirical evidence about the learning experiences, which have brought biographical trendsetters on their way, or about the more favourable contexts they benefit from (also Heinz, 2002, p. 61). Nor is there much theoretical work done on the subject (see also Hollands, 2002, p. 160 about this lack). Such young people are cursively referred to as the new entrepreneurs or 'independents' (Leadbeater and Oakley, 1999) or 'biographical designers' (Alheit, 1996), the winners of post-Fordist flexibilisation of labor markets and the individualisation of the life-course.

To find out biographical constellations and turning points in the educational and working careers of young people, we conducted explorative individual interviews as well as focus group interviews. The sample in each research country consisted of about 30 interviewees, males and females in even proportion, asking them about their learning and working experiences, difficulties in transiting from school to further education or the labour market, about support systems like professional counseling and family help, networks of friends and other significant persons (peers), and about their ideas concerning their future life plans. In comparison with the disengaged, the trendsetters were older. We assumed that *both groups* of young people despite their different starting positions and resources would share essentially the same desire to protect their individuality against overly standardized institutional learning and training arrangements.

Ideal-Typical Constructions

Our interview analysis of both groups of young people resulted in a collection of traits and constellations. The table pictures the multifaceted reality of young people in transition with special attention to learning:

Four Biographical Constellations

Differences in learning and working biographies of young people can be traced back to different personal and institutional resources and opportunities on the one hand, and to different personal engagement and attitudes on the other hand. The first refers to *structural factors* such as the social-economic and cultural background of the family, educational level, ethnicity, gender and labour market conditions (transition regimes), the second to the *individual* person's needs and capacities to use, or fail to use, resources and opportunities. On both dimensions a person can have many or few resources and opportunities, and can display much or little personal engagement.

Combining the structural dimension of high or low resources with the subjective dimension of high or low engagement, we arrive at four biographical constellations:

- Low resources – low engagement
- High resources – high engagement
- Low resources – high engagement
- High resources –low engagement

Table 8.1 Biographical constellations of trendsetters and disengaged young people

	Biographical trendsetters	Disengaged young people
Kind of trajectory	Open for (many) alternative routes	Routes institutionally defined, often leading into blind alleys
Meaning of learning	Learning of high personal importance; transversal learning abilities; intrinsic motivation	Restricted notions of learning; externally imposed; extrinsic motivation
Meaning of work	Work as a personal project; success not primarily defined in terms of money	Work mainly defined in terms of materialistic values; few possibilities to experience other kinds of success
Flexibility and mobility on the labour market	Forced as well as voluntary	Forced
Leisure-work relation	Blending/blurring	Clear distinction
Networks and networking	Strategic use of extensive, diverse and resource-rich networks	Networks can be dense but do not provide rich resources
Attitudes towards risks	Deliberate risk-taking and risk assessment	Risk avoidance or non-deliberate risk taking
Evaluation of experiences	Also failures evaluated as important for learning	Few experiences evaluated as important for learning
Self esteem	High	Low
Social recognition	Social acceptance by others even if alternative routes are followed	Little social acceptance of routes followed or rejection or discrimination
Future and adulthood	Future is now and open; mixture of optimism and realism; desirability of reaching the status of adulthood questioned; choice biographies	Future is felt as externally imposed and closed; pessimism about goal achievement, or unrealistic expectations; adulthood connected to gendered normal biography
Family support	Neutral or high	Neutral or low or impeding

Biographical trendsetters would be expected among the group with high resources and high engagement *and* among the group with low resources but high engagement. In contrast, *disengaged young people* would be rather expected in the low resources–low engagement group while the high resources–low engagement group would represent potentially disengaged but also less precarious types.

Obviously there is much more variation and ambiguity in the life-courses of the young people than can be captured by a division in four groups. This will become clear when we analyse turning points in the motivational careers of young people. For the now we concentrate on the two extreme groups, the biographical trendsetters and the disengaged young people. Later we will look at the structurally disadvantaged but with high agency potential. It is this group for whom participatory projects can make all the difference between misleading and successful trajectories.

Low Resources – Low Engagement

When low resources accumulate, they become factual disadvantages for the young people in question. Disadvantageous conditions are above all re-structuring or disappearing labor markets. Within our research this pertains to South Italy, East Germany and Spain, parts of Belfast (United Kingdom) and Turin (Italy). Segmented access to education and training, disadvantages due to gender or ethnicity and growing up in deprived neighborhoods may accumulate in one biography. Local context must be taken into account: for example young people of Palermo won't have a chance on a vanishing labor market despite of high educational levels; and although Stuttgart is located in one of the most stable labour market regions of Germany certain quarters of the city have such a bad reputation that young people living there are stigmatized and will not get any jobs.

In most of the cases, disadvantages include a family background with poor financial, cultural and social capital including, as in the case of Romania, sheer hunger, where some young people had spent their childhood and youth in extra-familial care institutions. There are big differences between transition regimes in Northern (universalistic) and Southern (sub-protective) countries, as well as between different types of family regimes. Most Italian respondents told us about warm and supportive family ties and family networks, which might help in getting work in absence of institutional support. Young people from the Northern countries stressed family support to a lesser degree, whilst benefiting from supportive transition regimes. The lowest feelings of being supported were to be found among young people from the United Kingdom and from Ireland – both countries endowed with liberal transition regimes.

Two groups in our sample – Romanian and East German young people – had experienced the change towards a post-socialist regime; they point to an almost unbridgeable gulf between the parent and youth generation after the fall of the Berlin Wall: *We are now living in a different world.* Gender and minority status often aggravate family dependence: young female gypsies or immigrants from Africa in Portugal, Turkish and Moroccan youth in Germany and the Netherlands, travellers in Ireland, experience sharp contradictions between family expectations and their own life plans which, due to that dependency, are likely to fail.

School plays a central role in creating and reproducing disadvantage as well as disengagement with learning. Due to a lack of adequate training and employment opportunities, this does not only concern low school achievers but also high achievers, like young males and females in South Italy, Spain or Romania who are pressed to stay at school as long as possible because of closed labour markets. Complaints about school and teachers were elicited in all countries: learning is experienced as cumbersome, boring and apparently leading nowhere. Young people voiced their grievances in almost identical complaints ('too much theory and too little practice') and lacking respect of teachers ('they don't give a damn'). Rarely was school reported as a place of motivated learning; career guidance and counseling services were described as totally insufficient ('we are left alone') for getting relevant information about the (regional) labour markets. Young people suffer from the growing tension between the educational and (pre-) vocational system and the shrinking labor markets for low (or even high) qualified work. This pertains particularly to East Germany where all young people finished vocational education in the much praised dual system, but faced unemployment afterwards.

Young people, even if full of resentments against formal education, are conscious of the absolute necessity to gain formal qualifications ('without training you will not make it'). But they also know that a diploma is no guarantee for getting a job – and this experience is an important factor for their de-motivation. Young people's criticism in most countries (except Denmark with exceptionally good provisions for young people) focuses on training or employment measures for not improving chances. Many young people blame themselves for getting unemployed; their self-esteem has been lowered through many negative experiences in school and training schemes, and although they are aware of the problem as being a structural problem, they nevertheless regard failure as their own fault. Lack of family support and supportive networks add to the feeling of being trapped ('I am not worth, I haven't fulfilled expectations'). Yet, there are also attitudes of rebellion against insurmountable obstacles to get a satisfying job, for example with some young West German males who would rather leave the job than being humiliated by their boss ('I said to him: since when do we have slavery again?'). Instrumental work attitudes seem to prevail: work is mainly associated with money. Without work one is worthless. Yet beyond materialistic motives there remains a yearning for a pleasant working climate and agreeable colleagues, social acceptance, a feeling of being integrated in society (Plug and du Bois-Reymond, in press).

Many young people mention informal networks and contacts as more important for making the transition into the labor market than any particular individual ability or qualification (especially confirmed by young men from Spain, Ireland and West Germany). This illustrates their distrust in what formal education and career counseling can give them. Usually they do not have rich personal networks, and if they have, they are restricted to peers who are in the same disadvantaged position, including criminal networks (as we were told by young men from North Ireland, Ireland and West Germany).

The majority of young people in this category just want one thing: get a stable and steady job and decent housing which allows them to build a family. In general it can be stated that within the group of the disengaged, young females from economically less fortune regions (Portugal, Spain, Romania, South Italy) are even more at a drawback than young men. Especially young (migrant) women with low education seem to profit most from non-formal settings where they feel safe and can develop their potentials.

Concerning transition countries like Romania, the relationship between formal education, family background and labour market is so unclear and unstable that hardly any reliable statement can be made, except that the majority of young people there suffer more drawbacks than their peers in North and West Europe. They are the most explicit about what they need: more information about developments on national and international labour markets, possibilities for self-employment and second chance education, especially in the field of ICT (see also Lauritzen and Guidikova, 2002).

High Resources – High Engagement

The opposite constellation refers to young people with considerably high resources and opportunities. They have faith in shaping their biographies according to their own wishes and ambitions. They share the severe criticism about school and formal education with the former group, they want *a fusion of learning and living.* Knowing that school cannot give that, they develop strategies of compensation by engaging in elaborate hobbies and learning in informal peer contexts. In the margins of the uninspiring (but safe) world of school, and often backed by the safe and stimulating environment of their families, they create their own worlds of activities.

Not all of them are high school-achievers; some even dropped out of school and continued their study in private and evening institutes where they were responsible for their own learning process and felt in charge of it. We found examples for combinations of formal and informal learning in Italy, Spain, Portugal and in Romania, where some young men and women prepared for flexible and incalculable labour markets by collecting a wide variety of qualifications and certificates, such as a young Romanian male who is active in music, has a job as a stoker, works in a catering business and follows foreign language courses. Despite greater resources and more active strategies for informal learning they know quite well how important formally acquired certificates are and would rather continue their educational courses after having finished obligatory education. But some of them would even quit university because they find learning there just as uninspiring as in school.

Against the backdrop of their diverse backgrounds and careers, these young people construct encouraging experiences that allow them to develop an intrinsic learning motivation early in life. They experience satisfaction in various forms of learning – formal learning in school in subjects they have a special interest in, non-formal and informal learning outside school in self-made projects and self-directed activities. They succeed in finding a balance between extrinsic and intrinsic motivation and push themselves to search for new fields of learning. They mention exploration as crucial for learning, surpassing limits and enlarging horizons. Like a German young man told us: 'I was a little bored with IT courses at school. Then I was allowed to build up the computer room together with my teacher. I set up the computer network for the school ... and gave classes in computer technology'.

Exploration as a learning strategy is closely (and reciprocally) related to communicative skills and competencies ('I'm a talker' – this is how a Dutch young man who is successful in catering characterized himself). Communicating, not only with their peers but with all kinds of people in different professions and positions, is part of their youth-cultural capital, which they have accumulated in various surroundings (cf. du Bois-Reymond, 2000; Stauber, 2003). The diversity of their networks has to do with the socio-economic and cultural milieux they come from as well as the range of their interests. The more diverse the latter, the more diverse and extensive their networks are, which run through all stages of their lives: mates from school to university; experts in special fields; family members who might provide them with valuable contacts; friends to discuss plans with; older siblings with whom they set up projects, often in the ICT or music field. Peer-learning for them is self-evident, simply because so much learning and working takes place with peers. They have possibly more trust in their own generation than in the generation of their parents and teachers, although they will use their advice and experience if it is offered and regarded as useful. Notably teachers and counselors are mentioned only by exception in this regard.

Like the disengaged, these young people have a flexible working attitude, which, however, does not spring from a necessity but from a more secure basis. Rather, changing jobs suits their needs. Because they trust in their abilities and capacities they endure a bad job with their mind open for change. If they have experienced unemployment, it has not been for long, which gives them the firm conviction that they will find another job and get into smoother fairway in time. Or they redefine the status of unemployment as actually being learning time: 'I have been unemployed for one year, but as a matter of fact I made music and prepared for the conservatory' (male, East Germany).

Self-blame has a different meaning for them than it has for the disengaged: they, too, blame themselves if things do not work out as they expected, but that does not affect their self-esteem: they know that they are good at what they are doing or plan to do. Work is an extremely significant part of their lives and of their identities. They describe it in terms of *fun, self-realisation, passion* and *curiosity*, which can be interpreted as sound critique of late capitalistic working conditions that neither correspond to personal needs and capacities nor use the possibilities of contemporary (information) societies (Sennett, 1998).

Most of them are self-employed or aim to set up their own enterprises, which originates in their rejection of others having power over their lives (*I won't let anyone make decisions for me*). In contrast to the disengaged, who share that dislike of authority but have to submit to it, trendsetters have more powerful strategies at their disposal; one of them is deliberate risk-taking: 'I decided I'd manage a bar full-time … they gave me a brilliant wage that I couldn't walk away from. So I went down, did the job, and ended up hating the job … I made a decision: I have to get out of here. I knew that I was walking away from a lot of money to nothing' (female, Ireland). Risk-taking needs self-consciousness and trust in one's own capacities as well as skills to use resources. Applying the principle of trial and error and developing multiple option strategies (i.e. combining a low-paid job with getting an own business started) requires perseverance and planning capacities and at the same time the flexibility to switch jobs or dismiss a project if it proves invalid. The main difference with the disengaged is that trendsetters acquire informal learning on the basis of formal qualifications, backed by family resources. Therefore they can afford to interpret possible failures as necessary experiences.

They are highly mobile, which also could be a totally virtual mobility, like in the case of a Dutch young man who buys and sells music via Internet, hardly ever leaving his flat somewhere in a little village. Their work schedules are flexible, apparently self-directed, they do not mind working eighty hours per week, as long as it is up to them to decide. They loath routine in all forms (as do the disengaged). Work and spare time are combined in many trendsetter careers in new ways.

Looking at their future prospects, biographical trendsetters are optimistic and realistic at the same time. Some have fairly extravagant ambitions, but they will realise them – or do something else (*my options are open*). Others would state that they live by the day, experimenting with this and that, but that eventually they will look for more structure and security in their life. Marriage and children are for most of them still far off, even for the older ones; what they do now or want to achieve in the near future is more urgent (Plug et al., in press). All feel self-responsible for what they do, yet many realise that they do not *only* depend on their own energy and initiative, but also on developments of the labour market which might destroy their enterprises. Adulthood for them is more open than for the disengaged, they worry less and describe this status in less concrete and more general terms, certainly not in terms of the gendered normal biography.

Biographical trendsetters could be identified in every national context, in advanced capitalist economies as well as in transition countries like Romania. Of course, booming or at least dynamic labor markets are advantageous for the transitions of *all* young people, not only for the trendsetter group. This becomes obvious from our material in the experiences from the Netherlands, Denmark, Portugal and Ireland, where dynamic labor markets provide potential niches in which individual activity could be developed, as opposed to (East) Germany, Spain and (Southern) Italy. Flexible regulations in terms of education and training (Denmark, United Kingdom, Ireland) or self-employment (Italy, United Kingdom, Ireland, Netherlands) might stimulate promising projects like in Italy, whereas rigid regulations impede such initiatives like in Germany.

With regard to gender differences we found among the trendsetters as many initiatives started by females as by males – females thus use very well the potentials of alternative trajectories. Many of them compensated disadvantages caused by gendered segmentation in training and labour market and lacking care facilities through a higher degree of biographical reflexivity compared to young men – which is confirmed by findings of other research (Peters and du Bois-Reymond, 1996; Leccardi 1996).

Turning Points in Young People's Motivational Careers

In the foregoing section we have singled out low and high motivational learning careers, and we have described the interplay between structural factors and biographical agency. All young people experience a growing tension between compulsory and voluntary forms of learning, and their motivation is higher in informal learning settings than in educational institutions. Especially the separation between 'theory' and 'practice' is felt as alien to one's own life and world experiences. Yet one should be aware that the split between the two does not parallel the split between general and vocational education, as the latter is not regarded as relevant practice either by many young people who follow it in schools or training schemes. Young people show a clear desire to be allowed to have a substantial say in making vocational decisions. They are frustrated if there are not enough alternatives. Feelings of irrelevance have precisely to do with the artificial division in learning and living, which is inherent in formal education institutions. Motivation proves in all cases the most important factor for successful or problematic learning careers (Csikszentmihaly, 1975).

The youth projects we chose as case studies for our research – different as they are in clientele scope, content and organisation – unite in their aim to give young people new learning and/or working chances by letting them participate in shaping their vocational trajectories. Finding an appropriate project is the first step young people have to take, and all activities and experiences around that step can represent the *first turning point* in their trajectories. For it means that a new relationship is going to be established between societal structure (i.e. lack of qualification; a restricted labor market) and biographical agency (passivity versus active search). Some of them are too frustrated and disappointed through earlier negative experiences with counseling and training measures to deliberately change routes and take risks; they have too little self-esteem to dare something else; too few contacts to hear about new initiatives. But if contact is made – through peers or local experts rather than formal institutions– change can get going.

Lydia, a 23 year old mother of a 7 month-old son from Northern Ireland, was raised in a family living on welfare benefits and was holding a part-time job in a supermarket. She had so little self-confidence that she thought she could never get out of her present situation. By pure chance she read an advertisement about a project especially meant for young mothers, which offered training in ICT skills. Already the ad gave her hope that now things might change. Mihail, a young Romanian, spent several years in care institutions, had no family support at all, but was determined and optimistic to change his situation. He worked himself up from plumber to chef assistant in a restaurant, worked on the black market, made enough money to live on, but he wanted to learn more and different things and therefore engaged in an NGO. In both cases the respective project changed the trajectory of the young person fundamentally.

When having found a project to their needs, young people experience a *second turning point* in their motivational careers. It is perhaps for the first time during transiting from school to work that they experience the pleasure of being accepted by others, co-participants as well as project workers. Re-motivation, initiated through project entry, can now be generalized and will enhance self-esteem and lead to a fresh look on the meaning of learning and work. The projects show the close relationship between self-esteem and motivation: the lower the 'entrance self-esteem', the more project activities must be oriented towards changing that psychological state – otherwise learning cannot take place. Non-formal and informal/peer learning are better learning modes to re-establish self-esteem than are formal courses. Through these learning modes young people who rejected formal/vocational education and were rejected by it can be re-activated even to re-accept formal education.

This is the case with an art project in Portugal which provides dance training for Afro-Portuguese young immigrants. Here the first turning point was immigration itself before finding the project and experiencing the pleasure of exercising dancing. In this project the participants must commit themselves to attend regular school. They accept this condition because they do not want to lose their right to perform and to travel with the dancing group. Formal education and informal learning are reconciled in the biographies of these young people.

In the course of the second turn, young people get the opportunity to accumulate social capital by building up networks and learning the art of networking. Networking has shown to be crucial for motivation, and positive in two ways: it *initiates* turning points in that existing networks enable young people to change their trajectory in a favorable direction, i.e. make good use of a project offer. And it *results* from turning points, when young people learn to use project resources to build up new networks.

The *third turning point* concerns the future of young people. For many of the disengaged young people their future causes negative associations and no-future-feelings. Project experiences can change such feelings by opening up concrete prospects through present learning motivation. Lydia, the young Irish mother, tells us: 'Lifting the Limits (project) has given me back the hope that I can achieve my ambitions and get the career I want. After finishing this program I want to go to university to get degree in Youth and Community Work. Lifting the Limits will not only give me qualification but also the experience, the drive and, most importantly, the confidence to be able to take that next step'.

There are some conditions in order for turning points in motivational careers to happen: first of all, projects must be entered voluntarily; most training schemes do not give that freedom of decision. Secondly, the participants must be able to see directly and immediately the connection between the project offer and her or his personal life situation. If it is an offer which serves only partial needs, i.e. offering training but no child care for young mothers, the measure is worthless. Thirdly there must be project workers who find a good balance between steering and leaving the young persons on their own to experiment with the consequences of their choices. In addition to that the participants must have trust in the staff. Finally – and that is the most crucial point – the project must give the participants a realistic prospect of their future, even if the labour market is closed. The much discussed concept/policy of 'flexicurity' accounts for this situation: if transition regimes demand of young people flexibility, they must guarantee a minimum of social/financial security (López Blasco et al., 2003).

Looking Back and Forth

We have, through the voices of different fractions in the young generation, demonstrated the alienation of young people from the formal educational and training systems and have pointed to the largely unused potentials of informal and non-formal learning. By analysing the trajectories of biographical trendsetters and disengaged young people, we discovered the contexts and constellations which enable young people to change from disengagement to re-engagement. The learning biographies of trendsetters are the product of the interplay of structural factors and agency forces; so are those of the disengaged, which means that they are not separated from each other by unsurmountable barriers; promising turning points in their motivational careers can make all the difference in the lives of young people, as we also have shown. That points to the need of transition policies which strive for a better integration of different modes of learning. Participatory approaches should be acknowledged for the 'hard' sectors of education, training and employment instead of being reserve for the areas of youth work, culture and leisure in order to enable young people to develop 'strong, effective, and above all fluid individualized systems of social capital' (Raffo and Reves, 2000, p. 154). It is our conviction that all the skills and facilitating conditions of biographical trendsetters could stimulate transition policies for young people with fewer resources, above all encouraging learning experiences which provide young people with self-esteem, helping them find a balance between flexibility and security, and being able to benefit from supporting networks. As European youth (policy) researchers, we should go on providing evidence for the necessity of developing meaningful concepts for such policies.

Notes

1 European Group for Integrated Social Research (EGRIS); www.iris-egris.de.
2 Youth Policy and Participation. Potentials of Participation and Informal Learning for the Transition of Young People to the Labour Market. A Comparision in Ten European Regions (YOYO), funded by the EU Fifth framework programme, Key Action 'Improving the Socio-economic Knowledge Base' (see http:www.iris-egris.de/yoyo).

References

Alheit, P. and Dausien, B. (2000), '"*Biographie*" *as a basic resource of lifelong learning*', in P. Alheit (ed.), *Lifelong Learning Inside and Outside of Schools*, Roskilde: Roskilde University, Universität Bremen and University of Leeds, pp. 400–422.

du Bois-Reymond, M. (2000), 'Jugendkulturelles Kapital in Wissensgesellschaften' (Youth-cultural capital in knowledge societies), in H.-H. Krüger and H. Wenzel (eds.), *Schule zwischen Effektivität und sozialer Verantwortung,* Opladen: Leske und Budrich, pp. 235–254.

Clausen, J. A. (1995), 'Gender, Contexts, and Turning Points in Adults' Lives', in P. Moen, G. H. Elder and K. Lüscher (eds.), *Examining Lives in Context: Perspectives on the Ecology of Human Development,* Washington D.C.: American Psychological Association, pp. 365–389.

Csikszentmihaly, M. (1975), *Beyond Boredom and Anxiety. The Experience of Play in Work and Games*, Jossey Bass Publishers.

Esping-Anderson, G. (1990), *The Three Worlds of Welfare Capitalism,* Cambridge: Cambridge University Press.

Gallie, D. and Paugham, S. (2000), *Welfare Regimes and the Experience of Unemployment in Europe,* Oxford: Oxford University Press.

Heinz, W. R. (2002), 'Self-socialisation and post-traditional society', *Advances in Life Course Research,* 7, 41–64.

Hollands, R. (2000), 'Divisions in the dark: youth cultures, transitions and segmented consumption spaces in the night-time economy', *Journal of Youth Studies,* **5** (2), 153–171.

Lauritzen, P. and Guidikova, I. (2002), 'European Youth Development and Policy: The Role of NGO's and Public Authority in the Making of the European Citizen', in R. Lerner, F. Jacobs and D. Wertlieb (eds.), *Handbook of Applied Developmental Science,* 3, London: Sage, pp. 363–382.

Leadbeater, C. and Oakley, K. (1999), *The Independents. Britain's New Cultural Entrepreneurs,* London: Demos.

Leccardi, C. (1996), *Futuro brese. Le giovani donne e il future,* Turin: Rosenberg and Sellier.

López Blasco, A., McNeish, W. and Walther, A. (eds.) (2003), *Between Cooling Out and Empowerment. Young People and Policies for Transition to Work in Europe,* Bristol: Polity Press.

Peters, E. and du Bois-Reymond, M. (1996), 'Zwischen Anpassung und Widerstand: Junge Frauen im Modernisierungsprozess', (Between Adaptation and Resistance: Young women in the process of modernization), in A. Walther (ed.), *Junge Erwachsene in Europa,* Opladen: Leske + Budrich, pp. 93–123.

Plug, W. and du Bois-Reymond, M. (2000), *Continuity and Discontinuity in the Attitudes of Dutch Young People About Work-Related Values in European Perspective,* Bristol Policy Press.

Raffo, C. and Reeves, M. (2000), 'Youth transitions and social exclusion: developments in social capital theory', *Journal of Youth Studies,* **3** (2), 147–166.

Sennett, R. (1998), *The Corrosion of Character,* New York: W.W. Norton.

Stauber, B. (2003), *Junge Frauen und Menner in Selbstinszenierungen und Handlungspotentiale* (Young Women and Men in Youth Cultures. Self-Performing Self and Potentials of Agency), Opladen: Leske and Budrich.

Stauber, B. and Walther, A. (2002), 'Young Adults in Europe – Transitions, Policies and Social Change', in A. Walther and B. Stauber (eds.), *Misleading Trajectories. Integration Policies for Young Adults in Europe?* An EGRIS Publication, Opladen: Leske and Budrich, pp. 11–26.

Wethington, E. (2002), 'The relationship of turning points at work to perceptions of psychological growth and change', *Advances in Life Course Research,* 7, pp. 111–131.

Chapter 9

Texting as Style: Preliminary Observations on Cellular Phone Use among Filipino College Students[1]

Clarence M. Batan

Cellular Phone, Texting and the Filipino Youth

The impact of new Information and Communication Technology on social life has interested many social scientists in recent years (Castells, 1996, 1997, 1998; Tomlinson, 1999). In the Philippines, local studies (Aguilar, 2000; Braid, 1998) show that these technological developments significantly affect the lives of Filipinos, particularly in the field of media and communications. One particular technological development which arguably improved, if not revolutionized, the state of telecommunications in the Philippines, is the cellular phone with its short message service, popularly known in the country as 'texting'. How this technological phenomenon has come about in a developing country like the Philippines, and the ways by which it reproduces identity and social status, and how it influences and develops the character of cultural communications among Filipinos have become fascinating sociological questions that local social scientists are grappling with at present. The apparent cultural affinity between Filipino social norms and the technology of texting has perhaps made the Philippines, the texting capital of the world, with young people as its most prolific users.

This study presents a sociological perspective on understanding the implications of cellular phones among young Filipino college students, and their propensity to interact, connect and develop links through texting. Although the effects of texting, in general, extend beyond age groups, and may not be specific to Filipino youth, the aim of this study is limited to the cultural practice of these youths engaged with this new technology. How far their identities and relationships have been reproduced, enhanced or altered, and to what extent has texting influenced their behaviour towards their peers, family and school, are central to this analysis.

Methods

The research uses quantitative data collected from a sample of 337 college students, from 16 private non-sectarian post-secondary schools in Metro Manila. Self-administered questionnaires were randomly distributed to students who, at the time of the survey (September to October, 2001), owned cellular phones and are involved with texting. This is combined with the qualitative data from 16 individual in-depth interviews and five focus group discussions (each composed of four to eight persons), also with college students from similar schools, who agreed to share their experiences on texting. Quantitative data analysis was undertaken using descriptive statistics (frequencies and percentages) and thematic analysis was employed to analyse the qualitative data.

Texting as 'Style' and its Cultural Implications

Cultural analysis of youth phenomena has long been used in the social sciences (Bourdieu, 1977; MacLeod, 1987; McRobbie, 2000; Willis, 1977; Brake, 1985). These studies focus on questions about how young persons participate or resist adult culture, and how they develop their own subcultures in relation to identity formation and 'coming to age' processes. Culture, as a concept, offers a sociological understanding of human interaction, which corresponds to both cohesive and divisive processes that construct the nexus of social relations and identity.

To demonstrate how this cultural process occurs among the lives of upper-middle class Filipino youths, I perceive the communication gadgets such as the cellular phones, as a new form of material culture, which is potent to create images and differentiates social relationships. Texting is the particular cultural practice, which links this material culture with these youths. In order to show this empirically, I use Brake's (1985) notion of 'style' to understand the cultural elements of texting. My concern is to pursue the question on the relationship of social structure to social interaction.

Brake offers a discussion of 'style' (1985, pp. 11–15) that makes it useful as a conceptual tool in this attempt to understand the cultural practice of texting in the Philippines. He defines 'style' as consisting of three main elements:

a. 'Image', appearance composed of costume, accessories such as hairstyle, jewellery and artefacts.
b. 'Demeanour', made up of expression, gait and posture.
c. 'Argot', a special vocabulary and how it is delivered. (Brake, 1985)

I propose that the cellular phone, as a material culture, generates these three elements. An image of the cellular phone, for instance, positions the person within the cultural space (Hall and Jefferson, 1976) based on the brand, model and accessories it overtly manifests. Also, owning a cellular phone, and texting, produced modes of expression and behaviour, where its use has challenged generally accepted social etiquettes in public spaces (i.e., church, school, theatres). Moreover, texting has produced an 'argot' – a special vocabulary and language (i.e., texting lingo) which has alarmed some local educators, and spawned a growing academic interest in the field of linguistics (Rojo-Laurilla, May 15–17, 2003b). Later, I will discuss these elements further.

Two more points, however, are worth noting. First, my intention to see texting as a cultural practice among Filipino college students does not mean that it is resisted by their parents and teachers. On the contrary, I contend that texting builds, rather than breaks, relations and communications among these age groups. Texting, as I view it in this study, is a positive response to the changing demands of social and cultural structures which other researchers describe as 'Philippine modernity' and 'complex connectivity' (Pertierra, et.al., 2002). Second, Bourdieu's (1984) notion of 'cultural capital' becomes important in showing how cellular phone, as a material culture, defines tastes and distinctions of these youths. Thus the symbolic use of 'style' accomplishes social reproduction. Subsequently, I shall present a historical brief of cellular phones and texting in the Philippines and describe how these have affected the general social life of Filipinos.

The Birth of a Texting Society

The phenomenal growth of cellular phone users in the Philippines is attributed to different converging factors. One of these is the introduction of a new state policy, known as the *Public Telecommunications Policy Act in the Philippines* (Republic Act 7925, 1994), which responds to the country's inadequate telecommunications system. Its objective is to end the monopoly of a corporation giant, the Philippine Long Distance Telephone Company, over the country's telecommunications industry for decades. The new policy intends to liberalize the field to other telecommunication carriers. About the same time in the mid-1990s, global wireless technology has slowly penetrated telecommunications worldwide and RA 7925 brought new players in the Philippine cellular phone market.

Another significant factor, which caused the growth of cellular phone ownership and subscription in the Philippines, is the introduction of short message service, in the form of text messaging. This was an accidental success and took nearly everyone in the local mobile industry by surprise (Raciti, 1995). During the first quarter of 2002, the estimated number of cellular phone subscribers was 12 million. About 16 per cent of the entire Philippine population sent approximately 120 million messages per day, which comprises about ten per cent of text messages sent worldwide (ABS-CBN, March 24, 2002). This makes the Philippines, arguably, the text capital of the world, a *texting society,* in which the number of subscribers has steadily grown since. Where does this desire of the Filipinos to remain 'in touch', and be always accessible come from?

In establishments and places of Metro Manila, one would observe that many Filipinos carry a mobile cellular phone. In food houses, shopping malls, offices, schools, and even streets, the beeping and ringing tones have become natural noise. Even traffic signs have evolved, which now includes: 'Don't Text While Driving', 'Eyes on Your Wheels and Not on Your Text' and 'Don't Text While Crossing the Street'. Moreover, texting has even made newspaper headlines of national interest. For instance, texting is perceived to have contributed to the mobilization of the 2001 peaceful political revolution, which forced the resignation of former President Joseph Estrada (Perry, June 4, 2001; Rafael, 2001). Broadcast media, both in radio and television, use text messaging to generate opinion, and comments from viewers. Also, texting facilitates media-oriented game shows and contests. A cross-national survey conducted by *Siemens Mobile Lifestyle Survey* reports that cellular phones play an increasingly important role in social life (D'Bayan, February 11, 2002).

The two obvious reasons for the success of the cellular phone in the Philippines, with texting as its driving force, are its accessibility and affordability. Telephones, which were denied to the majority of the Filipinos for a long time, have suddenly become easily accessible. One need not wait for months to obtain a telephone line; instead immediate mobile access is provided in various business and shopping centres, and other establishments. In addition, the text messages cost less than telephone voice calls. For the first time, Filipinos have easy access to an affordable gadget, which allows sharing of information in the form of messages to everyone, from friends to loved ones or even to strangers. The cellular phone is now likened to a toy, a plaything. It gives one control to send and receive messages to new networks of communities unimagined by previous generations. This phenomenon has therefore caused the evolution of the *text generation,* in which young Filipinos are probably, its foremost members.

Two recent national surveys (Ateneo Youth Study, 2001; McCann Erickson-Philippines Youth Study, 2000), offer some insights about the Filipino youth's response to modern technologies which include findings on cellular phone use and texting. *McCann-Erickson Study* (2000) reports that Filipino youth is more empowered technologically, as compared to previous generations. It states that text messaging (12 per cent) ranks second to computer use (17 per cent) as a form of recreation/leisure. This study however, did not offer much information, other than to suggest that a growing number of Filipino youths are involved with texting. On the other hand, the *Ateneo Youth Study* (2001) offers some interesting insights about text messaging. This study explains that the youth respondents on average send less than 5 text messages per day. However, youth from the upper class send and receive over 11 text messages a day. In a week, the average amount spent by these youths for cellular phones and texting is Php 111.00 (about US$ 2.00). Further, the research suggests that those in the National Capital Region and urban areas spend a lot more than their rural counterparts. Those from the upper class spend an average of Php 383.00 (about US$ 7.00) a week compared to as low as Php 51.00 (about US$ 1.00) among the lower classes. These findings provide a broader backdrop that allows comparison with my own research results.

In the following section, I will discuss the experience of young college students with cellular phones, and their cultural practice of texting. Empirical evidence suggests that, texting has indeed become an important part of their everyday life, wherein new ways of social relations evolve, which builds intra and inter-generational communications. This is apparent especially with these youth's motivations and positive behavioural responses towards the process of texting.

Youth College Students as Texters

Table 9.1 gives the profile of the respondents. More than half (61 per cent) are females and 39 per cent are males, which reflects the current gender statistics of enrolment in post-secondary education in the Philippines. As expected, 81 per cent live in urban areas and a mere 17 per cent are from rural areas, which refer to the outskirt towns near Manila.

Forty-two per cent are taking courses in Social Sciences and Humanities, 39 per cent are in Natural Science and Technology courses, and 19 per cent are in the Health Sciences. Data on the father's education of these respondents indicate that more than

Table 9.1　Distribution of respondents by gender, locality, current course and father's education

	Frequency	%
Gender		
Female	206	61
Male	131	39
Total	*337*	*100*
Locality		
Urban	273	81
Rural	64	17
Total	*337*	*100*
Current Course		
Social Sciences & Humanities	142	42
Natural Science and Technology	130	39
Health Sciences	65	19
Total	*337*	*100*
Father's Education		
Primary	12	4
Secondary/Vocational	81	24
Post secondary	244	72
Total	*337*	*100*

two-thirds (72 per cent) are college graduates (Table 9.1). This suggests that most of the respondents are from upper-middle class families whose parents are formally educated, employed (especially the fathers), and earn modest incomes. The mean age of the respondents is 19.5 years. The profile of the respondents in the individual in-depth interviews and focus groups is similar except for a proportionate representation of both genders.

Survey data (table not shown) also indicate that more than two thirds of the respondents (64 per cent) acquired their cellular phones from their parents. Some important themes from interviews and focus groups, with regard to cell phone ownership, reflect two related issues. One is peer group influence, in which the cell phone serves as a symbol of "being in" and "trendy" among their peers. The other is family communication and parental control in which the cellular phone makes possible the easy monitoring of children by parents as well as communication of children with their parents. In interviews and focus group discussions, respondents also expressed that their parents felt that cellular phones are important for security purposes.

Texting as 'Style'

As earlier discussed above, Brake (1985) explains that 'style' consists of three cultural elements: image, demeanour, and argot. This section presents the empirical evidence describing these elements. Analysis of the data raises important sociological issues about the nature of social reproduction and relationships that evolve with these young college students among their peers (i.e. courtship language, school behaviour), and their parents; and the recent concern about texting as a corrupt language.

Image in Mobile Phones

Cellular phones have indeed become an important part of family life among Filipinos. Multiple responses (Table 9.2) from the survey data reveal that the two primary reasons for owning cellular phones are immediate communication with family (32 per cent) and emergency purposes (29 per cent). However, when asked about the actual practice of texting, more than half (60 per cent) usually sent messages to their friends and only about one-third to their parents or relatives.

Table 9.2 Multiple responses of reasons for owning a cellular phone and to whom text messages are usually sent

Reasons for Owning a Cellular Phone	Count	% of Responses
For immediate communication to family	298	32
For emergency purposes	266	29
For studying and other academic activities	124	13
To maintain communication with friends	165	18
To meet new friends	77	8
Total responses	*930*	*100*
To Whom Text Messages Are Usually Sent	**Count**	**% of Responses**
To friends, peers or classmates	300	60
To parents or relatives	163	33
To teachers, community leaders, etc.	31	6
Others	6	1
Total responses	*500*	*100*

The evidence suggests that the function of cellular phones, according to these college students, is to maintain identity with their group, which points to the notion of status. For instance, Kim, one of the interviewed female respondents, explains that having a cell phone adds to her style and fashion, which she considers important in maintaining identity with her group. Another respondent, Aaron remarks, 'I have a cell phone because of the social perception of my fellow classmates to those who don't have one. I think cell phone signifies one's social status. If you do not have it, you'll be left out'.

Thus, the respondents express both excitement and anxiety about the brand or models of their cellular phones. Cellular phone features, other than short message service, which includes games, ringing tones, logos, calculator, web-access capacity, and even accessories (i.e. cell casings/housing, backlights, keypads), are indices of how up-to-date, and sophisticated the cellular phone model is. Hence, cellular phones as a material culture, act as a symbol of status, as an addition to these youths' 'cultural capital' (Bourdieu, 1984), which forms a set of values that culturally distinguishes their tastes from those of lower class counterparts. This shows how the cellular phone has become a symbolic good, which positions these youths in the cultural space of social structure.

The Demeanour of Text as Expression

While the image of cellular phones may indicate social status among the respondents, their texting behaviour, that is, the various ways in which they send and receive text messages, give more insights on how this dynamic cultural practice builds and expands cultural communications among Filipinos.

Survey data (table not shown) reveal that college students are indeed enamoured with the sending and receiving of SMS text messages on their mobile phones. Seventy-four per cent of the respondents express that texting is part of their everyday life, and 73 per cent agree that it is a necessity. As one interview respondent, Franco affirms, 'You know I can't go out of the house without my cell. I make it a point that it is with me wherever I go. It is very important'.

Based on this survey, the college students send and receive about 22 messages a day, a figure that is double that reported in *Ateneo Youth Study* (2001). Furthermore, our data also reveal that these college students usually spend an amount of about Php 800.00 per month (about US $16.00), which compared to the same study, [2001 #23] is more than twice the amount spent for cellular phones by youth respondents who are from the upper class. What are the underlying cultural factors that make these young Filipino college students with upper-middle class background spend so much for texting?

Texting seems to emphasize and enhance the cultural character of communications among Filipinos, who love to talk and share stories. The process of texting reinvents this communication process and it serves as a new medium for telling stories. This phenomenon is considered a new form of communication and presents a unique way of social bonding with people. Thus texting has become an intrinsic part of Metro Manila youth culture, complete with new semantic terms, courting language and its own distinct social etiquette of responding and sending messages.

Survey data (table not shown) suggest that text messages are usually responses to inquiry (38 per cent); to keep 'in touch' (27 per cent) and greetings (26 per cent). Both focus groups and individual interviews note that these college students love to save messages, and always anticipate receiving one. This may be the reason why 50 per cent of the respondents express anxiety whenever they cannot send text messages. Further, evidence indicates how texting has facilitated a certain degree of bonding and friendship among their peers, in school activities and in extra-curricular situations such as courting.

Joy, for example, who stays in Metro Manila because she studies there, communicates with her friends in her native province through texting. She admits that without texting she would not have been able to keep her small town friendships because she is not fond of writing letters. Also, she thinks that in texting, one can show care and thoughtfulness. On the other hand, Edward, another interview respondent, uses texting not only to communicate with his peers but also for courtship. He explains that texting has become his way of expressing his feeling, saying that, 'A text message creates a bridge to every heart'.

Texting is effective in schools in dealing with assignments and projects as one respondent claims. Bernadeth explains, 'Whenever we need our teacher to deal with academic problems such as our thesis, we just text her. Often, we communicate with her only through texting'. Campus announcements, change of schedule, cancellation of classes and school campaigns are facilitated through texting. As a result, texting has also been used for cheating and caused disturbance in classrooms. Schools had to enforce new set of policies on how and when to use cellular phones to eliminate these problems.

Another emerging theme, which results from this cultural practice of texting, is parent-children interactions. Parents, who have provided these college students their cellular phones, are also enamoured, with the capacity of texting to monitor their children. Rather than being opposed to this parental control, the youths in this study admit that texting has improved their relationship with their parents and created a new level of closeness with them. Parents immediately know where their children are, and children in return are able to communicate with their parents more confidently through text, which avoids a confrontation that may arise from a face-to-face interaction. As expressed by one respondent, Kristin, 'Even though my parents are in the province, and I am here in Manila, I could maintain closeness and bonding, because I could text anytime. I could communicate with them anytime. It is as though I am close to them though in the real sense, we're far from each other'. BJ, another respondent, who for a long time did not have good communications with his father, reveals that, 'At least through texting, I can say what I feel, which I can't say to my father's face. Suddenly, a new line of communication has been opened up'.

In addition, given the state of overseas work in the Philippines, texting facilitates the exchanging of messages between some respondents and family members who work abroad. As one respondent, Norbert explains, 'Because of texting, I can send messages to my brother who is an overseas contract worker. It seems that he is just near'.

Texting in this sense has become a powerful tool of expressing ideas and feelings towards peers and parents. These expressions, as symbolized by text messages, illustrate how technology, in this case, the cellular phones and texting work as a bridge to enhance and expand intra and inter age groups communications, which may indicate the nature of relations in future generations.

Argot: New Texting Lingo

Texting in itself is an argot, the last cultural element in the notion of style (Brake, 1985), because this process produces a new form of vocabulary, a *texting lingo*. Instant text messaging have redefined language and spellings altogether (George, Online, n.d.). This has alarmed some educators in the Philippines who view text messages as 'corrupt language'.

Survey data (table not shown) indicate that 94.1 per cent of respondents abbreviate or cut words in their text messages. This technique is the result of the very logic of short messaging itself. Texting follows the principle of the old telegraph machine, with limited space for characters in each message, which necessitates the abbreviations of words. However, what is interesting about this texting lingo, its various combinations of letters, numbers and symbols is the way by which it creates a certain linguistic norm among these youths. For example, 'I love you' may be expressed in different forms, which combines letters, numerical numbers and symbols such as 'I LUV U', '143' or 'I ❤ U'. As Filipino linguist Rojo-Larilla (Rojo-Laurilla, May 15–17, 2003a) speculates, this combination of letters and numbers within a word, and the interspersing of number between letters to substitute for certain syllables (i.e. 'Do not worry too much' into text message: 'Dnt wori 2 mch') is naturally different and unique to Filipino culture. It seems that Filipinos have acquired a talent for logical abbreviations of words through texting.

In the focus groups, it seems though that some respondents know the differences between the language in the school, and texting lingo. In fact, while these college students use texting to communicate with their teachers, survey data (table not shown) reveal that 76 per cent do not use texting language in their research papers and other related writing projects. Kristin, one of the interview respondents, explains that, 'I do not think text language corrupts our English or Filipino spelling and grammar. I think the real issue depends on the school or the teacher with whom these languages are learned'.

The respondents, as I view it, while optimizing the use of texting in almost all dimensions of their youth life, apparently understand its limitations, and how it differs from the language taught in schools. Texting as characterized by the peculiarity of the lingo it produces, and the symbolic norms and rules it engages is, at present, still evolving, with the Filipino youth's active use of the process.

Conclusion

Mobile technologies have become a conduit to communities and communications, which explain young people's fascination to wireless technology (Easton, 2002; George, Online, n.d.). The whole amazing culture of texting in the Philippines, as examined within the experiences of young college students in private non-sectarian post-secondary schools in Metro Manila, affirms the current fascination of Filipinos with cellular phone technology.

Texting, using Brake's (1985) notion of 'style', consisting of the cultural elements of image, demeanour, and argot, gives a conceptual understanding of how the actions and behaviour of upper-middle class Filipino college students are influenced and enhanced by mobile technology. The study showed how cellular phones, in itself an evolving technology, position these youths in the cultural space of their peers and groups. Peer influence, the need to belong or to be in the 'in group', and the notion of identity, that is to be fashionable and 'in style', drives these young people's decisions and motivations to have cellular phones. In doing so, this mobile technology as a material form of symbolic good functions as cultural capital, which generates a 'stylistic technological taste'. The possession and use of the cellular phone further differentiates these youths from their lower class counterparts, and therefore reproduces their social position in the cultural space.

The expressive demeanour produced by texting is an interesting finding of this research. Texting has enhanced the cultural communications of Filipinos, who are enamoured by the power of sending and receiving messages. It has built bridges among friends and peers, as well as across generations, between parents and children. The notion of surveillance (Foucault, 1995) seems to provide an illustration of how parents' use of cellular phones has become a means of control. However, in these preliminary observations, parental monitoring in this cultural practice of texting has not been perceived by the respondents as obtrusive. This may be an indication of how communication technologies such as these 'panoptic' cellular phones, permeates and control individual lives, in a different way.

This study, which also documented the debates about text lingo and described how its current forms and usage, is perceived as a corruption of formal languages (i.e. Filipino and English). The youths in this research seem to know the extent to which texting may be used and, understand how it threatens formal education.

In conclusion, cellular phones in general, and texting, in particular, have indeed revolutionised the state of communications in the Philippines. This is a vivid example of how a society uses technology, and how this use could, in turn, shape and enhance cultural capital and the character of communications in society. These are only a few sociological implications enumerated in this paper. I expect that further research on the effects of information and communications technologies, such as cellular phones in a developing country like the Philippines will continue to raise questions on the notion of self, identity, culture and social reproduction in a global world, where young people are expected to play a significant role.

Notes

1   Work on this paper was supported by the Social Research Center, University of Santo Tomas, Manila Philippines. Some materials are adapted from a paper presented during the XV World Congress in Sociology, Research Committee – Sociology of Youth held at Brisbane Australia on July 7–13, 2002. I wish to acknowledge the exceptional research assistance provided by Frederick Rey, Riza Therese Santos and Julius Caesar Balagtas. I am particularly grateful to Dr. Victor Thiessen, Margaret Dechman and Gloria Sangalang for their detailed and helpful critique of an earlier draft.

References

ABS-CBN (March 24, 2002), OFF THE RECORD: a television forum on texting. Quezon City, Philippines.

Aguilar, C. (2000), 'The role of science and technology in national development.' Paper presented at the 6th International Philippine Studies Conference, Philippine Social Science Center, Quezon City.

Asian Institute of Journalism and Communication. (1998), *MEGATRENDS: The Future of the Filipino Children*. Quezon City: Katha Publishing.

Ateneo Youth Study (2001), Quezon City, Philippines: NFO Trends.

Bourdieu, P. (1984), *Distinction: A Social Critique of the Judgement of Taste*, Cambridge, Massachusetts: Harvard University Press.

Bourdieu, P. and Passeron, J.-C. (1977), *Reproduction in Education, Society and Culture*, London: SAGE.

Braid, F. R. and Tuazon, R. (1998), 'The Philippine communication sector in relation to national development: a historical critique', paper presented at the Philippine Social Science Council Pre-Congress, Philippine Social Science Center, Quezon City.

Brake, M. (1985), The use of subculture as an analytical tool in sociology, *Comparative youth culture: The Sociology of Youth Cultures and Youth Subcultures in America, Britain and Canada*. London: Routledge and Kegan Paul.

Castells, M. (1996), *The Information Age: Economy, Society and Culture 'The Rise of the Network Society'* (Vol. I), Massachusetts: Blackwell.

Castells, M. (1997), *The Information Age: Economy, Society and Culture 'The Power of Identity'* (Vol. II), Massachusetts: Blackwell.

Castells, M. (1998), *The Information Age: Economy, Society and Culture 'End of Millennium'* (Vol. III), Massachusetts: Blackwell.

D'Bayan, I. (February 11, 2002), Cell phones increasingly play an important role in social life, *Philippine Star,* p. 32.

Easton, J. (2002), *Going wireless: transform your business with mobile technology*. New York: HarperCollins.

Foucault, M. (1995), *Discipline and Punish: The Birth of the Prison*. New York: Vintage Books.

George, S. (Online, n.d.), *Emerging Youth Cultures in the Era of Globalization: TechnoCulture and TerrorCulture*, retrieved January 11, 2003, from www.tiplady.org.uk/pdfs/bookGeorgetechnoculture.pdf.

Hall, S. and Jefferson, T. (eds.) (1976), *Resistance through Rituals*. University of Birmingham: Centre for Contemporary Cultural Studies.

MacLeod, J. (1987), *Ain't No Makin' It: Leveled Aspirations in Low Income Neighborhood*, Boulder Colorado: Westview Press.

McCann Erickson-Philippines Youth Study (2000), Makati City, Philippines: McCann Erickson-Philippines.

McRobbie, A. (2000), *Feminism and Youth Culture,* London: Macmillan.

Perry, A. (June 4, 2001), 'Getting out of the message', *TIME (Asia Edition)*, p. 84.

Pertierra, R., Ugarte, E. F., Pingol, A., Hernandez, J. and Dacanay, N. L. (2002), *Txt-ing Selves: Cellphones and Philippine Modernity*. Manila: De La Salle University Press.

Raciti, R. C. (1995), '*Cellular technology*', retrieved August 23, 2001, from http://scis.nova.edu/~raciti/cellular.html.

Rafael, V. (2001), 'The cellphone and the crowd: messianic politics in recent Philippine history', San Diego: University of California, retrieved June 13, 2001, from http://communications.ucsd.edu/people/f_rafael.cellphone.htm.

Republic Act 7925 (1994), Public Telecommunications Policy Act of the Philippines. Republic of the Philippines.

Rojo-Laurilla, M. A. (May 15–17, 2003a), '"He Texts, She Texts": Gendered Conversational Styles in Philippine Text Messaging', Paper presented at the The Fifth National Social Science Congress, Quezon City, Philippines.

Rojo-Laurilla, M. A. (May 15–17, 2003b), 'A preliminary investigation on the socioliguistic aspect of text messaging', Paper presented at the The Fifth National Social Science Congress, Quezon City, Philippines.

Tomlinson, J. (1999), *Globalization and Culture,* Chicago: University of Chicago Press.

Willis, P. (1977), *Learning to Labour: How Working Class Kids Get Working Class Jobs,* New York: Columbia University Press.

Chapter 10

Risk Among Youth in Modern Russia: Problems and Trends[1]

Julia A. Zubok

Risk in a Changing Russian Society: Methodological Traits

Growing uncertainty and risks have become distinctive features of many societies in late modernity. In societies undergoing socio-economic, socio-political and socio-cultural modernization, risk has a particular meaning. This reflects a certain period of transition as society moves from one stage of development to another and is connected to innovations in different spheres of society. On this way the old social mechanisms and patterns of social relations have already lost their effectiveness but the new ones have not yet been fully worked out. This situation gives rise to uncertainty and risk.

Risk in a society in transition occurs alongside other social, economic and political contradictions, which are also on the increase. Long-term instability, deep social contradictions, conflicts and unclear social goals lead to the escalation of risks. In highly unstable societies, such as the former USSR and many East-Central European countries, where a larger proportion of young people are suffering from the consequences of economic and political crisis these and other risks are more pronounced. Such unfavourable conditions have had a significant influence on youth integration into society and social development of this social-demographic group. (Chuprov, Zubok and Williams, 2001; Chuprov and Zubok, 2003; Kovacheva, 2000; Machachek, 1998; Furlong and Cartmel, 1997; Roberts et al, 2000; Wallace and Kovacheva, 1998; Williams, Chuprov and Zubok, 2003).

Since the beginning of the reforms at the end of the 1980s Russian society survives expanding production of risk in accordance with economic, political, financial, technological and social indicators. If, following western scholars, it can be argued that modern and particularly post-modern societies face risks determined by the ambivalence of economic development and adverse sides of wealth production (Beck, 1992; Giddens, 1991; Turner, 1994), then Russia's risk society stems from 'reproduction of crisis'. The escalation of instability and crisis has increased the threshold of risk dramatically. Empirical data show that Russia's risk society has been developing as a consequence of the impact of economic decline during more than a decade that is often being characterised in terms of regression and *de*modernization. (Bogdanov, Kalinin and Rodionov, 1999; Osipov, Levashov, Lokosov and Sukhodeev, 2000; Yanitskiy, 1998). The latter has become a key feature of Russian society and involves the production and reproduction of risk in different spheres of the economy, politics and society. The environment itself is both a generator and distributor of risk. As a result of the accumulation of risks in different surroundings (both natural and social), the present determines future risks.

Due to the socio-economic, the socio-legal and the socio-political factors the definition of a risk society can be applied to contemporary Russia. Firstly, the socio-economic factor which includes the collapse of the industrial, technical and scientific potential of Russia, an over-reliance on imports, Russia's technological lag behind the West, Russian reliance on Western credits, commercial bank speculation, a lack of investment in industry and the misappropriation (redistribution) of state property and the creation of numerous financial schemes with no basis in reality. The consequence of this risk factor is an unprecedented fall in living standards, widespread economic, social and political differentiation and increased social tension.

Secondly, the socio-legal factor which is linked to the lack and breaches of various types of legislation as well as to the absence of a well-developed system of legislative and social protection of citizens. As a consequence, there has been a sharp divergence between rights in theory and rights in practice. This issue concerns all Russians, but especially the young. The lack of respect for the rule of law provides firm grounds for the development of the criminalization of society in different spheres of social life as well as at different levels of the power structure.

Finally, the socio-political factor is the product of the contradictions between the separation of powers and the fact that Presidential power is not sufficiently constrained. The government and parliament are weak. The politicians seem to have no clear idea in which direction the society is heading. The present political regime, which is based upon the 1993 Constitution, is actually guarded against major change. Thus any attempts at change are blocked by existing laws or by the President as arbiter of the Constitution. At the same time, as problems build up and attempts to resolve them fail, this produces a situation of constant uncertainty.

All of these risk factors and the ever-changing environment of risk have adversely affected the reproduction of life conditions and the physical, cultural and other resources, which determine the latter tend to fluctuate, thereby creating a risk production process.

Risk in Social Development of Youth

As a result of the replacement of one generation by another, a reproduction of the social structure takes place. During this process, the particular social functions of youth itself become more prominent. The most important function is young people's role in society's reproduction due to which the younger generation inherits and reproduces the existing social structure and relations. In fulfilling this function, every younger generation contributes to the maintenance of society's integration and development by bringing about innovation.

Taking part in the on-going process of societal reproduction, which is essential for the evolution and development of society as well as the social groups within the process, each younger generation integrates themselves into the social structure. In so far as social reproduction involves not only changes in economic variables, but also the reproduction of all kinds of social ties and relations, it is possible to talk about the evolution of the system of social relations and groups in terms of a cyclical reproduction. Reflecting this kind of cyclical reproduction of social relations, this process brings about changes in characteristics of youth and the place that young individuals occupy in the social structure. The positive nature of the changes in the quantitative and qualitative characteristics of youth is evidence of the social development of this socio-demographic group. Thus in this way youth development and society's reproduction are closely inter-linked.

The degree of social maturity is an indicator of the level of social development among young people. Social maturity of the younger generation is connected with achievements and changes in young persons' social status during the process of their integration into the social structure as well as with the nature of their identification with different social groups. Hence, this is closely linked to patterns of social mobility. In personal terms, social mobility is encouraged by an expression of young people's desire to achieve at least the same or higher status as their parents, older siblings and friends. Achieving desired positions brings satisfaction and encourages new endeavors. Conversely, the failure to achieve one's life plans or goals can lead to disappointment and a search for other ways of self-realization.

Achievements as well as the search for alternatives are closely connected with risk and risk-taking. In the first instance, risk is determined by the limited opportunities for upward mobility among young people provided by society. As a consequence of the prevailing risk environment, young individuals in many countries, including Russia, are permanently at risk of missing out, of not achieving their desired goal in life, be it a good vocational education, a job (let alone an interesting one), good career and promotion prospects, and living standards adequate enough to be able to start a family. In cases where young people fail to realize these ambitions, they naturally start the search for alternative ways to a better life but this also brings risks of failure, alienation and social exclusion.

However, in contemporary societies risk means more than just negative outcomes of the individual actions. Readiness to act under conditions of risk and ability to optimise results of risk-taking, to take motivated risk and predict its outcomes has become the main factor for self-realization in all spheres of the social life. For young people risk is the important factor that plays the role of the locomotive of their social mobility and social development. The latter allows examining risk as a typical characteristic of youth, and youth integration strategies model one type of risk called 'taking a chance' (Evans and Furlong, 1997). Thus, in this context *risk* means both a special attribute of one's activity i.e. risk-taking, and particular conditions of society, a group or a personal position.

Despite differences between various European societies convergence of risk conditions is occurring under the pressure of globalization. On the one hand, reproduction of risk is almost universal in character and involves such common trends as unemployment, inequality of opportunities in education and work, inability to compete in the business sector, collapse of traditional family and appearance of its surrogates (Williams, Chuprov and Zubok, 2003). On the other hand, convergence is also accompanied by certain unique features in these processes. In a broad sense young Russians are facing particular risks determined by current dramatic economic, political and cultural changes in the post socialist society.

Escalation of Risk Trends among Russian Youth[2]

Empirical data and official statistics indicate that an escalation of this kind of risk has and is taking place. Over the last few years, risk has extended its influence and entered new spheres of life. Taking into account the conditional character of any classification, there are three main directions in which risk is developing in modern Russia. *The first direction* refers to socio-demographic risks and the threat of destructive demographic reproduction – de-population. *The second direction* is linked with the threat of *de-*modernisation in Russia and caused by risk during socio-structural changes and finally, *the third direction* involves the risk of social exclusion and identity threatening disintegration on the societal level. Operating in parallel these risks affect youth as well societal development in the long-term.

Demographic reproduction is a significant aspect of societal reproduction, which plays an important role in the development of society. Birth and death rates, and health status are useful indicators of the wealth of a society as well of characteristics of youth development. Creating a family of distinction, having children, providing for the health and welfare of your family and ensuring that they are safe and have good prospects of development are among the greatest uncertainties in Russia. Although the country has passed the stage of stagnation of socio-demographic indicators, our analysis of the demographic situation among young people shows many unfavourable trends.

First of all they are related to health care. A wide spectrum of determinants has led to a gradual worsening of young people's health status ranging from poor ecological conditions, the bad quality of food and the neglect of the health of youth, its physical condition and the collapse of mass sport facilities to the unhealthy life styles with early tobacco, alcohol and drug use contribute to such socio-demographic risks. The general disease level among Russia's teenagers has increased by 21 per cent by the end of the 1990s. For example, the proportion of healthy teenagers in the Russian population only constitutes around 25 per cent (Kamaldinova, Rodionov, Kovrizjnikh and Kupriyanova, 2002). In the period 1999–2002 the number of young alcoholics increased by 17.3 per cent. Drug taking has increased by 10 per cent over the same period among all young people and 18.8 per cent among teenagers. 40 per cent of young males and 8 per cent of their female counterparts constantly smoke tobacco. The level of HIV has increased steadily; the number of infected has increased 25 times since 1996 and now constitutes 1 million people, of which 75 per cent are youth and children (Kamaldinova, Kovrizjnikh, Kupriyanova and Rodionov, 2002).

Mortality trends among the younger generation are unprecedented for peacetime and have become another indicator of social-demographic risk. In accordance with state statistics mortality rate varies in different age and gender groups. The older category of young Russians is particularly affected by risk of earlier death. Representatives of this cohort more often than others are losing their lives in criminal bickering. This particular age group has also been on the front line of the two Chechen wars. All in all in accordance with state annual statistics, every seventh person has died because of different kinds of accidents in 2001, which was 167 per cent more that at the beginning of the 1990s. Empirical data, collected in 2002 indicated that 30.5 per cent of young people in Russia are clearly aware of and concerned about the threats to their own health or that of one of their relatives.

The escalation of risk has affected marital trends in Russia. As a rule, when conditions are uncertain, people refrain from getting married or starting in a new family for reasons similar to those that cause increased tensions and destruction of family relations. According to the state statistics the rate of marriage in the Russian Federation is falling while the number of divorces is on the increase among young people. Statistics also show that in 1990 there were 423 divorces per 1000 marriages but by 2000, this had increased to 699 divorces per 1000 marriages. Since the beginning of 1990s liberalization more of the young people are rejecting marriage and children, preferring instead to simply live together.

The declining birth rate, especially in large cities, is another indicator of the social-demographic risk in Russian society. The birth coefficient rate by 1997 had fallen to 1.23, which is 0.91 less than the level required for simple reproduction (Osipov and Lokosov, 2001). Despite that 53.6 per cent and 51.4 per cent desired to have two children in 1999 and 2002 respectively and 7.1 per cent and 8.9 per cent of young Russians desired to have three or more children in 1999 and 2002 respectively, the reality is different. In 2002 most young couples had just one child (57.8 per cent), approximately ten percent had two children and less than one percent had three and more children. Many young people (21.7 per cent) are rejecting the idea of children for economic and financial reasons and 13 per cent do so because of uncertainty about the future. Thus, demographic decline has coincided with a new systemic crisis, which has accelerated since 1992. In a broad societal sense there is strong evidence of the escalation of risk of negative demographic reproduction especially with regard to Russia's constant de-population.

Risks in the Socio-Structural Changes

This type of risk comes into being alongside structural changes in employment, increasing social differentiation, fragmentation and restriction of opportunities for different categories of Russian youth. On an individual basis it expresses itself in uncertainty for putting into practice individual goals and life plans in accordance with one's inclinations and gifts in education and work, leisure and culture.

The developing social differentiation among young people affects their self-realization opportunities at the starting point of life course. Such opportunities in education are closely related to the material position of young people's families and to the type of settlement. (See Table 10.1).

While opportunities for better education are open for young people from high social status families (about one third), those young people born in or who have been living in small towns and particularly in the rural areas, as well as those with low living standards, are more likely to chose between education and work and so have fewer opportunities to gain a better education (two thirds). The connection between opportunities for self-realization and material differentiation is even closer. Poor young people that constitute the majority of Russian youth face lack of opportunities in comparison with those well off. In this way the poor young people are becoming poorer while the rich ones become richer. This makes social stratification deeper and produces social exclusion.

Table 10.1 Structure of the opportunities among youth aged 15–18 years in Russia in 2002 (in per cent)

Basis for stratification		Type of activity						
		A	B	C	D	E	F	G
Type of settlement	Moscow and Saint-Petersburg	5.1	39.1	25.7	20.6	5.9	2.4	1.2
	Other big city	3.2	46.9	30.9	13.6	2.1	1.1	2.2
	Small city	3.9	43.7	32.0	10.6	3.9	3.9	2.0
	Village	15.9	37.9	28.2	8.4	2.1	4.7	2.8
Incomes and living standards	Low	5.5	40.5	32.4	10.7	3.4	4.4	1.7
	High	2.5	52.7	24.3	15.7	1.6	3.2	0

Source: 'Social development of Russian youth' survey data (2002).

Table Key:
A – Work
B – Study at school
C – Study at technical college
D – Study at high education institutions
E – Work and study
F – Neither work nor study
G – Unemployed

As Table 10.1 shows the regional factor brings big differences into youth opportunities structure. This traditionally existing difference turns into a crude barrier for social mobility and becomes one of the most powerful risk generators for young people living on the periphery. The most unfavourable situation is observed in rural area where youth life chances are much narrower than among those living in urban areas. It is consequently reflected in youth consciousness as low estimated life-chances.

As a result of such differentiation, the commom model of life start and opportunities for self-realisation do not exist among youth in post-Soviet Russia. Instead of it, at least three models of life starts typical for Russian youth have been discovered on the basis of sociological survey. The *first model* applies to the 25–30 per cent of young individuals mainly oriented towards higher education. However, not all of them are motivated towards gaining better knowledge. One in three of them are driven by instrumental motives only: to avoid conscription or to have diploma as permission for a better occupation only.

In the *second model* (60–70 per cent of youth) life start is also connected with education but without any clear idea of its particular type and form. This group of young people depends on circumstances such as presence of educational establishments in their area, the level of knowledge provided by compulsory school, educational costs and family financial opportunities. They try to enter any specialized educational establishment and care less about future professional profile. This category is particularly concerned with the opportunity to enter university and graduate. Work is considered by this group as the undesirable consequence of failure in education.

The *third model* is common among 10 per cent of young Russians. Because of material needs they are oriented only towards work. Size of the salary is the leading criterion for this category of youth. They do not care about the content of their work or about working conditions. Without professional education this category can only hope for unqualified work in socially unprotected niches. Hence risk is a permanent feature for them. In fact all three models contain great risk that is determined by social and youth policy that has still not succeeded in decreasing inequality.

Analysis of the connection between the main indicators of young Russians' life start and social differences shows they are certainly dependent on economic, social and cultural factors. However, socio-cultural factors such as parental education (with mother's education being most important) as well as regional factors influence orientations towards different types of education. The traditionally determined distribution of roles in Russian family is reflected here; the mother is always closer to children and her influence is stronger. The regional factor is also among the leading ones and leaves the material factor behind. It is not by chance and it is linked to the great social differentiation among regions in the Russian Federation. Such differentiation causes cultural differentiation in the environment in which young people live. In addition, traditionally existing differences between urban and rural ways of life have been polarised over the years of crisis. All of this affects youth life chances and priorities in the Russian Federation. Paradoxical this connection appears to be natural under conditions of general decrease in living standards and socio-economic polarisation of the population. Hence, living standards are not much different in the majority of families that find they are drifting toward the poverty line. To be 'in need' is common amongst the majority of young people in Russia rather than typical of some sections of youth. This is why material position does not make a big difference between them. However material well being starts playing a significant role when comparisons of life start opportunities and the prospects of self-realization among the rich minority and poor majority are made. As for gender differences, this is determined by different male and female role structures that become clear quite early, i.e. at the stage of life start. However, in the Russian case gender factor among young people express itself not as strongly as other factors and is subordinated by previously mentioned socio-cultural and regional factors.

Opportunities for self-realization and upward social mobility are the main tools for risk control on the individual level. Data presented in Table 10.2 show considerable changes in their structure since 1999. Nowadays young people in Russia can find a job more easily and gain higher wages than was the case at the end of 1990s. At the same time, young peoples rights have failed to be protected, a good career is difficult to obtain and so the opportunity to set up their own business remains the same i.e. low. Under conditions of uncertainty the latter opportunities are at significant risk in Russia.

Table 10.2   Young people's opportunities for self-realization in the sphere of work (coefficient on a 7 point scale), 1999–2002

Opportunities of	1999			2002		
	low than average accordingly to a 7 point scale, in %	K	Rank	low than average accordingly to a 7 point scale, in %	K	Rank
Improving one's qualifications	23.0	4.54	1	24.6	4.59	1
Protecting one's social and legal rights	36.3	4.08	2	42.8	3.79	4
Finding a job	33.9	4.04	3	30.0	4.27	2
Making career	43.8	3.66	4/5	46.2	3.61	5
Better pay	44.6	3.66	4/5	39.3	3.86	3
Setting up one's own business	70.8	2.64	6	64.9	2.76	6

Source: 'Social development of Russian youth' survey data (1999–2002).

Despite that the general work opportunities remain below the average, there is a notable difference in such opportunities among those young people working in the state economy as opposed to the non-state economy (see Table 10.3).

Table 10.3   Degree of opportunities for self-realization according to different social factors (coefficient on a 7 point scale), 1999–2002

Factors		Opportunities of			
		Improving qualification	Better pay	Making career	Set up own business
Sector of the economy	State	4.21	2.89	3.02	2.26
	Private	3.97	3.70	3.31	3.09
Incomes and living standards	High	2.45	2.07	1.99	1.60
	Low	2.28	1.51	1.59	1.33
Area of settlement	Urban	2.64	2.06	2.04	1.69
	Rural	1.99	1.49	1.50	1.27

Source: 'Social development of Russian youth' survey data (1999–2002).

At the same time since the beginning of market reforms a contradiction exist: opportunity to improve one's qualification in the state sector does not lead to higher living standards of those employed by state enterprises while wider opportunities for career and incomes growth are not being supported by adequate level of one's qualification in the private economy. Thus skills do not lead to upward social mobility and do not always influence the process of self-realization of young people. Taken together these factors have already badly affected labour orientations of young people on an individual level. On the social level this has lead to the risk of decline in labour ethic of younger generation.

Thus, structural changes have lead to risks spreading into the main spheres of young people's self-realisation, which in turn crucially affects their integration into society. Lack of opportunities for satisfying the basic needs is leading to uncertainty in the civic identities among young people.

Risks of a Civic Identity Crisis

Under conditions of uncertainty young people's civil identities, attitudes towards the state and the views of citizenship as a whole have been affected by rational and mainly instrumental patterns. Relations between individuals and the state are more often seen from the point of view of rational exchange. However, great differentiation among young people has led to two different civic identity models (Chuprov, Zubok and Williams, 2001; Williams, Chuprov and Zubok, 2003). *The first model* is reminiscent of the Soviet civic model in which individuals serve the state. In this model individual rights are secondary in comparison with their citizenship obligations and duties associated with belonging to the state. Young advocates of this model expect the state to protect their rights in exchange for meeting such obligation. A sense of national pride together with a sense of security and safety result from and generate patriotic feelings among this category of Russian youth. Such types of civic identities can best be described as 'socio-centrism'. Under *the second model*, which has resulted from the liberalization process in Russia, the state serves the individual. Hence, constitutional rights for those young people who support the second model are prioritized and everything else follows. Citizenship therefore refers to belonging to the state, with citizens having obligations and duties to perform in exchange for the protection of their rights. All of this will be realized only if constitutional rights are observed. If this occurs a sense of security and safety will follow. The latter is the main means of strengthening the degree of patriotism among Russian youth. As opposed to the first model the last one reflects anthropocentrism as a particular value orientation.

Comparative data show these two models indicate different patterns of citizenship in which the individual-state relationship varies according to the degree of stability or risk prevailing in young person's individual life situation. The liberal model, with priority given to individual freedoms and rights ('state serves the individual'), is more popular among young people in Russia who are lucky enough to enjoy stability and certainty in everyday life. Among those young Russians who estimated that their lives are unstable and full of risk the reverse is true, namely 'the individual serves the state' model is more common. The latter has become a significant obstacle for successful adaptation of some categories of young people in a highly individualistic society.

Reproducing the old patterns of civic identity they fail in competition with their more egoistic and egocentric counterparts who have internalized the norms of a risk society and act in accordance with 'new forms of individualism, based on self and self-interests' (Turner, 1994). Correspondingly the nature of patriotism is also different in the two models. While in the first model patriotism comes into existence as an emotional reflection of citizenship; in second model the degree of patriotism is strongly dependent on how constitutional rights, security and safety are observed by the state. Thus, the growing rationalisation of civic relations and identities is a particular feature of the 'antropocentrist' pattern of citizenship.

This comparison of civic identities patterns show the first place is still being given to formal belonging to the state as the main attribute of citizenship, which is common for both models during the last five-seven years. At the same time, a negative trend can be observed with regards to security and safety as with other elements of citizenship. Such changes have indicated a state of uncertainty and risk with young Russians seeking to survive in social and personal life. (Table 10.4).

As sociological data show uncertainty is clearly reflected in young people's view of the current situation in the country. For 80.6 per cent of young Russians the current situation seems absolutely unclear, 86.1 per cent of them do not believe they have an opportunity to influence the social and political process. Together with rapid loss of trust in others (from 57 per cent in 1997 and 1999 up to 70.8 per cent in 2002) these trends have indicated an ontological insecurity that eventually encourages two thirds of young people to live each day as it comes and not care about the future.

Uncertainty and insecurity are shaking patriotic attitudes towards the country among 37 per cent of young people for whom citizenship is not closely associated with patriotism and does not encourage pride in the Motherland. The number of young people taking pride in their country has fallen down from 39.3 per cent in 1999 to 33.2 per cent in 2002. More than half of them (54 per cent) do not see legitimate basis for pride while the country survives long-term crisis; 48.8 per cent cannot feel

Table 10.4   **Russian youth civic identities dynamic, (coefficient on a 7 point scale), 1999–2002**

Civic identity indicators	1999		2002	
	κ	Rank	κ	Rank
Formal belonging to the state	5.09	1	5.19	1
Obligations and duty	4.87	2	4.78	2
National pride and self respect	4.84	3	4.76	3
Constitutional rights	4.69	4	4.52	4
Security, safety	4.52	5	4.25	6
Patriotism	4.37	6	4.37	5

Source: 'Social development of Russian youth' survey data. 1999–2002.

pride because the country does not respect its citizens. While a quarter of young people in Russia are proud of their country the rest (three-quarters) associate present-day Russia with the regime that plunged them into crisis and so their attitudes towards their country lack clarity. As a result, among those who estimated that their lives are unstable and full of risk, the proportion that was proud of their country was 1.5 times fewer than among those young people who estimated that their lives are stable. Thus, this analysis demonstrated that risk does not necessarily lead to the total breakdown of patriotism, instead it distorts it.

Hence, symptoms of an eroding citizenship and a civic identity crisis are the outcomes of a growing general insecurity, which in its turn is caused by the inability of the state to provide young citizens with social and legal protection. Finally a quarter of young Russians (25.2 per cent) is not pride of the country because it has done nothing personally for them. Such strong instrumental attitudes are built on the wrongly understood idea of priority of their own rights in opposition to obligations and have appeared along with a new type of extreme individualism in post-socialist Russia. This type has been brought about by a crucial contradiction between liberal rhetoric and lack of social, legal and political protection in reality over the last 15 years. Social differentiation in accordance with regional factors and material well being among young people strengthen the sense of individualism and egocentrism among young people.

Localization of Risk Trends

For the empirical analysis of risk localization trends the entire sample was divided into two groups – the first one is in accordance with one's self-estimations of the real life situation in terms stability and certainty or instability and risk and the second one is according with one's orientations towards stable and reliable or changeable and risky life (Zubok, 2003). Data show that the level of risk in everyday life for young Russians has changed in a positive way. In 1999 the group of those young Russians experiencing high risk in their life situation included 34.5 per cent of the sample whereas in 2002 this proportion has decreased by 8.4 per cent. Among 68.7 per cent of young people who described their life situation in terms of risk it has predominantly been caused by individual problems (47 per cent), professional risks (8 per cent) and taking unnecessary risk (13.7 per cent). This trend demonstrates an example of the individualization of risk when broad societal factors challenging risk give way to the individual factors connected with individual risk-taking. Although one in three young Russian citizens constantly experience danger coming from the current situation in the unstable society, a positive process of the localization of *objective* risk within certain categories of young people is evident.

Comparative data shows certain fluctuation in youth orientations towards risk, which overlaps with the periods of increased uncertainty and crisis in society as a whole, and correspond with the collapse of the USSR and the 1998 economic meltdown in Russia. Such *subjective* orientations towards risk taking have been not more than a response to objective risk among youth. Comparative data show a consistent increase in the number of young people who desired stability and rejected risk-taking since 1990. 'Risk orientation' have been significantly weakening giving place to 'stability orientation'. This reflects attempts of some sections of young people to resist the mounting crisis in Russian society and contributes to a sustainable societal development and changing the direction of risk. The latter is becoming more motivated and reasonable in character that localizes risk within relatively narrow social boundaries.

Conclusions

Making transition to adulthood in Russian risk society young people find themselves under pressure of risks posed by societal transformation. Thus, risk of unrealised possibilities in physical, cultural and social development is growing at the very stage of life start. As soon as these risks are caused by the current situation in the society they are *objective* in character apart from *subjective* which could be connected with a personal choice made in favour of risk-taking. The undertaken analysis has uncovered mainly objective risks as the most common conditions of youth transition and development in post-socialist Russia. This particular risk was produced by the social-economic, the social-legal and the social-political factors such as a fall in living standards, widespread economic and social differentiation, the lack of a well-developed system of legislation and social protection of young citizens with a divergence between rights in theory and in practice as a consequence, and an unpredictability of the political course when politics itself is becoming the main source of uncertainty and risk. Under such conditions risks of negative demographic reproduction, downward social mobility, social exclusion and identity crisis tend to reproduce themselves.

Together with an escalation of risk some indications of risk localization have also been found among Russian youth. On the objective level risk localization trends are linked to positive changes in social and individual life situations of some sections of young people. Such positive changes eventually lead to a reduction and narrowing of the social boundaries of risk. On the subjective level, young people's personal choices tend to favour stability rather than change and risk which also promotes the localisation of risk. The future prospects of risk trends in Russia will probably be determined by the active choice of young people themselves, their priorities and orientations as well as by the role of the state which is called up to provide young people with opportunities for self-realization. These are the main tools for risk control on the individual level in a risk society.

Notes

1   The author expresses gratitude to Christopher Williams and Gunilla Holm for their help in translating the text.
2   Current analysis is based on the national survey on social development of young people conducted by the Centre for Youth Sociology of the Institute for Socio-Political Research (Russian Academy of Sciences). The project was headed by Professor Vladimir I. Chuprov and assisted by Dr Julia A. Zubok. Samples of young people aged between 15–29 years as follows: 10.412 in 1990, 2.612 in 1994, 2.500 in 1997 and 2.004 in 1999, and 2.012 in 2002.

References

Beck, U. (1992), *Risk Society: Towards A New Modernity*. London, Sage.

Bogdanov, I. Y., Kalinin, A. P. and Rodionov, Y. N. (1999), *Economic Security in Russia: Figures and Facts,* Moscow.

Chuprov, V., Zubok, J. and Williams, C. (2001), *Youth In Risk Society*, Moscow: Nauka. (In Russian.)

Chuprov, V. and Zubok, J. (2003), 'Russian youth and work: social integration and exclusion under conditions of risk', in L. Roulleau-Berger (ed.), *Youth and Work in the Post-Industrial City of North America and Europe*, Leiden-Boston: Brill.

Furlong, A. and Cartmel, F. (1997), *Young People and Social Change. Individualization and Risk in Late Modernity,* Philadelphia: Open University Press.

Giddens, A. (1991), *The Consequences of Modernity*, Cambridge: Polity Press.

Kamaldinova, E.Sh., Kovrizjnikh, Yu. V., Kupriyanova, G. V. and Rodionov, V. A. (eds.) (2002), *Situation among Youth and Implementation of Youth Policy in the Russian Federation: 2000–2001.* Report presented by Department of Youth Policy to the Government of RF, Moscow. (In Russian.)

Kovacheva, S. (2000), *Sinking or Swimming on the Waves of Transformation? Young People and Social Protection in Central and Eastern Europe*, Brussels: European Youth Forum.

Machachek, L. (1998), *Youth In The Process of Transition and Modernization in Slovakia*, Bratislava, Institute for Sociology, Slovak Academy of Sciences.

Osipov G. V., Levashov S. K., Lokosov, V. V. and Sukhodeev, V.V. (eds.) (2000), *Russia Searching Strategies: Society and Power (Social and Political Situation in Russia in 1999)*, Moscow: Institute for Socio-Political Studies. (In Russian.)

Osipov, G.V. and Lokosov, V.V. (2001), *Social Costs of the Neo-Liberal Reforms*, Moscow: Institute of Socio-Political Research, Russian Academy of Sciences. (In Russian.)

Roberts, K., Clark, S. C., Fagan, C. and Tholen, J. (2000), *Surviving Post-Communism: Young People in the Former Soviet Union*, Cheltenham: Edward Elgar.

State Annual Statistics of the RF (1999–2002), Moscow: Goskomstat.

Turner, B. S. (1994), *Orientalism, Postmodernism and Globalism*, London: Routledge.

Wallace, C. and Kovacheva, S. (1998), *Youth in Society: The Construction and Deconstruction of Youth in East and West Europe*, London: Macmillan.

Williams, C., Chuprov, V. and Zubok, J. (2003), *Youth, Risk and Russian Modernity*, Aldershot: Ashgate.

Yanitskiy, O. N. (ed.) (1998), Russia: Risk And Hazards In 'Transitional' Society, Moscow: Institute of Sociology Publishing. (In Russian.)

Zubok J. (2003), *Risk as Problem in Sociology of Youth,* Moscow: MGSA Publishing. (In Russian.)

Chapter 11

An Attempt to Reverse the Failure
of Rural Youth Development
in South Africa

David Everatt, Sipho Shezi and Ross Jennings

Introduction

This article describes a programme designed to create sustainable employment for young people in rural South Africa. The Sirius Development Foundation (Sirius), a company involved in infrastructure provision, has designed a programme to create sustainable employment for rural youth. In partnership with Strategy & Tactics (S&T), a development agency, a formative evaluation has been completed and a pilot phase is about to commence. The article begins with a contextual overview to remind us where young South Africans have come from, historically, and then goes on to provide a detailed situation analysis of the site for the pilot programme, Shobashobane in the KwaZulu-Natal province, including opinions from local stakeholders about what is required for the programme to succeed. The article also outlines the youth development programme that is currently being implemented.

Young People in Rural Areas: The Context

Young people played a key role in the struggle against apartheid, providing hundreds of thousands of foot soldiers to challenge the South African police and defence forces, engage in schools boycotts, and enforce consumer boycotts. By the late 1980s, young people 'saw themselves as leading the older generation to freedom' (Straker, 1992). The media wrote them off as the 'Lost Generation', while the resistance movements lauded them as 'Young Lions'.

In 1990, liberation movements were unbanned, and the process of negotiating a democratic state began. The early 1990s saw a great deal of youth-focused research and policy development taking place, as youth structures and the churches sought to highlight the damage young people had suffered under apartheid and in resisting it, and to move them from victim to developmental actor. However, infighting amongst youth structures allowed political parties – notably the African National Congress (ANC) – to largely ignore youth as they finalised policies for post-apartheid South Africa (Everatt, 2000).

Every major youth initiative of the 1990s has collapsed. The National Youth Commission, hastily inaugurated to meet the twentieth anniversary of the 1976

Soweto uprisings, has consistently failed to mobilise youth or government resources for youth (Everatt, 2000). Young people, in turn, were able to be teenagers instead of cadres. A host of subcultures have developed, each with distinctive clothing, music preferences, and lifestyles. Although participation in the 1994 general election was universally high, by the time of the second general election in 1999, less than half (48 per cent) of those aged between 18 and 35 registered to vote. Age was a key variable: fully 97 per cent of South Africans aged 70 and above registered to vote (Levin, 2000).

Young people have travelled the full circle from social outcast through development partner back to outcast. But those in rural areas have simply disappeared from public discourse. This is particularly tragic given the massive rural mobilisation achieved by the United Democratic Front in the 1980s, when resistance to apartheid reached its apogee, and which demonstrated that spatial, communication, and other problems in rural areas could successfully be overcome.

Rural South Africa is synonymous with poverty. Some 75 per cent of South Africa's poor live in the rural areas, mainly concentrated in or near the old apartheid bantustans. Moreover, 'compared to the poor in urban and metropolitan areas, the rural poor suffer from higher unemployment rates, lower educational attainment, much lower access to services … [and] lower access to productive resources' (World Bank/South African Labour Development Research Unit, 1995).

The rate of poverty is also more severe in rural areas: some 74 per cent of the rural population is poor, compared to 41 per cent of the urban and 20 per cent of the metropolitan populations (World Bank/South African Labour Development Research Unit, 1995). South Africa is also strikingly unequal: the lowest 40 per cent of households (equivalent to 53 per cent of the population) account for less than 10 per cent of consumption. Poverty also has a strong racial dimension: 95 per cent of the poor are African and about 5 per cent are coloured; whites and Indians scarcely feature (World Bank/South African Labour Development Research Unit, 1995).

Youth is defined by law in the National Youth Commission Act of 1996 (in somewhat perplexing fashion), as all those aged between 14 and 35. Officially defined, youth comprise 40 per cent of the total population. Youth are more likely to live in urban areas (57 per cent do) than rural areas (43 per cent), but in only slightly greater numbers than the rest of the population (55 per cent of the total population live in urban areas) (Statistics South Africa 1998). Rural areas in South Africa were formerly the location of the bantustans, in which surplus black labour was expected to reside. These were also places of deep poverty. However, rural schools were often preferred by urban parents, because there was less political violence and fewer boycotts than in urban areas in the 1980s. In the 1990s, lower fees kept rural schools attractive. Many children born in urban areas were and still are sent 'home' to rural areas for their education, with older female relatives (normally grandmothers) taking responsibility for them.

The rural population is distinctly youthful. A fifth (18 per cent) of those defined as youth in urban areas are aged between 14 and 17 compared with over a quarter (27 per cent) of those in the same age cohort in rural areas. The trend is reversed in the upper age cohorts because of urban to rural migration (and presumably children returning to their urban birthplaces): 21 per cent of urban youth are aged between 31 and 35, compared with 16 per cent of those in rural areas (Statistics South Africa, 1998).

But behind the statistics are messy, complex, local realities, and real people. In order to better understand youth in rural areas, the remainder of the article steadily narrows our focus from the general to the specifics of our pilot site. We begin with a statistical analysis of Ugu District Municipality and then focus on Eziqoleni Local Municipality (where Shobashobane is located), using available data.

Where We Are ...

The October Household Survey (OHS)[1] conducted annually by the government's statistical agency Statistics South Africa found in 1997 that 27 per cent of urban and 34 per cent of young people in rural areas were unemployed (Statistics South Africa, 1998). In rural areas, unemployment is far higher among young women (at 42 per cent) than among young men (29 per cent). If these figures are recalculated to measure the rate of unemployment (by excluding those not in the labour market such as students and recalculating accordingly), the figures rise to 39 per cent in urban areas and a massive 58 per cent in rural areas. This is compounded by the growing impact of HIV/AIDS on all aspects of life, dragging rural youth in South Africa in a downward spiral. Although 'crisis' is among the most overused words in the South African lexicon, it seems appropriate when discussing young people in rural areas.

Something must be done to break out of the *status quo*. Waiting for 'market forces' to transform the rural economy is akin to waiting for Godot; moreover, young people in rural areas represent the least attractive sector for investment in the eyes of the financial and business sectors, and will be among the last to benefit from economic growth. Government has expressed much support for youth development, but has only managed to mount some *ad hoc* projects.

To break out of the *status quo* requires two main outputs:

- an efficient and effective project model that can be replicated
- a monitoring and evaluation strategy and a robust communication strategy in order to show that youth development can be done, and to help break down the mental barriers that can be found across much of South African society.

This was the point of departure for the design of the sustainable employment programme.

... And Where We Want To Be

The ultimate goal is a programme that works through faith-based structures to:

- recruit and train young people
- organize them in their own, formally constituted structures
- facilitate the process through which local municipalities will employ them to maintain the infrastructure provided by government's development and anti-poverty programmes (a growing area of need – see for example Everatt, 2001).

By following in the footsteps of government programmes, the programme will be located in poor rural communities. The model is flexible: providing maintenance services is the first area to be explored (see below), but this could be followed by training youth to operate and manage directly productive assets provided by programmes such as the Community Based Public Works Programme. Many other possibilities exist.

The programme seeks to match two needs – jobs for youth, and maintenance suppliers for local authorities – by providing youth with the skills for asset maintenance, and negotiating with the relevant local authorities to employ the youth group to perform the required maintenance.

The overall ethos of the programme is essentially service-based. Young people will be recruited through local faith-based structures to participate in a programme where they are provided with a range of skills that they use to enhance the sustainability of assets provided to their communities. Faith-based structures continue to enjoy high levels of youth participation (Everatt, 2000), and are less open to outside interference than many other organs of civil society.

The key intervention will be the training provided to young people, which must account for psycho-social as well as technical and related needs. A detailed scoping exercise will specify the type and level of required inputs. It is probably safe to assume that alongside technical skills, training will include life skills, HIV/AIDS issues, organisational skills, negotiation and conflict resolution skills, and so on. It is probably also safe to assume that some recruits will need more specialised assistance, such as trauma counselling, and the programme will include a referral function. The target group will fall within the parameters of youth but will be locally determined.

Youth Service: An Idea Whose Time Never Seems to Come

Youth service has been on the national development agenda since the early 1990s. Since then, youth service has been on a see-saw: topping the agenda at one moment (usually when elections are imminent) and forgotten the next. Despite the fact that youth structures have consistently expressed clear support for youth service (see National Youth Commission 1999) government departments and state structures such as the National Youth Commission have failed to put in place a national youth service programme.

Youth service was one of the key proposals to emerge from the 1990–1993 consultation process managed by the Joint Enrichment Project (Everatt, 1993). It appeared as a recommendation in the Reconstruction and Development Programme. It re-appeared as a key demand emanating from a consultative youth conference organized by the National Youth Commission in 1997. The National Youth Commission managed a lengthy process to draft first a Green Paper on youth service, and then a White Paper. The latter was submitted to the Presidency in 2001, but no response has yet been forthcoming (Everatt, 2000).

The context may be changing. The issue of youth service was discussed when former United States President Bill Clinton met President Mbeki in 2001, both publicly and privately. The Ford Foundation has created an international centre focusing on service – primarily but not exclusively youth-focused – with resources for information-sharing, research, and policy and programme development. Domestically, the Department of Public Works with the Independent Development Trust implemented a R150million programme using aspects of a youth service approach – youth were recruited, trained, and deployed in a programme that made public buildings accessible to people with disabilities. No evaluation of the programme has taken place, and is sorely needed to inform discussions around youth service schemes.

The Sirius initiative we are discussing here stems in part from frustration at the lack of progress, and in part from the clear need and ongoing demand for youth service programmes. The frustration, need, and demand may also prove to be problematic: precisely because service has been so frequently promised but not delivered, we may encounter scepticism among potential partners and/or recruits. But the programme is more than a service initiative: it shares many aspects of traditional service initiatives, but the specific goal is to situate youth so that they can exploit opportunities for employment that exist in otherwise economically stagnant rural communities. In other words, the programme seeks to balance a service ethos with a hard-headed business approach: youth will be trained and organized to serve specific community needs (maintenance), but the key to success will be providing graduates of the programme with sustainable employment opportunities.

The Sirius initiative is small-scale and focused. The aim is straightforward (if ambitious): to show that youth service can work, can add real value to both participants and their communities, is economically sustainable, and is viable on a large scale. By so doing, we hope to break the log jam that currently exists.

The Model

The basic model will be familiar to anyone from the youth sector. In the diagram below, showing the model in stripped down form, there are three main areas of work:

- Consultation;
- Engaging the local authority;
- Project level.

The design team has drawn on its members' experience in the youth sector and lessons from past failures to improve the programme's design. Government-sponsored development programmes have been successful in many areas, but youth development is not one of them (see for example Everatt and Zulu, 2001). We believe one of the key reasons for this is an insistence on treating youth as an undifferentiated entity, which has led to:

- A failure to identify specific target groups within the overarching youth age cohort and design programmes to meet their specific needs;
- A failure to develop communication strategies tailored to the needs and idiom of the target group;
- A failure to work with youth on their own terms and provide for their various and multiple needs (that is integrated youth development);
- A failure to mount youth-only programmes.

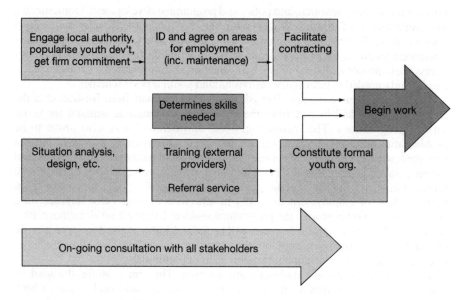

Figure 11.1 The model

These assertions are based on our experience in the youth sector as well as evaluations of youth projects and other development programmes, such as the Community Based Public Works Programme and Consolidated Municipal Infrastructure Programme, which recruit large numbers of youth as part of their workforce (See *inter alia* Everatt *et al.*,2002; Jennings and Everatt, 2001; Everatt, Mulaudzi and Ntsime, 2001; Atkinson, 2002; Unit for Housing and Urbanization, 1999).

If we turn the failings identified above into programmatic guides, they tell us the following:

- Identifying and understanding the needs of specific target groups of young people is a vital first step.
- Communication strategies must be tailored to suit the needs of that target group, including the messages being transmitted, the media used to do so, and the 'public face' of the programme.
- Youth is a transition phase, and young people have various needs, which must (as far as possible) be met. Merely providing skills training may benefit some youth, but many others will need additional inputs covering a wide range of issues and needs. Some youth may have been exposed to various forms of violence, leaving them with unresolved trauma, and professional assistance must be provided.
- A large body of literature argues that youth work best – and their needs are best met – in youth-only programmes (Foley, 2000). Some have gone further to argue for single-sex programmes.

These four points are critical: define the target group, develop an appropriate communication strategy, provide an integrated set of services, and create youth-only projects. They form the basis of the Sirius initiative. But there are two additional aspects of the programme that deserve emphasising.

Partnering Faith-Based Organisations

Firstly, the organisational home of the programme will comprise faith-based structures. In the pilot phase, we have formed a partnership with St John's Faith Mission Apostolic Church, an independent church of some 4 million members. Youth research since 1993 has consistently shown that faith-based organisations are key vehicles for reaching youth – especially rural, unemployed, and female youth. St John's gives the current phase of the programme a particular ethos that emphasises the value of service, and is considerably less likely to generate.political conflict than other potential partners.

Ensuring Access to Employment

As we noted earlier, the programme will train youth to take up specific employment opportunities – asset maintenance (and possibly asset utilisation). Identifying opportunities and securing agreement with local authorities is a programme deliverable.

Rolling Out Slowly

Given the failure of youth development programmes in South Africa since 1990, the programme's approach is slow and incremental. This is important for a variety of reasons, including to learn the right lessons at each step; to test ideas without rushing them; to work at a pace determined by local conditions; and the need for continuous, broad-based consultation with stakeholders and the community more generally.

Furthermore, we do not know enough about the push and pull factors at local level – those that attract youth or act as a disincentive, as well as those impacting on older peoples' attitudes towards youth participation in development programmes. Trying to understand these will be an important component of the pilot phase.

Situation Analysis: Youth in Shobashobane

Shobashobane is located within the Ugu District Municipality in KwaZulu-Natal. Ugu stretches from Port Edward in the south to Umzinto in the north, and from inland areas past Harding in the west to the coastal border in the east. The area is predominantly rural, with an urban strip hugging the coastline and some urban areas in the hinterland. The average monthly household income stands at R1,344. Africans comprise 89 per cent of the population, with women outnumbering men – in part reflecting the impact of migrant labour. The population of the district – like most of the rest of the country – has a large proportion of children and youth, and has the classic pyramid shape common to developing countries.

Table 11.1 Steps in the process

Formative phase

Situation analysis
- Analyse existing data.
- Site visits.
- Stakeholder interviews.

Establish partnerships
- Faith-based partner.
- Brief national structure.
- Meet and brief local representative.

Local authority
- Meet & brief local authority.
- Secure support for project and agreement over employment.

Select pilot site
- Identify area with inadequate maintenance.
- Consult stakeholders and partners.
- Agree on specific site for pilot.

Programme design

Field Visit I: Assess local conditions.
- interview local stakeholders.
- identify and interview local youth structures.
- prepare risk analysis.

Field Visit II: Youth input on design.
- Focus groups among target group.
- Test overall approach.
- Test specifics (content, methods, etc.)
- Draft curriculum for training inputs and overall programme *modus operandi*.

Field Visit III: identify providers.
- Identify local providers with track-record in working with youth.
- Identify providers for referral service.

Finalise design
- Prepare draft implementation strategy.
- Circulate among partners & stakeholders.
- Revise & finalise implementation strategy.

Pilot phase
- Test all aspects of programme.
- Monitor, evaluate, disseminate findings.

For the purposes of our programme, we defined youth to include all those between the ages of 15 and 35 years (since youth can work from age 15), and the focus was restricted to African youth living in the rural areas of the district. There were 226624 people meeting these criteria (15–35 years old, African, and rural-based) in Ugu. As with the total population in the district, rural African young women outnumber young men by 54 per cent to 46 per cent. The cohort is extremely broad and includes people at very different life stages.

Relationship to Head of Household

Many young people – of all ages – are already heading up households, while the majority live in the households of older relatives; just less than half of 31- to 35-year-olds are still living in their parents' households. It is also important to note the percentage living with their grandparents (which drops from 14 per cent of the youngest age group (15–17 year-olds) to 4 per cent of the oldest (31–35 year-olds). Pensions are likely to be the key income in these households, and for youth to contribute to the household financially could prove difficult.

These figures will be important to track over time, particularly as the impact of HIV/AIDS becomes clearer. There are a growing number of child-headed households in KwaZulu-Natal, resulting from the premature deaths of parents through HIV/AIDS. Child- or youth-headed households should be considered as a specific target group for the programme, although no reliable figures exist yet.

Unemployment

Unemployment is a key challenge in the district. Using the official definition of unemployment (which requires the respondent to be out of work and to have actively sought work in the seven days prior to being interviewed), 42 per cent of the total population of Ugu is unemployed. Research has shown that unemployment is commonly higher among youth. Ugu is no different: 55 per cent of African 15–35 year-olds in the rural areas of Ugu are unemployed.

The rate of unemployment is calculated by excluding those who are unavailable for work and working out the percentage of unemployed as a proportion of the remaining economically active population. The rate of unemployment amongst rural African youth of Ugu was a massive 71 per cent. It is important to note that unemployment is gendered: the rate of unemployment among young men was 64 per cent, rising steeply to 77 per cent among young women.

Education

38 per cent of our target group were full-time students (one per cent were part-time students). Among the remaining 61 per cent, almost half (47 per cent) wanted to further their education. This was higher among younger respondents: 52 per cent of 15- to 17-year-olds wanted to further their studies compared to 36 per cent of 31- to 35-year-olds. The older the person the lower their present education level is likely to be, reflecting the impact of post-1994 education. Of our total target group, 70,219 are unemployed and not studying, 45 per cent of whom are men and 55 per cent women. The group shows a wide variation in levels of education, reflected in the table below.

Table 11.2 Levels of education for unemployed, not studying, as a percentage of age group for men and women

	15–17	18–20	21–25	26–30	30–35
Male					
None	20	10	7	13	27
Primary	50	33	36	45	39
Junior secondary	30	29	16	15	27
Senior secondary	0	28	41	27	6
Female					
None	12	4	7	23	11
Primary	76	28	27	28	32
Junior secondary	12	42	27	24	29
Senior secondary	0	25	40	25	28

Source: Statistics South Africa (1998)

Younger respondents as a whole have higher levels of education than their older counterparts – but a significant proportion of the youngest age group has no formal education at all. This is dramatically higher than the proportion of the population of the whole district with no formal education, and is particularly pronounced among young men. Although the number of young people between 15 and 17 years old who were neither at work nor at school is relatively small – 2,440 – in large part they have never gone to school. So while they require urgent assistance, they will also need to spend longer being trained if they are to benefit from developmental and other opportunities.

Training needs to be designed so that it can maximise opportunities for success, thus encouraging others to support and join youth development programmes. Targeting uneducated or less educated youth creates a series of challenges. Youth who are illiterate and/or innumerate will take longer to train in some key areas – bookkeeping, financial management, organisational management, and so on. If a development programme succeeds in linking youth to opportunities for the maintenance of its assets, they will have to have sufficient capacity to understand tender documents, prepare and submit invoices and financial reports, and so on. Youth with relatively high levels of education may, however, become dissatisfied with maintenance and related work, and leave a development programme in search of more lucrative employment. Mixing participants with low and high education may also create tensions within the group.

Membership of Civil Society Organisations

Assessing the involvement of youth in civil society organisations (CSOs) provides an indicator of their social engagement and identifies potential vehicles for reaching youth. Figure 11.2 below shows the important role that religious organisations can play, with almost half (46 per cent) of our target group belonging to a religious organisation. Young women are far more likely to belong to such a group than young men (55 per cent compared to 19 per cent). Age does not influence membership of religious organisations.

At the other end of the spectrum, 28 per cent of rural African youth in Ugu were not members of any organisation, with insignificant differences between the proportions of men and women in this regard. However, 31 per cent of youth aged 18 to 25 years had no organisational affiliation compared to 24 per cent of youth aged 26 to 35.

Religious organisations thus emerge as one of the key vehicles for accessing rural youth, particularly young women. However, the fact that over a quarter of youth have no organisational affiliation means that other measures must also be employed to reach them.

One of the main concerns raised by leaders about the future of young people is the lack of structures among them. The fact that the majority of young people in Eziqoleni are apparently unorganized hampers chances of mobilising them around issues that affect them, but underscores the importance of working through religious organisations. The local council indicated that when they address youth issues they rely on traditional authorities, who are not seen to be the most effective in dealing with young people.

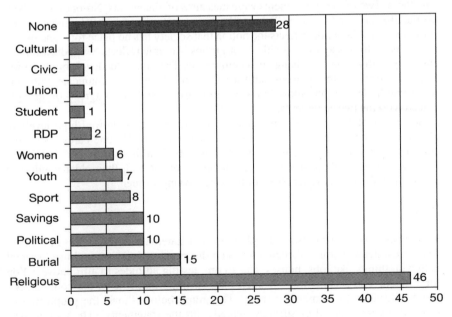

Figure 11.2 Membership of civil society organisations
Source: Strategy & Tactics (2000)

HIV/AIDS

The HIV/AIDS epidemic is likely to impact on development projects where the focus is on creating sustainable assets and the community plays a central role in the maintenance of these assets. In our survey of rural African youth in Ugu we asked questions about their awareness of anyone in their community who suffered from and who has died of HIV/AIDS.

One in three (33 per cent) of our respondents knows someone in their community with HIV/AIDS, while a slightly higher proportion (37 per cent) knows of someone who had died as a result. The need for any developmental intervention targeting youth to encompass some HIV/AIDS education is very clear. However, education around this issue on its own is inadequate. Given that the young, and women in particular, are at risk, youth development programmes need to be based on the blunt assumption that a significant proportion of those youth who enrol for the programme will already be infected. They need to be planned to address stigmatising within the programme and in the community at large, to facilitate support and care if needed, and so on. Programmes would also have to make provision for the likelihood that participants tasked with project maintenance or implementation may well become unable to continue with their tasks.

'Headspace'

To explore attitudes and perceptions in our target group, a series of statements was read out and respondents were asked to give their level of agreement or disagreement with them. Two of these statements were measures of alienation ('No-one cares about people like me') and anomie ('People like me cannot influence developments in my community'). Alienation reflects the notion that society has no place for – and makes no provision for – specific individuals or groups. Anomie reflects a withdrawal from engaging with action and change in a community. The higher the levels of alienation and/or anomie are, the more difficult it will be to identify, communicate with, and reach youth. The graph below looks at those respondents who agreed or strongly agreed with the two statements.

Seven out of every ten (70 per cent) of our respondents showed high levels of alienation, either agreeing or strongly agreeing with the 'No-one cares about me' statement. Levels of anomie were slightly lower, but still high at 64 per cent. Youth from the younger age group displayed higher levels of both than older youth, and young men displayed higher levels of both than young women.

Women

Respondents were also presented with a series of statements on the status of women. The first statement was 'Women have been discriminated against and need special help with things like jobs, houses, and so on', testing attitudes to affirmative action for women. The second was 'Women play an important role in the community', testing attitudes to women generally. The graph below shows the proportion of respondents that agreed or strongly agreed with the statements. (The two gender-related statements are reflected in the middle and bottom sets of bars.)

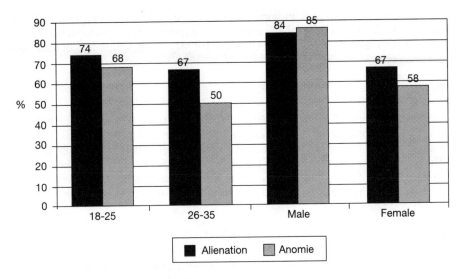

Figure 11.3 Alienation and anomie
Source: Strategy & Tactics (2000)

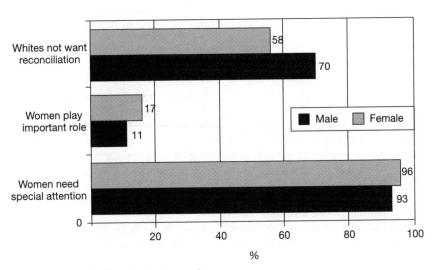

Figure 11.4 Attitudes to gender and race
Source: Strategy & Tactics (2000)

It is positive to note that the overwhelming majority of male and female respondents agreed with the statement on affirmative action for women. It is, however, startling (and somewhat counter-intuitive) that so few men and women agreed with the second statement, that women play an important role in the community. This may reflect a problem with the phrasing of the question, confusion among respondents, or the belief that women do not (or are not allowed to) play an important role in their own community.

Race

Respondents were also asked to respond to the statement 'Whites in South Africa don't want reconciliation'. This was less to judge whether people are racist or not than an attempt to find out whether there might be obstacles to using white trainers. The results show that two-thirds of our target group (64 per cent) do not believe that white South Africans want reconciliation. This is considerably higher among men than women. The findings suggest that members of the target group share strong race-based attitudes.

Crime

A further statement – 'Criminals have too many rights' – was intended to gauge respondents' opinions on crime and human rights. The overwhelming majority of respondents (79 per cent) agreed or strongly agreed with the statement. The point is not about crime and the criminal justice system specifically, but rather that the majority of the group share conservative views on some key issues, and that civic education should be considered amongst youth. This could cover a wide range of issues, but the data suggest that human rights and their place in the South African Constitution should feature quite strongly.

Development Priorities

Respondents were asked to imagine that they were in government and facing financial limitations on what they could deliver, and to prioritise the issues that needed to be addressed in their community. Water was by far the most common issue mentioned, followed by electricity, and housing. This well reflects the fact that over half (52 per cent) of residents in Ugu rely on rivers, streams, or dams for their water, and less than half (42 per cent) have access to electricity (Statistics South Africa 1998). The data reflect the real need in rural areas of KwaZulu-Natal as a whole for access to basic services and infrastructure. Only one in twenty five of the young people mentioned education as a priority.

Male and female respondents prioritised issues in the same way. This indicates the pressing nature of the needs, and that youth are consistent judges of their communities' needs.

Respondents were asked what one thing would make their lives better. Jobs were mentioned by over a quarter (28 per cent). Given the high levels of unemployment among youth in Ugu, this is not surprising. A quarter (25 per cent) mentioned having their own house as important, followed by education (15 per cent), water (14 per cent), and the need to fight poverty (9 per cent). The table below details the findings by age group.

Table 11.3 What one thing would make your life better?

Age	Jobs	Education	Houses	Water	Fight poverty
18–25	38%	22%	15%	11%	9%
26–35	16%	7%	35%	18%	9%

Source: Strategy & Tactics (2000)

For the younger age group, jobs and education were the two main things that they felt would make their lives better. For the older age group, it was houses and water. This reflects the point made earlier: the 15–35 age group includes people at different life-stages and with differing needs and perspectives.

Attitudes Towards Development

While the majority of local leaders and church organisations in Eziqoleni supported youth development projects for the area, most expressed their concern about what they perceived as a lack of interest among young people in developing their communities, and a lack of interest in embarking on creative, short-term job-creation projects such as those provided by youth development projects. Some of the local leaders were particularly critical of what they termed a lack of purpose and interest among male youth in their area. As one leader put it: 'Most young people do not know what they want, often they are less interested in development initiatives. If they are not involved in local activities we would not know what their needs and immediate priorities are.'

However, during a visit to one of the local church organisations we discovered a number of projects in which young people were playing a pivotal role, including communal gardens, youth choirs, and candle-making projects. Development programmes could link with organisations like these and build on their activities. Amongst other things, they could provide the opportunity for peer training, a powerful tool for youth development in particular. Local church leaders indicated that female youth are most likely to participate actively in church affairs and attend church services.

One local priest said that young people in church-initiated projects often change the agenda and focus on issues and programmes for political gain. According to him, political intolerance remains one of the challenges facing young people in the area. The municipal manager corroborated this view when she indicated that the lack of exposure to developed areas and how they function, coupled with low levels of education, compounded the intensity of political intolerance. She also raised the concern that at times it appears that some of the local political leaders fuel this behaviour.

Local Voices

In late 2001, S&T partner Moagi Ntsime undertook a lengthy field trip to Eziqoleni and Shobashobane itself. He interviewed a wide range of stakeholders, and we briefly summarise the key findings here.

Eziqoleni is predominantly rural, lacks an industrial base and employment opportunities, and the area is generally underdeveloped. Poverty and unemployment are key issues for local residents. When presented with the proposed youth development project, respondents overwhelmingly welcomed the idea. People argued that it is one of the most relevant types of project for their area in addressing unemployment among young people. The role of the church was also welcomed as both important and appropriate. Local examples already exist where the youth of Shobashobane are involved in projects of local church organisations.

Most people stressed the need to include all relevant stakeholders during the consultation and/or implementation of the project. Local leaders indicated that it would be very important, for example, to inform and consult a particular *inkhosi*[2] under whose area of jurisdiction the project would be implemented. While there could be some resistance among certain *amakhosi* in the beginning, most people indicated that normally they would come to accept the project over time, and be of assistance should they be required to do so. Co-ordination with the local council was identified as a weakness.

There is a low level of youth organisation in Shobashobane. The fact that the majority of young people in Eziqoleni are said not to be organized limits chances of mobilising them around issues that affect them; but underscores the importance of working through churches. The local council indicated that when they address youth issues they rely on traditional authorities, which they accept is not the most effective way of dealing with young people. Concerns were raised about the number of projects built by government and not being used in the area. Some of the local leadership argued that this would jeopardise their chances when they apply in the future to national government departments for additional development projects. As a result, they welcomed the notion that the proposed youth development project would ensure that some of these unused assets would be utilised.

There is political tension between the local traditional authorities and the newly elected councillors in some of the rural areas, which places strain on their relationship. It is, however, encouraging to note that the council leadership has taken this as one of the issues, which needs to be addressed in order to ensure that development initiatives become the responsibility of all stakeholders, including the *amakhosi*.

Conclusion

The development needs of rural communities in Ugu are enormous. The majority of young people in the area are unemployed and lack the skills to enter the world of work. The local leadership and community mostly welcome creative proposals or suggestions geared towards dealing with the challenges facing young people in the area. Most leaders raised the question about what would be the best way to convince young people to be involved in local community initiatives. Involvement of youth in development programmes is affected by both youth's lack of motivation and changing adult attitudes to youth. The majority of the leaders in the area view involving young people as the beginning of a long process to unlock their talents and potential. This is one of the critical challenges that they are faced with, and it is going to be a long and hard exercise to undertake. There are no quick-fix solutions to problems of poverty and development.

Youth development projects must be locally based. They must understand the local youth cultures and their participants, so as to understand the value base and cultural milieu in which they operate. Projects also need to gear themselves towards providing multiple services, directly or indirectly. Young people have multiple needs – providing them with a technical skill will not meet those needs, and referral services should be a component of the project.

Finally, it may once again be time for the youth sector to organize itself around the need for government policies and programmes to be revisited and revised. The current approach has failed. The generation that brought apartheid to the negotiating table was left to fend for itself. Its successors have faced the same socio-economic problems, coupled with the impact HIV/AIDS is already having. The next generation will include huge numbers of HIV/AIDS orphans and others who have been directly or indirectly affected by the epidemic. Can South Africa afford to leave things as they are, and hope that youth somehow find the resources to navigate their way to the future?

Postscript

Since this article was written, the Sirius Development Foundation has been awarded a 3-year grant from AusAid to implement the programme. By the time this book appears, youth in Shobashobane will have been recruited into the programme.

Notes

1 Data used in this section come from the 1997 October Household Survey conducted by Statistics South Africa (Statistics South Africa 1998), and the Community Based Public Works Programme Community Profile Survey (Strategy & Tactics 2000). We are grateful to Bongani More of the National Department of Public Works for granting permission to re-analyse the latter survey data.

2 Zulu word for a traditional authority. *Amakhosi* is the plural form.

References

Atkinson, D. (2002), 'Special employment projects in the Department of Water Affairs', Johannesburg: Strategy & Tactics photocopy.

Everatt, D. (1993), 'Putting youth on the national agenda', Johannesburg: Community Agency for Social Enquiry.

Everatt, D. (2000), 'From urban warrior to market segment?: Youth in South Africa 1990–2000', *Development Update*, **3** (2), pp. 1–39.

Everatt, D. (2001), 'Implementing special employment programmes in South Africa', Pretoria: Department of Public Works.

Everatt, D., Jennings, R., Dube, N., Mulaudzi, J. and Ntsime, M. (2002), 'Poverty alleviation in rural South Africa: Evaluating the Community Based Public Works Programme 1999/2000/2001', Johannesburg: Strategy & Tactics.

Everatt, D., Mulaudzi, J. and Ntsime, M. (2001), 'Can sustainable rural development be fast-tracked? An evaluation of the rural anti-poverty programme (RAP-85)', Johannesburg: Strategy & Tactics.

Everatt, D. and Zulu S. (2001), 'Analysing rural development programmes in South Africa 1994–2000', *Development Update,* 3 (4), 1–38.

Foley, P. (2000), 'Exploring the opaque: Working with young people – the Joint Enrichment Project 1986–2000', *Development Update,* 3 (2), pp. 116–130.

Jennings, R. and Everatt, D. (2001), 'Evaluation of the 1998/99 Community Based Public Works Programme: Consolidated report', Johannesburg: Strategy & Tactics.

Levin, M. (2000), 'Opting out of organized politics: Youth and the elections', *Development Update,* 3 (2), pp. 89–100.

National Youth Commission (1999), 'National Youth Service Summit: Final report', Johannesburg: Strategy & Tactics photocopy.

Strategy & Tactics (2000), 'Community Based Public Works Programme Community Profile Survey', Pretoria: Department of Public Works.

Statistics South Africa (1998), '1997 October Household Survey', Statistical Release P0317, Pretoria: Statistics South Africa.

Straker, G. (1992), *Faces in the Revolution: The Psychological Effects of Violence on Township Youth in South Africa,* Cape Town: David Phillip Publishers.

Unit for Housing and Urbanization (1999), 'Review of the South African government's grant-funded Municipal Infrastructure Programs: Summary document', Boston, Harvard University Graduate School of Design.

World Bank/South African Labour Development Research Unit (1995), 'Key indicators of poverty in South Africa', Pretoria: Reconstruction and Development Programme Office.

Chapter 12

Cross-Cultural Understanding:
Service-Learning in College Coursework

Gunilla Holm and Paul Farber

Universities provide a brief interlude between a young person's initial immersion in some local, particular culture and their subsequent immersion in more inclusive, cosmopolitan and global domains of adult life. Across a range of fields, disciplines, and domains of work, young people find themselves in post-university settings that welcome, if not positively demand, cross-cultural openness and understanding. Young scientists, for example, enter into a global community of scientific inquiry and communication, business school and liberal arts graduates alike work to overcome parochial borders, and so on. This is not to say that disciplines do not also foment status barriers (see Jeff Schmidt, 2000). But the point is that diverse kinds of highly skilled work and expertise take place in settings that explicitly tout the value cultural openness and communication and the harms associated with cultural exclusivity. Cross-cultural understanding is a guiding ideal of university studies. (See, for example, Martha Nussbaum, 1997)

If that is so in such domains as business and the arts and sciences, it is especially true for those preparing for careers in public service professions such as teaching and social work. Here the transition from one's local frames of meaning, the cultural constraints of childhood, to an enlarged capacity to overcome cultural differences in effective and sympathetic ways is particularly crucial. A scientist or scholar can, in the end, live in a global community of like-minded peers; a teacher or social worker cannot. Many, if not most, graduates of such programs will not return to settings like the ones they grew up in. Rather, they will emerge as young professionals working with students not their mirror image, young people they are obliged to work with but with whom they do not feel at home.

Across a wide spectrum of programs, then, university studies implicitly or explicitly engage the highly charged territory of cultural diversity, the disconcerting need to confront the otherness of people whose looks, lives and experience are distinctly alien in some variety of ways. The hope of many observers of higher education is that young college-age students will manage the transition in a way that opens up prospects for a lifetime of cross-cultural understanding and communication. Their lives will almost certainly feature countless occasions for such understanding and communication to unfold, or fail to do so. What experiences at a university contribute to the possibilities of moral growth in this sense?

Academic service learning is an emerging field of applied theoretical and practical work that has entered into higher education practice with such concerns in view (Koulish, 2000; Langseth, 2000; Martin and Wheeler, 2000). In this chapter, we provide an overview of academic service learning, then go on to examine its impact on a particular group of university students, in this case young people aspiring to be teachers. Our principal aim will be to clarify what is at stake during the sensitive, transitional period between the somewhat sheltered life of a teenager and the exposed, culturally contested role of the kind young professionals or other college graduates enter in contemporary culturally diverse society. What is the pertinence and possible value of academic service learning with respect to such unavoidable, and often crucial transitions.

The Idea of Academic Service-Learning

To be very honest, I was quite intimidated when I first met the students at the school. I come from a very small town without violence problems within the school. I have never seen school officials walk around with walkie-talkies in their hands [and have them] worried about visitors in the school. My experience with minorities is pretty much nonexistent so I was worried about being able to relate to the student I was placed with. When I first met my student I wasn't sure what to talk to her about. I was trying to think of things to ask her in order to get to know her better. I was quite surprised though at how easy it was.

This comment comes from a student taking part in an academic service-learning course as part of a professional program in teacher education. In this case, the course was entirely structured around the service-learning component (Ward and Nitschke-Shaw, 2001; Anderson and Hill, 2001). Readings, assignments and evaluation were tied to the required service-learning experience. The university students served as mentors to students in an alternative high school for one semester. A central purpose of this mentoring experience was for the university students to develop a personal relationship with a student whose cultural background and educational experience was significantly different from their own. Since most of the university students in question will one day be teaching in culturally diverse classrooms, this mentoring experience was intended to enhance their ability to build relationships and learning communities on the basis of cross-cultural understanding. School officials were pleased that the high school students would have contact with young people who went to college and had a job. The mentors also did some tutoring of the high school students when deemed useful or necessary.

The features of this particular course – which provides the focus of our discussion in this chapter – exemplify central components of academic service-learning. A growing literature testifies to interest concerning academic service-learning at this time. Indeed, some, such as Claus and Ogden (2001), would go so far as to say that service-learning or community learning now is a full-fledged movement in the US for connecting young people to their communities and for making their lives more meaningful and for developing a commitment to social change. Or as O'Grady (2000) puts it, service learning is guided by the notion that university students engaged in such courses, learn to work collaboratively, to reflect critically on what they do, and to promote civic responsibility. For many university instructors implementing such courses, the intention is that students will feel a civic responsibility to carry on in their professional lives working in areas where they are truly needed, with a heightened awareness of the need to take action in a democracy.

The political component of service learning is sometimes explicit and intentional. At other times, it is downplayed. One of the deepest issues at this stage in the development of service learning coursework is in fact the question of political intent (Deans, 1999). There are practitioners of service learning who emphasize only common, explicit purposes, and for whom social issues concerning power are subjects to be avoided. But this perspective is increasingly difficult to maintain given the highly charged terrain of issues and insights service learning centers on.

The most prominent voices espousing service learning at this time address a core set of critical issues at the intersection of social structure and personal identity that they would have university students in a wide array of program areas better understand. And they see the point of this understanding in the promise that young people so educated will be better equipped and more likely predisposed to participate in forms of constructive social change grounded in such cross-cultural understanding. (Parsons, 2001; Kahne and Westheimer, 2001)

In the next section, centred on a case study of community service learning designed for prospective teachers, it will become evident how strong the political underpinnings and ramifications of this orientation are. As we will show, this is particularly the case where the cross-cultural communication in question links university students with students for whom schooling has been largely an experience of failure, pointlessness, resistance and mutual antagonism.

A Case Study of Service-Learning

As a case in point, we will focus on a service-learning course in a professional teacher education program. In this instance, twenty teacher education students were involved. All were white, lower middle and middle class, mostly from suburban, small-town, or rural areas; half of them self-identified as Christians. They all wanted to teach in schools similar to the ones they had attended. No one wanted to teach in an inner-city school and certainly not in an urban alternative school. The high school students were very diverse with about equal proportions of white and African American students and a smaller number of Latino/a students. Most of these students had a history of school failure, absenteeism, unstable home situations, and various experiences with abuse and violence. Some were there because they had been harassed in their regular schools due to their sexual orientation, or their physical or psychological characteristics. Some found it easier to attend this school because they had care-taking responsibilities for siblings or for their own children.

The nature of the service learning course and its impact on the university students will be explored here. It should be noted first that the case involves an approach to service learning that Rhoads (1997) calls critical community service learning. As he notes (Rhoads 1997), 'community service without reflection does not challenge students' perceptions of social inequalities and therefore is unlikely to achieve far reaching social change (p. 9). In this project the service was closely connected to writing and reflection individually as well as within a group. Students challenged each other and connected their work and thinking to readings related to social justice and equality.

At the beginning of the semester the students were asked to reflect on and write about their experiences encountering prejudice, discrimination, and the sense of cultural difference. They also explored the kind of schooling they had had and in what kind of schools and what kind of students they hoped to teach. They wrote a reflection paper based upon a set of readings focusing on the social and educational circumstances of youth similar to the alternative high school students. They also wrote biweekly critical incident journals and participated weekly in an electronic class discussion about their mentoring experience. Finally, they explored, analysed, and wrote an account of the life story of their mentee in the light of additional course readings. The complete set of written work was examined for each student in the class. These writings were explored with regard to changes in their thinking about and views of the students they mentored, as well as their more general understanding of and reflections on issues of cultural difference. The analysis of these documents reveals that the students in this course underwent a considerable change of perspective in several respects.

Initial Self-Reflections

In their initial self-reflections it became clear that half of the university students had never noticed, or noticed first as young adults when coming to the university, the presence of distinct cultural differences. A few had noticed physical differences in elementary school when they had seen African American children play soccer or the like. Only one student, whose father had been in the army, had attended culturally diverse elementary and secondary schools. Hence, they were a very homogeneous group similar to other teacher education students in their educational institution. They had, for the most part, been raised in ways that provided limited opportunities to reflect upon the range and nature of cultural differences comprising American society as a whole.

In response to whether they had ever thought about how others perceived them, nine of twenty had never considered this. Three thought that they could not be described with any kind of traits because they are unique individuals, which showed that they really did not understand that they and others always classify people at least to some extent (male, female, etc.) One woman stated that she had never thought about this because she had never noticed others as having particular cultural characteristics, and another stated that she hadn't thought about this because she had never thought about other cultures. Five thought they would be thought of as Christian because they were very active in campus ministry. Three thought that others might think that they believe themselves to be superior or to classify them as white, middle class and Protestant. One thought of herself as privileged. Hence, students conceived of themselves for the most part as 'normal, regular, average Americans.'

Despite the expressed view that they had not experienced what it is to be regarded as different, sixteen of the twenty university students claimed that they had been discriminated against. The kind of discrimination perceived included not being taught about car engines by one's father on account of being a girl, not being treated well in a restaurant because of one's young age, not receiving financial aid, and being treated badly in a car repair shop. Three white students reported being mistreated by African Americans.

Interestingly, the discrimination perceived seemed in several instances to be related to social class and gender. All the students who reported discrimination could refer to one particular instance even if it referred to something that happened many years ago. This indicates the power of mistreatment. It stays with young people and is not easily forgotten. Only one student said he thought he had received privileges on the basis of his social standing.

With regard to the question of whether they had seen others being discriminated against, three said that they had never seen this occur. One had seen a gay student harassed in school but most (13) gave examples related to race and ethnicity. The examples ranged from a girl who had herself told an African American boy not to touch her in case the colour would rub off, to several students being told not to date African Americans. Overall, their conceptions both of discrimination and of privilege were thin, anecdotal, and largely unexamined.

Regarding what kind of school they wanted to teach in the students were somewhat confused. Many stated that they wanted to teach in a diverse school, but they wanted this diverse school to be small and rural or suburban. Sometimes they wanted these schools to have mostly middle and upper middle class students of the kind likely to be college bound and to have supportive and engaged parents. Several stated straight out that they want to teach in a conservative, middle class or upper middle class school like the one they went to. Furthermore, some expressed the desire to teach in Christian schools or in all-white schools.

Prominent Issues that Emerged

By way of discussions, journals, and papers a record of significant issues arising during the service-learning course emerges. As noted above, the university students were not well disposed initially to work with students of the kind they encountered in their service work. But over time, the university students developed a better understanding of the difficulties the high school students struggled with. They learned what it meant, for example, to live with ten other people in a very small house or not to live with your parents or to bring up your own children when you are fifteen or sixteen years old yourself. They themselves had for the most part been well supported and had had someone to turn to with difficulties and they simply had assumed that that was the case for others as well. The importance of gangs for young people with no family support or friends became clearer. Many of the high school students had extensive family responsibilities that interfered with their school attendance and work, such as taking care of younger siblings.

The high school students' drug, alcohol, and sex habits were shocking for the university students and most of all they could not understand why the students talked with a wide array of people about these things as much as they seemed to do. For them, these were very private issues, not something to be discussed in a classroom. The most unsettling insight for them was the high school students' apparently desensitized view of violence. For example, the high school girls' indifferent response to a girl who said she had been raped was not understandable for the university students. They found the response of fellow high school students that 'she asked for it' objectionable and outdated. The high school students considered violence to be part of everyday life and often a functional way to solve conflicts. The mentees saw suicide and running away as, sometimes, the only alternatives to violence. The university students had minimal experience with violence while about 60 per cent of the students in the school had been involved with the court system and many in the school had participated in violent acts.

Most of all the university students learned about how little they knew about the lives of students like those they encountered while mentoring students in this school. As a corollary of this, they also learned to recognize the extent of the privileges they had enjoyed in their own childhood and education.

> As I drove into her neighbourhood there were empty lots, rundown houses, boarded up houses with caution signs on them, and old beat up cars in the street. I didn't really know how to react so I just kept driving and continued to talk and smile … As I drove away I started thinking. I realized how fortunate I was to have grown up where I did. I lived in a nice home, in a predominantly white neighbourhood where no one had fences. My parents gave me a car to drive … I lived with both my mother and father, who supported and encouraged me in everything I did … My mother didn't work, so that she could stay home with my brother and I. My father made enough money so we could still live comfortably with only one income. But does my father make as much as he does because he is a white male? Did I do as well as I did in school because of my family's SES?

The university students in this course began in earnest to question their own privileged background and common stereotypes. In addition, as a result of their experiences, the university students became passionate about teaching kids facing difficult life circumstances and realized that they want and need to be involved in their students' lives outside of school time. They began to question the extent to which they had lived a sheltered life. 'I learned that I am not as educated about social issues as I would like to think. In fact, I am quite naïve when it comes to some of the issues that educators are dealing with.'

As the semester progressed and the mentors learned more about how classes were conducted they became frustrated with what they saw as a clear example of what Haberman (1991) calls 'the pedagogy of the poor.' For example, they started to question the relevance of the materials and methods used. Books were old, and examples did not connect to the students' lives. There was an endless stream of worksheets and no homework. They found that the expectations of the students were very low. Some mentors pointed out that perhaps those working in the school were simply struggling to improve badly bruised self-images and raise the self-esteem of students, but wondered to what end. Questions were raised about the purpose of this alternative high school with its teacher-control, classroom management-oriented curriculum. As some of the mentors asked, since the school seemed neither to give students a vocational education nor to prepare students for college, what did it do? Some concluded that it was best regarded as a holding tank for problematic students. Some of the students stayed there for a couple of years while others left for the regular high school as soon as they could earn the chance to do so on the basis of good behaviour and passing grades. A major concern of the mentors was whether the school prepared the mentees for going to a regular high school. Some of the mentors talked extensively with their mentees about what a regular high school requires of students for them to be successful. Some even taught note-taking skills and how to communicate with teachers. The mentors, overall, came to believe that the alternative school students need most of all to learn how to communicate better. But as it is now, the curriculum always focused on the individual. Many suggested intensive cooperative learning where students would learn how to work with others and work out conflicts and how not to become offended by the slightest provocation. Some of the mentors noted though that the school probably works for some of the students because they get the individual attention they need in the very small classes. It might in the best of cases prevent some of them from dropping out.

One student started a discussion about the Alternative school in the following way:

> I feel like the Powers that be at [the alternative high school] have missed the boat. We're told that these are kids who can't succeed for one reason or another in a normal school setting, right? Well, then why not give them a very different setting instead of this watered down version of a traditional school? It's like they're going to School Lite because they can't handle the real thing. But is this what an 'Alternative School' should be? Why don't they really shake things up? Students are crying for something different. Are they crying out for worksheets? These are kids who need a radically new pedagogy the most, but it sadly seems that they're the last who are going to get it.

The mentors often reported that they believed their mentees could accomplish more academically than they did.

> I know that the situations students bring to [the alternative high school] are extremely difficult. Sometimes all a teacher can hope to do is to have a student complete a worksheet and learn some basic ideas. But – if students are consistently allowed to contribute ... if they come to school *expecting* to be listened to and valued in meaningful ways, won't they attend more and participate more?

Another student said,

> I never saw students being challenged. The attitude seemed to be that alternative meant 'less' or 'easier.' I do not believe that the students are unteachable ... I think some educators' attitudes towards [this school] is more akin to baby-sitter than to teacher. Those who traditional schooling has failed receive an alternative education, which retains the very worst that traditional schooling, has to offer.

The mentors describe the joy they experienced when, for example, they tried algebra with their mentees, and the mentees could grasp it. These kinds of examples, which were frequently mentioned, confirmed the mentors' views that the school's prevailing expectations for these students were much too low.

However, the mentors also developed a better understanding of the difficulties the teachers struggled with. The students were at very different levels academically and had a wide variety of difficulties and problems that they brought with them to school. Their chronic absenteeism made it difficult for teachers to try anything other than worksheets. Some of the mentors also encountered difficulties in understanding their African American mentees and other students. A mentor commented: 'When I first got together with my mentee I could not understand about 50 per cent of what he was saying ... Listening to him takes concentration because he talks softly and speaks in Ebonics.' They had not thought before about how to deal with a situation where they as a teacher could not understand their students. For some mentors it was the first time in their lives that they had a personal relationship with an African American or Latino/a person.

Despite their deepened understanding of the students and their background the mentors were still frustrated and angry because the mentoring relationship did not always go smoothly. They were angry when students were absent or suspended. 'Our time is valuable, and I felt frustrated when my time wasn't used well.' Or, 'the mentees who don't come to school basically waste our time.' Even though they admitted to learning a lot from the students, and appreciating the need for patience, they still did not want to accept the fact that work with these students was quite unpredictable. The priority issue for the mentees was not whether they wasted the mentor's time or not. The mentors demanded that the next semester the mentees would have to sign a contract committing to always being in school when the mentor arrived. It was difficult for the mentors to step outside their own highly organized and orderly lives and to reflect upon the fact that many live in a very different way.

The challenge of cross-cultural understanding, particularly in the context of social class, is evident also in the university students' way of attributing causes and apportioning blame for the hardships they began to see. Despite their better understanding of the alternative school students' impoverished home lives and education, some still saw the cause of all the problems as 'the broken family.' One mentor, for example, expressed this notion in the following way: 'Her family was broken and had both Hispanic and Black members, along with several teen pregnancies ... She could not relate to my own personal experiences of a solid home life, moral upbringing, and a solid educational background.'

The temptation to blame the family, evident in this remark, undercuts the insight that the school does not provide the students a meaningful education, or that while we (typically the beneficiaries of much better schooling circumstances) cannot change the home life we can strive to change the education the students receive. Interestingly, she also considered it problematic that the family had both Hispanic and Black members.

But such limiting formulations did not predominate. By the end of the semester expressions along the lines of 'This has been an eye opening experience' appeared in most journals and discussions. The students entered the high school with trepidation and harbouring preconceived notions about the high school students. 'I entered the school thinking these kids were dangerous, low-ability, and had a negative outlook on school.' They discovered that 'these kids are not bad kids' and that 'no human being is trash.' But many stated that they had been afraid of going to the school: 'I was very apprehensive about going to [the alternative high school] at first because of the stereotypes I had formed about the school. Of course I had never even been in or met anyone from [there] and was merely scared from what I had heard from others.'

When asked what they had learned from their mentoring experience, students mentioned that 'my eyes were opened to a whole other side of life that I have never had direct contact with.' They had learned not to judge people by their first impression and felt that they had been 'forced to step outside of [my] limited life experiences and [my] judgmental tendencies.' Several of the students underwent fundamental changes with regard to their views on teaching and what kind of students they wanted to teach.

I have learned that I could work with high school students from an alternative high school on a regular basis. I thought I would struggle in a high school setting and one that was alternative on top of it. I was very wrong. This is probably one of the best–if not the best–and most meaningful experiences that I have had at the university.

I have gained a sense of confidence that I never knew I had ... Tutoring at [the alternative high school] has opened my eyes to a whole new career option. I can now see myself teaching in a high school. I am confident that I can make a difference in the lives of the students I am about to teach.

I used to think that teaching and learning consisted of a series of semi-inspirational moments leading to divine change in the lives of students. However, I now recognize that good teaching requires humility and discernment–and most importantly, a willingness to learn from your students and your many mistakes.

I've learned that I can be comfortable in a school setting like [this] ... I have come to realize that I have a love for these kids that I didn't think I could have. I never thought I would have the patience to deal with them or the ability to relate to them. I discovered that I could be a teacher in that setting and I wouldn't be frightened ... I also realized that I might not want to be a teacher in a nice, rural, middle-class school, but that I might want to teach in a school like [this].

To conclude, let us take one further, rather detailed account of what one of the university students experienced as a telling instance of the kind of change process service learning can represent. Her first mentee refused to meet with her after a couple of meetings and she was reassigned to another student. The second relationship was very successful.

How I chose to approach Christina was learned through failed interactions with my first assigned student at [the alternative school]. My first assigned student was a fourteen-year old student of African American origin. He too had expressed a willingness to participate in the tutoring/mentoring sessions, but my level of success with him was far from positive. I had been given information about his low academic abilities and his family situation prior to meeting with him, and had approached him with an attitude that I was the more 'knowledgeable other' that was going to fix everything *for him*. I read books *to him*, I solved math problems *for him*, and I even talked down to him rather than *with him*. My expectations were lower for this student from the beginning, and I soon found his resistance far from acceptable. I took it personally that our tutoring/mentoring relationship had not succeeded, fearing that I was prejudiced toward his ethnicity and gender even though I've always claimed not to be. After careful inner reflection and analysis, I determined that my actions and attitudes had displayed a 'hidden curriculum.' Based on the personal information I was given, combined with his ethnicity and gender, my actions had conveyed my low expectations for this student. After my assignment to Christina, I was able to observe my first student's interactions with another tutor/mentor. I sat in amazement as I listened to him read aloud and engage in a discussion about his reading material. I realized at that time how academically capable this student truly was and I regretted that I had not encouraged him to show me his talent.

Summary

We began by noting the increasingly significant transition that must be made between the particular culture of childhood and the cosmopolitan, culturally diverse contexts of adult life. Service learning experiences at the university level represent a promising development in promoting such transitions in the fullest possible ways. In the case study described here, the university students came to admire the alternative high school students for at least showing up in school occasionally despite their difficult lives and repeated failure in school. What bothered them most, however, was the understanding that despite the mentoring, the friendship, the individual attention, and a caring teacher, many of the high school students would drop out before graduation. They came to question why these alternative high school students received an education resembling a 'holding tank' when they themselves had all kinds of opportunities and challenges. The university students' understanding of students whose lives were very different from their own grew in complexity. At the end of the semester they could not use the simplistic labels they had used to categorize students at the beginning. They had begun their journey to understand 'the other America' and the role of teachers whether in perpetuating or striving to overcome societal divisions. As many students said about the high school students, 'they live in another world.' This study documents their efforts to bring that world into focus and open channels of communication they will need to develop as teachers of culturally diverse groups of students. The university students had come to understand the structural inequalities shaping both their own and the alternative high school students' lives.

In this regard, the students depicted here exemplify a process of broad contemporary interest and importance. In the context of this university course, the mentoring relationships that were forged represent small, but perhaps decisive, steps in the direction of their developing a sense of civic responsibility in a democratic society. They began to understand what it means to work with others very different from oneself, without succumbing to the temptations to categorize, and thereby marginalize, them in terms of their 'otherness.' This is the essence of what Burbules and Rice (1991) refer to as the creation of a 'dialogue across difference,' a process that opens up horizons of meaning that is unpredictable and difficult to gauge.

This case study is suggestive with respect to the ubiquitous contemporary experience of confronting others and developing one's conceptions of otherness; it suggests the hope and challenge of cross-cultural understanding. The students in this case, both the university students and those in the alternative high school, entered into the kinds of learning involved in bridging cultural differences by way of dialogue. In this sense, they participated in the kind of process we all face if we are to take part in communities of difference (Tierney, 1993). If service learning contributes to the building of such community, it is important that the service is beneficial for all participants and as the university students indicated they learned as much as the mentees had. University students learned to care about people strikingly different from themselves and they learned more about themselves in the process. While the experience of the students in this case is but a small step toward far-reaching change, it does suggest the promise of pursuing further the sometimes arduous, often rewarding practice of service-learning in university coursework. And importantly, while clearly this kind of change has deep significance for a life in teaching, the larger implications are evident. As university experience mediates the transition from the cultural particularity of childhood to the cultural diversity of contemporary society, service-learning opportunities may come to serve an increasingly prominent and valuable role in cross-cultural learning for adolescents and young adults.

References

Anderson, J. B. and Hill, D. (2001), 'Principles of good practice for service-learning in preservice education', in J. B. Anderson, K. J. Swick and J. Yff (eds.), *Service-learning in higher education. Enhancing the growth of new teachers, their students, and communities,* Washington: AACTE Publications, pp. 69–84.

Burbules, N. C. and Rice, S. (1991), 'Dialogue across differences: Continuing the conversation', *Harvard Educational Review,* **61**, (4), 393–416.

Claus, J. and Ogden, C. (2001), 'Service learning for youth empowerment and social change: an introduction', in J. Claus and C. Ogden (eds.), *Service learning for youth empowerment and social change,* New York: Peter Lang, pp. 1–7.

Deans, T. (1999), 'Service-learning in two keys: Paulo Freire's critical pedagogy in relation to John Dewey's pragmatism', *Michigan Journal of Community Service Learning,* **6**, 15–29.

Haberman, M. (1991), 'The pedagogy of poverty versus good teaching', *Phi Delta Kappan,* **73**, 290–294.

Kahne, J. and Westheimer, J. (2001), 'In the service of what? The politics of service learning', in J. Claus and C. Ogden (eds.), *Service learning for youth empowerment and social change,* New York: Peter Lang, pp. 9–24.

Koulish, R. E. (2000), 'Teaching diversity through service-learning immigrant assistance', in C. R. O'Grady (ed.), *Integrating service learning and multicultural education in colleges and universities,* Mahwah, NJ: Lawrence Erlbaum, pp. 169–187.

Langseth, M. (2000), 'Maximizing impact, minimizing harm: why service-learning must more fully integrate multicultural education', in C. R. O'Grady (ed.), *Integrating service learning and multicultural education in colleges and universities,* Mahwah, NJ: Lawrence Erlbaum, pp. 247–262.

Martin, H. L. and Wheeler, T. A. (2000), 'Social justice, service learning, multiculturalism as inseparable companions', in C. R. O'Grady (ed.) *Integrating service learning and multicultural education in colleges and universities,* Mahwah, NJ: Lawrence Erlbaum, pp. 135–151.

Nussbaum, M. (1997*), Cultivating humanity: A classical defense of reform in liberal education,* Cambridge, MA: Harvard University Press.

O'Grady, C. R. (2000), 'Integrating service learning and multicultural education: an overview', in C. R. O'Grady (ed.), *Integrating service learning and multicultural education in colleges and universities,* Mahwah, NJ: Lawrence Erlbaum, pp. 1–19.

Parsons, C. (2001), 'Service learning and the making of small 'd' democrats', in J. Claus and C. Ogden (eds.), *Service learning for youth empowerment and social change,* New York: Peter Lang, pp. 135–141.

Rhoads, R. A. (1997), *Community service and higher learning: explorations of the caring self,* Albany: SUNY Press.

Schmidt, J. (2000), *Disciplined minds: A critical look at salaried professionals and the soul-battering education that shapes their lives,* Lanham, MD: Rowman and Littlefield.

Tierney, W. G. (1993), *Building communities of difference: higher education in the twenty-first century,* Westport, Conn.: Bergin and Garvey.

Ward, K. and Nitschke-Shaw, D. (2001), 'Institutionalizing service-learning in teacher education: the perspective from feminist phase theory', in J. B. Anderson, K. J. Swick and J. Yff (eds.), *Service-learning in higher education. Enhancing the growth of new teachers, their students, and communities.* Washington: AACTE Publications, pp. 39–52.

Topic Area 2:
Youth Engagement

Chapter 13

Latina/o Youth Contest for Equity in the Public School System in Boyle Heights, Los Angeles: A Political and Theoretical Perspective

Fazila Bhimji

Introduction

There has been a recent surge of urban Latina/o[1] youth movement in California. Rather than being the product of universities with a reputation for student resistance, this form of activism has its roots in places such as Eastside Los Angeles, Oakland, and other inner-city neighbourhoods in California with most group members being under 21 and attending high schools. This marks the birth of a new youth movement, which works very closely with various movements, community based organizations, and Latina/o politicians in California. In 1993, primarily Latino/a youth were training and demonstrating in California against racist policies in schools, demanding La Raza Studies at the high school level and other educational rights. When, in the year 2000, California's proposition 21, the Juvenile Crime Initiative, passed with 62 per cent of the vote, an initiative which gives prosecutors (instead of judges) the option to file juveniles in adult court, and put 14-year-olds into adult prisons, appeared on the ballot, the youth were further politicized and young people in California birthed a new civil rights movement going by the slogan 'Schools Not Jails.' Youth Organizing Communities (YOC) are based in urban disenfranchised areas. These communities have a high level of participation of Latina/o high school students who forge alliances with politically conscious white students, other conscious students of colour, and organizing communities such as labour unions and teachers unions. Although there has been a resurgence of Latina/o youth movement, it has not been addressed by youth studies, or Latino/Chicano studies, or social movement studies. By tracing their narratives of political struggles as they shift meanings of race, class, and community, the study aims to extend the literature in all three areas and argue the diversity of urban Latina/o youth. More specifically, I will map the socio-political context that Latina/o youth of poor working families encounter. Second, this chapter will discuss the ways in which Latina/o youth work to restructure their educational experiences. Third, the chapter will discuss the formation of political identities of Latina/o youth.

Theoretical Framework

Youth Studies

Much of the recent ethnography on inner-city youth has attended to explaining their deviant coded behaviours. As Steven Gregory points out 'despite the emphasis on the diversity of racial identity in contemporary theory and criticism, scholarly and mass-mediated narratives of black urban life have rarely attended to this complexity' (Gregory, 1998, p. 12). As early as in the1940s and the 1950s academic research on urban youth was dominated by deviancy theories. These studies have mainly focused on urban street gangs (e.g. A.K. Cohen, 1955; Clowird and Ohlin, 1960; Becker, 1963). Becker and others contest the polarizations between 'delinquent youth' and 'non delinquent youth' and argue that young people who engage in 'delinquent activities' are represented as conforming to the values of relatively powerless sub-cultural groups, which would not label such activities as criminal or wrong. Although, these studies oppose the deficit views, which link crime and delinquency to family disorder, they do not take into account the complexity of behaviours among inner-city youth, which may include conformity with and accommodation to mainstream society. Similarly, contemporary research on urban youth continues to link youth culture with deviance and gangs (e.g. Sheldon et al, 1997). Alexander argues that while there has been an emphasis on viewing youth category as being in transition, the representations of black youth have proved remarkably resilient in changing where 'black youth' have remained then the epitome of oppositional youth culture, defined through disadvantage and alienation' (Alexander, 2000, p. 19). By tracing their struggles for enfranchisement, I will argue the diversity of Latina/o youth experience such that it goes beyond binary constructions of youth/adult, youth/authority, and deviance/conformity.

Chicana/o/Latina/o Studies

Recent work by Latina/o scholars has greatly contributed to our knowledge of Latina/o social movements as in the past several decades; Latinos in the United States have emerged as strategic actors in major processes of social transformation (Torres and Katsiaficas, 1999). Many of these studies focus on varying forms of political struggles. Navarro (1995) provides a historical analysis of the Latino Youth Movement-MAYO's participation in educational change and other social change activities from its inception in 1967 to its demise in 1972. Muñoz (1988) presents a critical study of Chicano youth movement in the sixties and the lesson that one can learn in order to shape future struggles. Many scholars examine the role that Chicanas and other Latinas have played in labour organizing (e.g. Flores, 1997; Melville 1998; Mora and del Castillo, 1980; Ruiz 1987; Zavella, 1987, 1988). Pardo focuses on the stories of Chicana American women from two Los Angeles communities and the ways in which they transformed the everyday problems they confronted in their neighbourhoods into political concerns (Pardo, 1998). Weber (2001) explores how activism of street vendors are affected by the role of the state, organizational strategies, and social and gender locations of the vendors. Although there has been much diversity in the scholarship of Latina/o social movements, there has not been any study, which focuses exclusively on the recent resurgence of Latina/o youth activism. This study aims to extend the literature by indicating ways in which Latina/o youth participate in social change and the ways in which their socio-political order helps construct their collective identities.

Social Movement Studies

There has been much discussion within the social movement literature about the formation of collective identities of political actors. Polleta and Jasper (2001) define 'collective identity [as] an individual's cognitive, moral, and emotional connection with a broader community, category, practice, or institution' (p. 285). It is particularly useful to consider Gamson's perspective on collective identity as he considers identity to be fluid, unstable, and permeable (Gamson, 1995). It is also important to take into account Taylor and Whittier's work on negotiation of identities. They point out that 'groups negotiate new ways of thinking in public and private spheres and attempt to free the group from dominant representations (Taylor and Whittier, 1992). These studies bear significant light when discussing urban youth activism since many of the young people do not strictly adhere to a single identity but assume multiple identities. Fantasia's (1988) study 'Cultures of Solidarity: Consciousness, Action, and Contemporary American Workers' examines the creation of solidarity between workers as they organize against the factory owners thus viewing collective identity to be an emergent process. Missing from these studies is a discussion of collective identities of younger generations and particularly of young people of colour. By including an analysis of one collective identity of high school age and college age populations of colour, I will argue that political structures can also affect and influence young people's identities.

Methodology

The principal research strategy for my study is ethnographic fieldwork, which includes semi-structured and structured interviews with students and adult leaders, participant observation/video-taped analyses of rallies, meetings, and hearings, and review of archival data and related newspaper and television coverage over a period of one year in youth community organizations based in Eastside Los Angeles. According to the US census bureau Latinos have recently surpassed African-Americans and are now the largest minority group in the US (Los Angeles Times, June 19, 2003, A1). More significantly, Latinos under age 18 make up 17 per cent of the under-18 population (Hernández et al., 2001). In addition to facing the challenge of 'burden of support' for the aging white and African-American population, Latino/a youth face the additional challenge of being treated as foreign-born immigrants in a society with growing xenophobia. Mainstream discourses often locate difficulties Latina/o youth encounter within family structures. By exploring the role of Latina/o youth, as they participate in the political process, this study aims to show ways in which Latina/o youth contest the dominant culture's interpretation of them and expand our knowledge of Latino/a youth identities.

The Political Economy of Latina/o Youth

In 1968, students at a major high school in Boyle Heights staged a walkout that called for a better education. This movement for quality education occurred in the section of Los Angeles, which was home to a hundred thousand Mexican Americans. It was (as is now) completely separated from the rest of Los Angeles. Only one out of four Chicanos completed high school. The drop out rate was viewed as a 'push out' rate as Mexican Americans' language and culture were not given due respect. Unemployment rate in the community was high. These conditions had a dramatic effect on Mexican American's children and youth. Mexican Americans students called for Bilingual Education, Mexican-American history courses, hiring of more Mexican American teachers and counsellors, and the end of corporal punishment. Today many of these issues remain. On May 18, 2000 the Los Angeles Times reported that the American Civil Liberties Union (ACLU) and other civil rights groups acting on behalf of nearly 70 students in eighteen California Public Schools, filed the most comprehensive lawsuit to date ever to be brought against a state concerning the bare minimum requirements for education. The legal director of the ACLU described some of the California schools as 'schools that shame the conscience.' According to Los Angeles Times report these schools were found to lack basic resources such as textbooks, regular instruction, school nurses on premises, and working bathrooms and water fountains. Furthermore, the schools experienced massive overcrowding with not enough seats available for students.

The distancing of voters, who are mostly white, from public institutions which largely serve minorities and recent immigrants from Mexico, Central America, Southeast Asia, and the Soviet Union, has also resulted in the passage of propositions and reforms which serve to further cause disparities in education. A property tax initiative (Proposition 13), was passed in California in 1978 which resulted in draining the public schools of its money forcing teachers to leave the teaching profession and causing libraries and municipal services to shut down. In more recent times, a series of propositions have passed which affect poor urban children and youth's educational rights. These propositions included 187 (which denied undocumented children health and education), 209 (the anti-affirmative action), 227 (anti-bilingual education), and 21 (where youth as young as 14 could be tried as adults). Gutiérrez et. al (2000) consider these reforms to be a 'backlash pedagogy.' These scholars argue that 'backlash pedagogy' does not harness diversity and difference as resources for learning; instead, it is characterized by its reductive notions of learning, particularly literacy and language learning, that define diversity and difference as problems to be eliminated or 'remediated.' However, these political actions did not go unheeded instead it politicized many of the youth-largely of colour, largely Latino.

One of the significant ways that the youth responded to what they describe as 'anti-youth and anti-immigrant initiatives' was by forming youth movement which actively campaigned for educational equity and basic rights for youth of colour. This study gives an insight into some of the ways in which the youth strive to change their unfair conditions.

Inner City Struggles: Transforming Educational Structures

In response to the varied social problems in Boyle Heights (a predominantly Latina/o neighbourhood in Eastside Los Angeles) such as educational disparities and housing inequities Inner-City Struggles was formed. This community based organization, the staff of which is predominantly second generation Mexican-Americans and Central Americans youth between the ages 17 to 25, defines itself as dedicated to promoting social and economic justice for youth and families in Boyle Heights and the surrounding communities of East Los Angeles. People who live in Boyle Heights are poor, low-income blue-collar workers, and the vast majority of them Spanish speaking. In the 1940s the neighbourhood experienced several changes. Up until the 1940s this section of Los Angeles included Japanese American, Jewish and Mexican American residents. However with the Jewish flight for suburban neighbourhoods and the internment of the Japanese American residents, Boyle Heights is now primarily a Latino immigrant community. In the 1940s also began the construction of five freeways and other public projects, which uprooted ten thousand residents, and noise air pollution, and traffic congestion and disrupted the lives of the rest of the people living in the area. (Escobedo, 1979 quoted in Prado p. 26.)

Inner City Struggles was originally part of a Catholic church in the community-the Project Pastoral at Dolores Mission-but later became an independent centre and has been in existence for eight years. The office is located on Whittier Boulevard, one of the major streets in Boyle Heights. The signs in Spanish language and the nature of the businesses on the street are highly characteristic of Latino Los Angeles. The *tortillerias* (bread-making), *carnicerias* (meat stores), *panaderias* (bakeries), *taquarias* (small-sized Mexican restaurants), and occasional street vendors create a lively atmosphere. The office space of Inner City Struggles is nestled in this colourful and lively setting. Adding to this colourful atmosphere is a beautiful, brightly coloured mural, which is painted at the entrance of the building. The sun, the Aztec Pyramid, and cacti decorate the façade of the building. One of the staff members explained to me 'this mural shows that we want to reclaim our culture – it represents a certain world-view.'

The radical political tone of the space is most evident by the posters adorning the walls of the office space. Posters of political leaders such as Malcolm X, Steve Biko, Che Gueverra and masked Zapatista leaders of Chiapas, Mexico, show that this community-based organization is interested in social change and transformation.

Inner City Struggles follow the philosophy that change happens when individuals, groups, and communities are well trained and well organized. This group has an active youth component to it. This youth component called 'Youth Organizing Communities' was formed in the year 2000 mainly in response to a campaign against a proposition which aimed to try youth as young as 14 as adults for major crimes. Youth Organizing Communities staff includes mainly Latina/o high school students, college students, and two recent college graduates. The programme consists of three main components-Academic Services which assists students with academic training, the Learning Academy where the staff works with youth residing in public housing in the local area and produce a self published magazine and the United Students which is the youth organizing component of the organization. The following paragraph describes in detail this division of the group.

The United Students

In the spring of 2002, United Students began a student-led research process to identify the main problems at Roosevelt High School located in Boyle Heights. Currently, United Students includes students from Garfield High School as well as Roosevelt High School. These two schools are among the largest high schools in the United States, so over-populated with about 5,500 students in each school that they have to run year round with 3 separate tracks to accommodate all of the students. These two East Los Angeles high schools, rank very low on the Statewide Academic Performance Index i.e. 1 out of 10 with 10 being the highest. The main purpose of the United Students is to help bring change in the educational structures of the public schools. This group composed of two site organizers and students at Roosevelt and Garfield high schools engage in a series of multifold activities. One activity that the students and the site staff do is they work with students to raise political and ethnic consciousness. Much of the time the site coordinator works with the students to develop a curriculum around current political issues and issues relevant to the community. Students design flyers and conduct outreach to ensure increased participation of the students at the meetings. This particular aspect of the program aims to raise political consciousness of the students. Topics such as 'Globalization,' 'Non-Violent Movements,' and 'Achievements of Political Leaders' are discussed. In addition, in these meetings, students see films with political messages such as *Chicano!*, *El Norte*, *The Bus Riders Union*. The aim of these films is to increase political awareness among the high school students. It is significant that although these political education classes are held during after school hours on a Friday, and lasting for two hours, is attended by 15 to 20 students. The students living in Boyle Heights often have multiple commitments since many of them work part time, take care of their younger siblings, or have other family commitments. By participating in these meetings, during after school hours, the young people (re)define what it means to be an urban youth, thus challenging monolithic representations. In addition to these meetings, the United Students meet once a week at the high school during lunch hour as well as in the office space. In these meetings, the students and the staff work together to develop strategies and plans for their respective campaigns. Additionally, the students also meet annually with other youth groups in California, where the various youth groups provide workshops concerning educational justice issues to/with students in public schools in California, which now consists of mainly of poor students of colour.

Some of the campaigns that the United Students work on include creating new policies for addressing attendance and tardiness, providing a purposeful and culturally relevant curriculum, and implementing policies that provide equitable opportunities for students to be eligible for entering into a university system. By working on this issues, which could lead to students' academic enhancement the students once again resist stereotypical discourses, which always define them as being unconcerned with their education. The students and the coordinators of United Students rely on multiple strategies to get their plans implemented. The students meet with teachers, principal, and school administrators on a regular basis, hold hour long after school forums with school administrators and students, conduct surveys, the results of which is used to convince administrators to meet their demands. The students also do political outreach on their school campuses by conducting weeklong teach-ins, skits, and mini-lectures on educational justice issues two to three times a year. In doing so, they involve their teachers, school administrators, and the students in their respective school campuses. In addition, the United Students also work in coalition with newspaper columnists on an ongoing basis. The director of the Youth Organizing Communities explained to me that the organization believes that it is important to build a continued relationship with newspaper columnists so that their voices and opinions get included in the paper. Indeed the efforts of the group did not end in vain. The Los Angeles Times featured a number of articles related to academic inequalities at Roosevelt High School.

These efforts by the students and young people to transform their under-resourced educational experience gained much recognition. On November 2002, the United Students reported winning significant parts of the student demands, such as the implementation of two Mexican American Studies classes, the addition to guidance counsellors, and the elimination of the tardy room.

What is noteworthy here is that the youth group in their struggles to change their institutional arrangements works in conjunction with the school staff, faculty, and administrator rather than in strictly oppositional ways. For example, the young men and women expressed to me that much of the time they found their school administrators and teachers to be quite supportive of their activities, allowing them to hold meetings, forums, and teach-ins during and after school hours on school grounds. When the United Students held their forum to start a discussion in regards to their grievances regarding school policies with school administrators, teachers, and students, they expressed clearly their intents in 'working with' the larger school community rather than against it. Moreover on the flyer announcing the meeting, the group expressed their acknowledgments to the school principal, the assistant principal, and the entire administrative team. On the front cover, however, the United Students had their radical logo printed, which included sketches of a masked Zapatista leader and Malcolm X. Thus, the young people assume multiple identities. On the one hand they express that they want to see radical social change, but on the other hand they show their willingness to work in coalition with the larger institutions, which discriminate against them. In this way the young people serve as intermediaries between the institution and the community of students they represent. Inner City Struggles is also community based serving community members in the form of tutoring, counselling, and providing access to computers. On the other hand, as was discussed above, the group demands social change in their educational structures and works diligently towards obtaining them. In sum, the way in which the young men and women who form part of the Inner City Struggles group strive to obtain social change cannot be described in monolithic ways but rather the group uses multiple strategies and forms to express their demands. More importantly, it is significant that young people engage in such levels of community work. Often enough, particularly in California, young people's engagement in 'community service' is often equated with acts of fulfilling probation requirements. However, in these cases the young people display engagement with their community in order to bring about social change thus dispelling myths about inner city youth of colour. The next section discusses the political identity formation of some of the students and some of the staff members.

The Political Socialization of the Youth

Social Networks

Many of the students and staff members stated that they either knew somebody who were involved in politics or that they were involved in some peripheral way and met people who were much more intensely involved who influenced them to assume a larger role in changing their every day realities. For example the following excerpts by students and staff members articulate their experiences.

> When I was in high school my friends told me about this group which meets at lunchtime. I really didn't even know what United Students was at that time. So I went there one time. And they were asking students what is wrong with your schools and we told them the books and everything. And they told us that we could do this and this and this to try to make it better. That's what held my attention. Because nobody else was trying to help the students.

In this narrative, Gloria explains that at first it was a friend who introduced the idea to her of joining the group. It is significant that she states that she didn't even know the group at the outset but that it was only later by attending the meetings she was in a position to make sense of her experiences, which led her to wanting to create change. Similarly, Jaime reports that initially he was involved with a church group and doing more community service:

> I think with myself before YOC [Youth organizing communities] I was already involved with a church group at the church I attended and through that it was doing more community service. You know trying to help out the community. Then when I was a junior at a high school I got involved with this after school training on environmental justice issues.

Thus, Jaime links his political development to his social networks First, he was involved with a church group where he was simply involved with community issues, which led him to be involved in other groups which were concerned with issues of justice. It is significant here that Jaime makes distinctions between critical issues of justice versus community service. He does not view his involvement in the church as very political but rather views his after school training on environmental justice issues as an activity, which helped develop his political identity. This contrasts with Prado's work on Mothers of East L.A. where 'they link family, community, and community activism as one entity.'

Other staff members describe that they were peripherally involved politically in other organizations and later became part of Inner City Struggles and became much more politically conscious. For example, a few of the current staff members reported that through their political activism around propositions they met the current director of Inner City Struggles Victor López and the coordinator of the United Students. Upon meeting him, they got more involved in educational campaigns and social justice issues. Many of the students stated that they had older siblings who were involved in social justice issues or were part of Chicano groups who socialized them politically. Although the students do not initially describe macrosocial structures as directly responsible for their initial political involvement, it is these very everyday realities that sustain their political involvement. The following paragraphs discuss this point of view.

The Everyday Struggles of Young People

Many of the students reported that their everyday political experiences were one of the biggest motivating factors that led to them be intensely involved with social change. Juana, the current director of Youth Organizing Communities reported that she became politically conscious when she was in high school as she faced expulsion charges because of her family's residential status:

> ... our community of Mexican border commuter students[2] were politically attacked by white parents from the district that we attended. Because some of the elementary schools started getting overcrowded and technically the students who did not live in the area were not supposed to go to school outside the country and we lived outside the country. And the reason our parents did not live in the United States is because they could not afford to live in the United States. And we were all US citizens and documented. We had grown up on the border. So it was more affordable for us. Technically we were not supposed to be going to school in the US but our parents thought it was okay since we were citizens ... So the [US]. parents organized a republican politician to do an investigation because we all used borrowed addresses or fake addresses and the school did not question it because the school received ADA [monies received from Average Daily Attendance]. And then my family rented a small trailer to say we had an address in the US. So then this thing was initiated by the parents and by the politicians where they came out of nowhere and was recording and getting them into school buses. And there was the media for about two weeks where the message was 'illegal aliens stealing taxpayers money to get an education.' When it was not true because most of us were citizens ... And so then things happened to us-like the federal police interrogated us. They stopped the school buses. Vigilante residents started following us ... So me and my family organized the parents. We had meetings at our house. And then we got lawyers from Mexico. The school hired a private investigator to find out where we lived. So this was my first experience with blatant institutional racism.

This rather intense narrative aptly reflects the educational experiences of many students of colour, thus politicizing many at an early age. When most white middle class youth may not start becoming politically conscious until they start going to college, the young people because of their struggles such as in these cases become politically aware at a much earlier age. Another staff member who went to Roosevelt High School and is currently attending a college campus (the ethnic composition of which is fairly mixed) reported:

> And there was this woman from Hermosa beach [in my class] who talked about of how they walked out of the high school ... and I asked what did you all walk out for and her answer was that they cancelled the pep rally or something like that before homecoming and this just spoke to me the differences in the community. Whereas, *I* participated in walk outs against proposition 21 or proposition 227 which took away bilingual education Prop 21 which was just an overt attack on young people of colour and you know it is just a different reality because here they are walking out because you have a pep rally whereas we are fighting for our lives basically to save our education and or to create a quality education.

In this excerpt, Leo makes clear that the realities for a student from Hermosa Beach (a predominantly white middle class area in Los Angeles) is clearly different than for somebody like himself who grew up in Eastside Los Angeles. While the student from Hermosa Beach is concerned about a pep rally, the student from Boyle Heights is concerned about legislations, which would directly affect his education in alarming ways.

Hence, it is such direct confrontations with racist legislations, disparities in education, health, and housing issues that the students and staff members attribute to their political development. However, it is important to recognize that these are not the *only* factors, which, affect and influence the young people's engagement in social change.

Political Socialization in Schools and Colleges

In addition to the direct experiences, and social networks, many of the staff members and students reported being exposed to issues which led to their political consciousness in Chicano Studies classes, symposiums, conferences, and lectures in their high school and college classes. For example, Victor López, the director of ICS reported that he gained his political awareness when Father Boyle, a priest very well-known for his work on community activism visited his high school. Jaime who is currently taking classes at a community college told me that he is also part of a program called Community Planning Economic Development Program (CPEDP) which trains students on community planning and development and students got introduced to the idea of how to improve the conditions of the community. Leo Sanchez who coordinates the United Students is currently taking Chicano/Latino studies at the university he attends. These classes often cover social issues in Latino communities. Maria, another staff member, reported going to a Chicano conference one summer while she was in high school as where she got politicized.

Concluding Remarks

The political development of the young people needs to be recognized as ongoing process with multiple factors contributing to the formation of their political identities. As Melucci (1996) aptly states: 'while this [varied] cultural experience has today come to concern all social categories and all age groups in differing ways, it is the young people who are more immediately exposed than others to the polarization of life opportunities (p. 125)'.

Hence, Inner City Struggles being primarily a youth network, it is not surprising that the young men and women report a multitude of life experiences, which lead to their political socialization. More importantly, the young people's political identity formation needs to be viewed as an ongoing process. Everyday macrostructural issues play a significant role in the young people's political development but many of the young people despite these structural constraints move on and enjoy varied experiences. When in universities and colleges, because of their particular everyday life experiences, they get involved in political groups and activism, take courses, which concern issues of inequity and even seek like-minded professors who in turn reinforce their awareness of equity and justice.

Hence, the youth attribute several factors for their political consciousness- the structural problems that the students who form part of this study encounter appears to be an important factor which sustains their political involvement. In this regard, the political experiences and opportunity structures of young disenfranchised men and women of colour may differ considerably from their white middle class peers and thus may have important bearings on future political participation of the youth.

Notes

1 Latina/os are assumed to descend from the brown indigenous Indians of the Americas south of the United States and in the Caribbean, conquered by Spain centuries ago. Latina/o is an ethnic category in which people can be of any race. The term Chicano has evolved to define the uprising of Mexican American reformers and rights activists as well as farm labourers and other workers who lived in squalor while toiling for low pay. The term Méxicano denotes the country of origin (Mexican in this context). The youth who form part of this study expressed their identities as Chicana/o, Latina/o, and Méxicana/o.
2 Border commuter students include students who may attend schools in the border cities of the United States and live in the border cities of México.

References

Alexander, C. E. (2000), *The Asian Gang: Ethnicity Identity and Masculinity,* Oxford: Berg.
Alonso-Zaldivar, R. (2003, June 19), Latinos Now Top Minority. *Los Angeles Times,* retrieved September 27, 2003, from http://pqasb.pqarchiver.com/latimes/349329721.html?MAC=bf6ded4a0737205a0962a794eff66763&did=349329721&FMT=FT&FMTS=FT&PMID=&printformat=&desc=THE+NATION%3b+Latinos+Now+Top+Minority.
Becker, H. (1963), *Outsiders: Studies in the Sociology of Deviance,* New York: Free Press.
Cohen, A. K. (1955), *Delinquent Boys: The Culture of the Gang* (Vol. Free Press), Glencoe.
Fantasia, R. (1988), *Cultures of Solidarity: Consciousness, Action, and Contemporary American Workers,* Berkeley and Los Angeles: University of California Press.
Flores, W. V. (1997), 'Mujeres en Huelga: cultural citizenship and gender empowerment in a cannery strike', in. W. V. Flores and R. Benmayor (eds.), *Latino Cultural Citizenship: Claiming Identity, Space, and Rights,* Boston: Beacon Press.
Gamson, J. A. (1995), 'Must identity movements self-destruct? A queer dilemma', *Social Problems,* **42** (3), 391–406.
Gregory, S. (1998), *Black Corona: Race and the Politics of Place in an Urban Community,* New Jersey: Princeton.
Gutiérrez, K. D., Asato, J., Santos, M. and Gotanda, N. *Backlash Pedagogy: Language and Culture and the Politics of Reform.* (In Press)
Ricardo, Alonso-Zaldivar (2003, June 19), 'Latinos now top minority', *Los Angeles Times,* retrieved June 19, 2003, from http:pqasb.pqarchiver.com/latimes/349329721.html?MAC=bf6ded4a0737205a0962a794eff66763&did=349329721&FMT=FT&FMTS=FT&PMID=& printformat=&desc=THE+NATION%3b+Latinos+Now+Top+Minority.
Hernández, R., Siles, M. and Rochín, R. (2001), 'Latino Youth: Converting Challenging to Opportunities.' Working Paper #50, The Julian Samora Research Institute, retrieved December 12, 2001, from http: //www.jsri.msu.edu/RandS/research/wps/wp50.html.
Melucci, A. (1996), *Challenging Codes: Collective Action in the Information Age.* Cambridge: Cambridge University Press.
Muñoz, C. (1988), *Youth, Identity, Power: The Chicano Movement:* New York: Verso.

Melville, M. (ed.) (1988), *Mexicans at Work in the United States*. Houston: University of Houston Press.

Mora, M., and Castillo, A. D. (eds.) (1980), *Mexican Women in the United States*. Los Angeles: UCLA Chicano Studies Research Centre Publication.

Navarro, A. (1995), *Mexican American youth organization: avant-garde of the Chicano movement in Texas*: Austin: University of Texas Press.

Polletta, F. and Jasper, J. M. (2001), Collective Identity and Social Movements. *Annual Review of Sociology,* 27, 283–305.

Prado, M. S. (1998), *Mexican American Women Activists: Identity and Resistance in Two Los Angeles Communities*. Temple: Temple University Press.

Ruiz, V. L. (1987), *Cannery Women, Cannery Lives: Mexican Women, Unionization and the California Food Processing Industry 1930–1950*. Albuquerque: University of New Mexico Press.

Ruiz, V. L. and Tiano, S. (eds.) (1987), *Women on the U.S. Mexico Border: Responses to Change*. Boston: Allen and Unwin.

Shahgun, L. and Helfand, D. (2000, May 18), ACLU Sues State over Conditions in Poor Schools. *Los Angeles Times*, retrieved March 10, 2003, from http://pqasb.pqarchiver.com/latimes/53904383.html?MAC=f0db385c69d7345176d98ce46f5363cc&did=53904383&FMT=FT&FMTS=FT&PMID=&printformat=&desc=ACLU+Sues+State+Over+Conditions+in+Poor+Schools.

Shelden, R. G., Tracy, S. K. and Brown, W. B. (1997), *Youth Gangs in American Society,* Belmont, California: Wadsworth Publishers.

Taylor, V. and Whittier, N. (1992), Collective Identity in Social Movement Communities, *Frontiers in Social Movement Research*. New Haven, Yale: UP.

Torres, R. and Katsiaficas (1999), *Latino Social Movements: Historical and Theoretical Perspectives*, New York: Routledge.

Weber, C. M. (2001), 'Latino street vendors in Los Angeles: heterogeneous alliances, community-based activism, and the state', in M. López-Garza and D. R. Diaz (eds.), *Asian and Latino Immigrants in a Restructuring Economy: The Metamorphosis of Southern California,* Stanford: Stanford University Press.

Zavella, P. (1987), *Women's Work and Chicano Families: Cannery Workers of the Santa Clara Valley,* Ithaca: Cornell University Press.

Zavella, P. (1988), 'The politics of race and gender: organizing Chicana cannery workers in Northern California', in A. Bookman and S. Morgen (eds.), *Women and the Politics of Empowerment*, Philadelphia: Temple University Press, pp. 202–224.

Chapter 14

Young People's Civic Engagement. The Need for New Perspectives

Henk Vinken[1]

The Erosion of Citizenship

At the beginning of the third millennium the concern with the 'collapse' of community is, once again, at the heart of the social science research agenda. The number of publications by social scientists dealing with the crumbling of community identity and engagement, often framed as the loss or erosion of social capital, is booming (see Dekker, 2002; Dekker et al., 2003). We witness a significant growth of studies on trends in citizens' civic virtues, political participation, volunteering, and involvement in informal social networks, which a few years ago accumulated in Robert Putnam's both much applauded and criticized book *Bowling Alone* (2000). In this chapter, I aim to show that it is important for youth research to take note of the cumulating tradition of civil society analyses. I will focus on some necessary perspectives for studying young people's citizenship. Following a more broad and dynamic approach this chapter focuses on citizenship defined as the process in which (young) people develop trust in others and in society's institutions and produce competences to participate in social networks, institutions, and associations that to some degree serve a public cause.[2] It is important to stress that civic socialization does include (young) people's capacity to react, respond and adapt to social participation proposals formulated in society (cf. Feixa et al., 2001). Young people's production of civic competences, therefore, is a key facet of civic socialization.

I believe that the emerging tradition of civil society studies does point at major weaknesses of contemporary communities and the way young citizens advance the common good. At the same time many of these studies have serious weaknesses themselves. These weaknesses should be taken into account before valid conclusions on the decline in civic virtues and civic engagement and its correlates can be drawn at all. These weaknesses especially relate to the need for a better understanding of the emergence of new forms of citizenship that go beyond the classic, 'modern' twentieth century forms. I aim to show that the debate should tune in more to contemporary forms of engagement among young people, especially those related to the leisure and consumption domain. Furthermore, the debate lacks a serious approach of the position of young people from the context of socialization and generation sociology. Finally, the debate has a profound North American origin and cannot be transplanted to other countries with impunity. It is very likely that young people in distinct cultural settings will develop their own ways of civic engagement, political involvement, and social connectedness. It is time, therefore, to take account of societies' basic cultural, institutional and political diversities.

Reading the 'Signs of the Time'

It is *bon ton* among the vast majority of civil society theorists to sketch the contemporary moral climate in pessimistic terms. The general idea in the contemporary concern about what constitutes the good life, the good citizen, and the good society is that prime social institutions no longer fulfil essential functions in providing young people with basic values and meaning structures. These mediating institutions between the individual and society have lost their significance, led to a fraying of the social fabric, de-unification of moral standards, and fragmentation of individual pursuits. The social capital as embedded in primary social institutions has inflated and the post-modern citizen becomes detached, non-affiliated, and feels no personal loyalty to the wider community. Malcontent is said to boom. '[N]umerous signs – unstable voting patterns, a return to religious orthodoxy, increases in antisocial behaviour, opposition to scientific and technological advance, a withdrawal from public issues into private worlds, and the rise of irrationality – indicate, for reasons both sound and unsound, a feeling of discontent with progress' (Wolfe, 2000, p. 51).

The present debate on community decline, civic decay, political disengagement, spiritual chaos, and the like, is at its crescendo and today includes all social problems known to contemporary society: divorce, juvenile delinquency, alcohol and drugs abuse, school drop out, intolerance, inner-city degradation, widespread cynicism, etc. It is crucial to address a set of basic issues central to this debate and answer the questions what it means today to be civically engaged, to be a good citizen, to foster the good society, to counter the erosion of community in a post-modern, highly individualized, fragmented, and technologically highly developed society which just entered the twenty-first century. These issues especially relate to the need for a better understanding of the emergence of new forms of civic, political and social participation that go beyond the classic 'modern' twentieth century ways of civic engagement, political involvement and social connectedness.

Mainstream political science survey research on quantitative trends in political participation is conservative as it typically lacks a sharp eye for new and innovative forms of political action particularly among younger generations. The 'signs of time', it seems, are not well read or covered in customary empirical studies of developments in civic political engagement. This has to do with the very nature of political trend studies itself. In order to be able to detect trends and trend changes, political scientists – as well as many other social science researchers prefer to measure the *same* longitudinal quantitative indicators of political participation. Mainstream political science survey research thus favours to focus on the longitudinal study of rather traditional indicators of political participation such as voting behaviour, writing letters to congress, attending political meetings, signing petitions, etc. By analysing these data over time, political scientists are likely to simply miss novel forms of political participation. The cultural dynamics of political engagement are simply underrepresented in the toolbox of the average political scientist who is interested in longitudinal data on political action using repeated measures.

Classic indicators of civic involvement may very well have less significance to young generations whose members are likely to express alternative forms of engagement that are both more meaningful and more functional to them. New generations will invent new forms of citizenship. The social parameters of what constitutes a good citizen are not culturally invariant but do change over time. New eras witness new definitions of meaningful community involvement. Sticking to the old parameters leads to serious misperceptions of what is going on in youth's citizenship. The world has changed and so have the ways in which citizens pursue and express their involvement in the public sphere.

Still, scientists, professional educators, and youth policy-makers focus mainly on citizenship that involves traditional, formally organized civic institutions (e.g., political parties, unions) and classic civic activities (e.g., writing letters to congress, signing paper petitions, reading about politics) that are appropriate for older generations. The same goes for forms of behaviour generating social connectedness and creating social networks: the emphasis in these studies is on classic forms of leisure behaviour, for instance on organized sports, giving parties, playing cards, visiting family, having dinner with friends (e.g. Putnam, 2000). Many of these studies fail to acknowledge that probably every generation has it's own forms of socializing. Card playing, for instance, seems not the best match of entertainment in the contemporary digital world. Young generations, in other words, today voice their public concern, show their political involvement and create social capital in new ways, especially in ways that allow more reflexivity, and through new channels, especially in the leisure and consumption domains.

Let me briefly illustrate this with focusing on the scholarly literature and social science research on the Internet (Ester and Vinken, 2003). These sources suggest that Internet has strong ties to the basic cultural, social, and political characteristics of contemporary society. The Internet emerges from the typical cultural, social, and political realities of today's society, as well as strongly contributes to these realities. *Culturally*, today's society provides space for more autonomous construction of meaning and builds on individuals who function within multiple cultures. The Internet is an almost perfect match in this respect: it is a constitutive force as it adds to the creation of multiple identities and symbolization of fluid selves in a setting where by definition no culture has central control. *Socially*, contemporary society and its permeable institutions allows and demands people to develop partial commitments, establish weak tie relationships and to combine diverse sets of social identities and roles based on shared interests more than on social categorizations. The Internet is the space that promotes and pressures people to connect and disconnect relationships at high speed, to experience heterogeneity and multiplicity in these relationships, and indulge in supportive environments and communities without social burdens or inhibiting social cues. *Politically*, present-day society confronts the citizen with a wide variety of agencies and organizations (political movements, parties, and interest groups) each with divergent repertoires of action and political expression, and each targeted to influence a diversified set of political actors. Internet offers alternative avenues of engagement. It is a new public sphere, a tool for boosting real life politics, as well as a new reality in itself. When the political system and political culture are less open for alternative political views, the Internet functions more as an alternative reality, benefiting non-mainstream political actors, preliminary findings show.

The promise of the Internet for civil society is culturally located in its vigour to bring down central control over truths and values and to involve citizens in the criticism and creation of what civil society should consist of. Socially, this promise is found in its power to counterbalance the trend of declining classic community involvement and contacts in public space. Politically, the promise lies in its potency to give a lucid voice to alternative political agencies, repertoires and targets.[3]

It can be argued that the main focus of civic socialization could be put at the leisure and consumption domains. This not only goes for media use or the involvement in Internet, but also for other types of activities in these domains. Small-scale qualitative studies suggest that shared consumer interests, shared fashions, shared musical tastes, etc., instead of for instance involvement in traditional political or ideological interest groups, create the strongest sense of collectivity and are the ultimate factor of sociality for younger generations (Willis, 1990; Laermans, 1993; Feixa et al., 2001; Micheletti, 2000; De Léséleuc et al., 2002). Consumer and shopping activities, activities that take up a large part of the time spent by younger generations, can have the same civic result as Internet use: yield new forms of solidarity, community life, and involvement in the common good. Most notable is politically inspired consumerism where buying ecologically, politically and socially sound and just produced goods and boycotting goods with the contrary traits are central. Through these consumer channels people build trust, share collective interests, and more directly hope to solve common (public) problems. Sports activities and cultural activities (e.g., music-, movie-, video-making, -buying and -listening) may have similar value. In these forms of participation strong civic links between people are created, in many cases aimed at deliberately counterbalancing, criticizing and contesting existing disengagement and political balances in society (De Léséleuc et al., 2002). Even when only smaller groups of young people engage in these types of activities, these activities might well point to a transition away from the 'biography' of citizenship that was 'normal' for the older generation, one that needed stable identities, strong-tie relationships, and life-long commitments in formal institutions and associations. Arguments for the emergence of a 'new biography' in citizenship can be found in contemporary youth sociology as well as in generation sociology, as the next section aims to show.

Birth of a Reflexive Generation

The rise of a new biography of citizenship can be linked to the youth sociological debate. Prominent in this debate is the issue of other- or self-socialization in which either the over-socialized man of modernity or the over-individualized person of post-modernity is emphasized. German youth sociologist Zinnecker (2000) has fuelled the debate by downplaying the relevance of the formal pedagogic environment of young people in their process of growing to adulthood. He states that socialization has become primarily self-directed and predominantly dealing with issues of self-realisation. Zinnecker argues that formal and more indirect social circles fail to connect to modern-day young people and have retreated in favour of the self and the peer group of contemporaries with whom young people filter socialization efforts by the wider social environment. Bauer (2002), Hurrelmann (2002), and others have criticized Zinnecker for his predominantly subject-oriented perspective of socialization.[4] The point in Zinnecker's assessment on self-socialization is, in my opinion, unjustly underrated: the role of consumption and media use. According to

Zinnecker (2000: 277, translation HV): 'Agencies of the market, of consumption, offer to and demand from children and young people other forms of participation as the small-spaced, neighbourhood-like environments of adult society did'. Through consumption and media use by young people (both children and adolescents), their traditional status of civic incapability (the idea of being a 'minor' itself) is transferred into, if not replaced by a model of equal competence of action, Zinnecker continues. In other words, especially the leisure and consumption domain is the domain where young people can themselves explore, develop, and maintain competences needed for today's growth into adulthood. It is *the* domain of self-socialization, to put it differently, *and* the domain where young people can meet their contemporaries relatively free of control by formal socialization agencies. It is the domain, therefore, where socialization is co-figurative *par excellence*. A major weakness of Zinnecker's perception is that he does not dwell on this co-figurative character of socialization much. Here is where generation sociology comes in.

The generational perspective in sociology builds on reflexivity. Central in a truly sociological view of generations is the reflexivity of those who, in their formative years, have experienced disruptive socio-historical events or discontinuous change in society. It was Karl Mannheim (1928/1929) who first framed generations in a sociological way. Though Mannheim has become the inevitable reference when focusing on generations, it is surprising to note that present-day sociology, including youth sociology, has drifted away from his notions, that is, from the purely sociological notions of generations.[5] Though the generational perspective is widely used in many value and life chance studies, methodologically the 'intergenerational' in these studies is usually analysed by comparing different birth cohorts. A crucial sociological notion emphasized by Karl Mannheim has been lost along the way. It is the notion that a generation is not simply a numerical clustering of birth cohorts, but a group of contemporaries who *share a sense of belonging* to a generation whose members have experienced common societal events and circumstances that marked their formative period and has lasting effects on their life course. From a sociological perspective, birth cohorts as such are not equivalent to generations. Consciousness of the shared history and destiny is a necessary condition if a generation is to emerge, a generational consciousness that separates one generation from the others. Mannheim made this very clear in his distinction between generation location, generation as an actuality, and generation unit. The sociological concept of generations originally refers to individuals who think of themselves as members of a generation and who (either implicitly or explicitly) express the extent to which this sense of belonging leads to unique experiences and endeavours (see Diepstraten et al., 1999).

The key concept that underpins both the self-socialization perspective and the generational perspective is the concept of reflexivity, the competence to recognize and signal the communality of experiences. Reflexivity is also prominent in the self-socialization debate. As Veith (2002) argues, the socialization process is no longer a matter of individuation through social integration (*Vergesellschaftung*) but vice versa can be understood only through the 'subjective observation of individually offered options to integrate framed as production of a future in self-control' (Veith, 2002, p. 169, translation HV). The aim of socialization, to put it more simply, shifted from developing individuality by taking part in society to developing a competence that allows one to make personal choices from the wide range of options to participate in society. As a consequence, Veith claims, the life course undergoes a certain 'reflexive biographisation' (Veith, 2002, p. 173). The ability to project one's own life course, to plan one's future, to evaluate different options, to think about the consequences of choices, has become thé central theme in the life course, more than taking the different transitions in the life course itself, transitions with which one gradually becomes aware of one's individuality and one's history and destiny as the life course evolves. Participation is not the key-issue, reflection on participation is. Veith's reflexive biographisation of the life course requires young generations to develop the competence of reflexivity, a competence to continuously project, plan, and evaluate one's choices and commitments. I suggest that for young people this is a kind of *anticipatory* reflexivity, considering that especially young people are required to look ahead and to anticipate to a broad ranged future. The key issue for young people is, in my opinion, not the 'choice biography' as such, but the rise of the reflexive biographisation of the life course. Not making choices on your own, or making a particular type of choices is what is relevant, but the development of skills and competences to project, plan, and evaluate one's choices. The choice biography suggests young people no longer make traditional life course choices and no longer follow structured paths to and through adulthood (Du Bois-Reymond, 1998). In the case of the reflexive biographisation of the life course, the issue is not whether people can or will make traditional choices or follow structured paths or not, but that increasing numbers of people are engaged in the projection, planning and evaluation of their life course. This, of course, still allows people to make traditional choices and follow structured paths, albeit that making these choices and following these paths are now more seen as a result of self-socialization or, more precisely, of their own anticipatory reflexivity competence.

This anticipatory reflexivity competence is not getting shape in a social void. The development of this competence is essentially co-figurative, arising more and more in coalition with significant others from the direct social circles of the young. A series of Dutch studies on future orientations of young people shows that Dutch young people are well aware of the wide range of life course options, possible transitions, and accompanying life course cultures (being orientations and aspirations related to particular choices). They choose for a dynamic life course model directed not at progress (getting ahead) or self-development (broadening one's capabilities), but at variation, change, and continuous experimentation (Vinken et al., 2002, 2003). At the same time, at least as far as their future career life within this dynamic life course model goes, their prime supporters are people, and only people from the direct social circle of intimates (girl and boy friends, and to a lesser extent parents and peers). Professional educators, teachers, career consultants and others with an explicit pedagogic agenda are remarkably absent in the career life course perceptions of young people. Only with their direct confidants – which in these days include parents who have more become equal to friends than to formal educators (Du Bois-Reymond et al., 1994) – they plan, negotiate, and project their life course, a life course aimed at dynamics as an end *an sich*, a type of life course, that in turn promotes the continuous process of reflexivity with close associates. With the company of intimates they might well develop a common consciousness of a shared history and destiny, a history and destiny in which autonomously, but with the help of close relatives, directing the dynamics of one's biography is and persists to be the central issue. This might result in the rise of a *reflexive generation*, not only *having* formative experiences regarding their relationship with their life course that are fundamentally different from the experiences of the previous generations, but also – and necessarily so, given the rise of the reflexive biographisation of their life course – *being aware* of the distinctiveness of their formative experiences.

The previously mentioned allows one to believe that especially the domains of leisure and consumption might well be the playing fields where young people and their closest associates exercise their generational consciousness. It is a playing field, especially when focusing on new media, where numerous contemporaries flock together, where social ties between young people are weak but non-hierarchical, informal and supportive, where there are no formal educators who can impose the truth, where young people bond on the basis of common interest, and where young people who interact are the ones in control and can choose from a wide range of other young people – virtual or real – to socialize, and identify with. Exactly the leisure and consumption domain, and the new media in this domain in the first place, we might argue, allows a reflexive generation to interact with supportive and like-minded contemporaries and allows this generation to develop their necessary competences that promote their self-socialization.

Exactly that is the domain too, of which we, in line with a number of theorists and researchers, expect that young people shape new forms of citizenship. As stated, this domain may even have become the main playing field for expressions of political voices, for the driving forces of new senses of belonging to society, and promotion of social connectedness. It is clear that if we aim to address young people's civic socialization the key is to look at leisure and consumption as domains where young people, if not a young generation in Mannheimian terms, materialize their anticipatory reflexivity competences with the help of their generation co-members, in this case competences that deal with issues of their idea of contemporary citizenship.

Taking Account of Cultural Diversity

Another important feature of the present-day negatively framed discussions on young people's civic engagement, political participation, and social connectedness is the dominance of the American perspective. Within the framework of this chapter I will only shortly touch upon this issue.

The vast bulk of studies on the assumed decline of civic engagement and the erosion of community bonding is from American political scientists and sociologists surveying American society. And there is, of course, nothing wrong with that. But the lack of a cross-national perspective becomes pressing. Is the prevailing malaise with American civil society to be generalized to other advanced Western societies as well? Is the loss of commitment to the public cause a phenomenon that cuts across national cultural and political boundaries? Answering this fundamental question is not an easy one but a highly relevant one. Other Western societies differ in many respects from American society but also share much of the American societal order. They also have strong market economies, are also believed to have changed into mass consumer cultures on the waves of globalization, their political arenas are also dominated by the prevalence of economic issues and special interest groups, and they too are thought to be confronted by the weakening of the triad of the citizen, the community, and the state. But at the same time there are marked differences too. America has a very special tradition and quite unique history of voluntarism, is much less of a classic welfare state then most European societies, and has a public philosophy of the role of the state that is not that pronounced in Europe. This mixture of similarities and dissimilarities calls for a cross-national analysis of civic engagement in Europe and the United States. Studying young people's citizenship should take basic diversities in societal contexts, institutional arrangements and especially cultural traditions into account.

It is clear that especially civic socialization studies need a cross-cultural comparison. Cross-cultural comparisons (e.g. Hofstede, 2001) show that a particular set of nations differs strongly on a core set of social capital indicators (memberships, voluntary work, interpersonal trust). It should be aimed in studying youth's civic socialization to at least address the consequences of cultural features (at different levels, e.g. national, regional or among subgroups), features that impact not only the way young people behave and interact, and thus what the practices of agencies involved in socialization process are, but also how institutions involved in this process are structured and organized (cf. Hofstede, 2001).

This perspective becomes even more relevant when we realize that the leisure and consumption domain might be a pivotal domain for young people to produce their forms of citizenship. Culture is most vividly underpinning this domain and especially elements such as the commodities, symbols, and heroes prominent in this domain. Moreover, these elements are believed to derive from the USA. Alarming notions of globalisation, or more specifically, in reference to consumer culture, notions of Americanisation and 'McDonaldisation' argue that the young around the globe uncritically copy US-models in leisure and consumption. Real large-scale evidence to back these claims is not available, on the contrary, cross-cultural consumer studies (De Mooij, 2003), show the young hardly divert from consumer patterns well established in respective countries. There does not seem to be much proof that the young form a globally uniform 'McWorld'-culture (Berger and Huntington, 2002). Still, this first evidence relates to consumption and media use as such, not to the sense of meaning young (or older) people address to it, let alone the meaning of this use in terms of citizenship. Considering the still existing fundamental cultural distinctions – not only between the US and Europe, but also within Europe – it seems obvious that young people in diverse cultural settings will develop their own forms of citizenship, within and beyond the domains of leisure and consumption. The conclusion still stands, however, that cross-culturally data on civic socialization taking account of the cultural and the political and institutional diversities are highly fragmented and underdeveloped.

Discussion

A number of claims regarding the declining willingness of young generations to participate in forms of citizenship invented by previous generations, need an answer from imaginative social science. Especially a better understanding of the emergence of new forms of citizenship, particularly those found in the leisure and consumption domain, is needed. Furthermore, a serious assessment is required of the position of young people from the perspective of self- or other-socialization, but also from the context of generation formation. Moreover, one should take account of basic diversities in societal contexts, institutional arrangements and especially cultural traditions.

A socialization and co-figurative or generational perspective can be of help to address young people's engagement in new forms of citizenship, forms that allow for more reflexivity and are located in the leisure and consumption domain. As the aim of socialization seems to have shifted from individuation through social participation or integration to the development of competences to make personal choices, to evaluate options and think about its consequences, reflexivity becomes a key competence. For young people this competence is best framed as an anticipatory reflexivity competence, which is firmly socially embedded, especially in the direct social circle of intimates. With this company of close associates, young people are engaged in continuous reflexivity on their life course. This is likely to result in an awareness of a shared biographical history and destiny in which developing and continuously reflecting on the dynamics of one's biography is a crucial element. Being aware of this commonness may well result in the rise of a 'reflexive generation' whose members recognize each other's attempts to produce the anticipatory reflexivity competences to deal with the dynamics of their biography. Specified for the issue of citizenship: This may lead to a generation formation around the recognition of a new and dynamic biography of citizenship, one that diverts from the normal biography of citizenship prevalent among older generations. The normal biography of citizenship required stable identities, strong-tie relationships, life-long commitments in formal and non-transparent institutions and associations and thus, in other words, little reflection. The new biography of citizenship is characterized by dynamic identities, open, weak-tie relationships, and more fluid, short-lived commitments in informal, permeable institutions and associations. Reflection in this biography of citizenship is a condition *sine qua non*. Continuous projection, planning, and evaluation of one's engagement and commitment are called for. It is precisely the leisure and consumption domain, the ultimate peer domain, that best facilitates the development of this co-figurative reflection and boosts these types of identities, relationships, and commitments. For young people, one might argue, the leisure and consumption domain is the ultimate domain with which to build a new community identity, a new 'among their own', as well as alternative routes to establish solidarity, community life and involvement in the common good.

One should be aware, finally, that many notions on citizenship of young people derive from a particular cultural setting. Concepts and detailed analyses available now are profoundly American. Nations, and regions and social groups within nations, vary strongly on basic structural and cultural features. As culture is a driving force for the way people interact, also as regards citizenship, and as it lays the groundwork for institutional arrangements and political contexts, and as culture plays a particularly strong role in the leisure and consumption domain (through heroes, symbols and other culturally induced practices) where the new forms of citizenships are to be found, it is argued that civic socialization studies make the necessary efforts to come up with cross-cultural comparisons that allow the assessment of the cultural make-up of young people's new forms of citizenship. It is highly likely that young people in diverse cultural settings will develop their own ways of civic engagement. Instead of copying concepts and analyses of a particular country's origin it is time to address the cultural diversity of civic socialization practices among young people, and in doing so focus on their new biography of citizenship, a biography that is taking place in the leisure and consumption domain, requires high levels of reflexivity, and is constructed with generation co-members.

Notes

1 I wish to thank Peter Ester and Paul Dekker (Tilburg University, the Netherlands), attendees of the 2003 Meeting of the Youth Sociology Section of the German Sociological Society at the Free University of Berlin, Germany, and members of CCGS, Consortium for Culture and Generation Studies, for their helpful comments.
2 See Dekker et al. (2003) for similar and more definitions (e.g. regarding civil society).
3 See Ester and Vinken (2003) for an overview.
4 This perspective is sharply criticized by the Brussels' sociologist Elchardus (1999), for instance, who warns for a 'self-ideology' leading to the underestimation of the social inequalities determining people's life chances as well as to the sole transfer of responsibilities for overcoming life's difficulties to the individual, which, in turn, relieves pedagogic institutions from their obligation to help those less capable to successfully deal with social demands in their life course.
5 The meeting of the Research Committee on Sociology of Youth of the International Sociological Association at the 2002 World Congress of Sociology started with a tribute to Karl Mannheim, and was presented as a true re-invention of the relevance of his thought for youth sociology (Chisholm, 2002). This tribute displayed the gap grown between youth sociology and Mannheim's sociological concept of generations.

References

Bauer, U. (2002), 'Selbst- und/oder Fremdsozialisation. Zur Theoriedebatte in der Sozialisationsforschung. Eine Entgegnung auf Jürgen Zinnecker', *Zeitschrift für Soziologie der Erziehung und Sozialisation,* **22** (2), 118–142.
Berger, P. L. and Huntington, S. P. (2002), *Many globalizations. Cultural diversity in the contemporary world,* Oxford: Oxford University Press.
Chisholm, L. (2002), 'Mannheim revisited. Youth, generation and life-course', paper presented at the ISA XV World Congress of Sociology, Brisbane, Australia, 7–13 July 2002.
De Léséleuc, E., Gleyse, J. and Marcellini, A. (2002), 'The practice of sports as political expression? Rock climbing at Claret, France', *International Sociology,* **17** (1), 73–90.
De Mooij, M. (2003), *Consumer behavior and culture. Consequences for global marketing and advertising,* Thousand Oaks: Sage.
Dekker, P. (2002), *De oplossing van de civil society* [The end of civil society], Den Haag: Social and Cultural Planning Office.
Dekker, P., Ester, P. and Vinken, H. (2003), 'Civil society, social trust and democratic involvement', in W. Arts, J. Hagenaars and L. Halman (eds.), *The Cultural Diversity of European Unity; Explanations, Findings and Reflections from the European Values Study,* Leiden and Boston: Brill, pp. 217–253.
Diepstraten, I., Ester, P. and Vinken, H. (1999), 'Talkin' 'bout my generation', *Netherlands' Journal of Social Sciences,* **35** (2), 91–109.

Du Bois-Reymond, M. (1998), '"I don't want to commit myself yet"; Young people's life concepts', *Journal of Youth Studies*, **1** (1), 63–79.

Du Bois-Reymond, M., Peters, E. and Ravesloot, J. (1994), *Keuzeprocessen van jongeren; Een longitudinale studie naar veranderignen in de jeugdfase en de rol van de ouders* [Young people's processes of choice. A longitudinal study on changes in the youth phase and the role of parents.], Den Haag: VUGA.

Elchardus, M. (ed.) (1999), *Zonder maskers; Een actueel portret van jongeren en hun leraren* [Without masks; A current portrait of young people and their teachers], Gent: Globe.

Ester, P. and Vinken, H. (2003), 'Debating civil society; On the fear of civic decline and hope for the Internet alternative', *International Sociology*, **18** (4), 659–680.

Feixa, C., Costa, C. and Pallarés, J. (2001), 'From okupas to makineros; Citizenship and youth cultures in Spain', in A. Furlong and I. Guidikova (eds.), *Transitions of youth citizenship in Europe; Culture, subculture and identity*, Strasbourg: Council of Europe Publishing, pp. 289–304.

Hofstede, G. (2001), *Culture's consequences; Comparing values, behaviors, institutions, and organizations across nations*, Thousand Oaks: Sage.

Hurrelmann, K. (2002), 'Selbstsozialisation oder Selbstorganisation? Ein sympathisierender, aber kritischen Kommentar', *Zeitschrift für Soziologie der Erziehung und Sozialisation*, **22** (2), 155–166.

Laermans, R. (1993), 'Bringing the consumer back in', *Theory, Culture & Society*, 10, 153–161.

Mannheim, K. (1928/1929), 'Das Problem der Generationen', *Kölner Vierteljahresheft für Soziologie*, 7, 157–185/309–330.

Micheletti, M. (2000), 'Shopping and the reinvention of democracy; Green consumerism and the accumulation of social capital in Sweden', paper presented at the ECPR Joint Sessions, Copenhagen, Denmark, 14–19 April 2000.

Putnam, R. D. (2000), *Bowling Alone; The collapse and revival of American community*, New York, Simon and Schuster.

Veith, H. (2002), 'Sozialisation als reflexiven Vergesellschaftung', *Zeitschrift für Soziologie der Erziehung und Sozialisation*, **22** (2), 167–177.

Vinken, H., Ester, P., Dekkers, H. and van Dun, L. (2002), *Aan ons de toekomst; Toekomstverwachtingen van jongeren in Nederland*. [To us the future; Future expectations of young people in the Netherlands], Assen: Van Gorcum.

Vinken, H., Ester, P., van Dun, L. and van Poppel, H. (2003), *Arbeidswaarden, toekomstbeelden en loopbanen; Een pilot-study onder jonge Nederlanders* [Labor values, future images and career courses; A pilot-study among young Dutch people], Tilburg: OSA.

Willis, P. (1990), *Common culture; Symbolic work at play in everyday cultures of the young*, Milton Keynes, Open University Press.

Wolfe, A. (2000), 'Whose keeper? Social science and moral obligations', in D. Eberly (ed.), *The Essential Civil Society Reader; Classic essays in the American civil society debate*, Lanham: Rowman and Littlefield, pp. 51–68.

Zinnecker, J. (2000), 'Selbstsozialisation; Essay über ein aktuelles Konzept', *ZSE, Zeitschrift für Soziologie der Erziehung und Sozialisation*, **20** (3), 272–290.

Chapter 15

Learning to Destroy the World: Western Schooling and the Natural Environment

Thomas Ray

Introduction

In the United States, anyone who reads a daily newspaper is aware of many of the consequences of our environmentally deleterious behaviours – depleted aquifers, toxic brownfields, loss of forest cover, species extinction, and ozone depletion for only a few commonly recognized examples. Nonetheless, few of us have begun to moderate in any significant way our various consumption and waste habits so as to effectively mitigate problems we know to exist. It is this strange and dangerous contradiction between what we know and how we act that is a principal root source of environmental disarray: we know what the problems are, but we fail to act on that knowledge in any but comfortable and superficial ways. Along this line, solutions to environmental problems are not to be found in technological innovation (solar and wind power, fuel cells, recycling, etc.). Rather, what is required is a radical rethinking of what it means to be a human being in relationship to other members of the biotic community so as to bring into congruence conscious thought and habituated behaviour.

If we take this reasoning seriously, two lines of inquiry are necessary. First, what are some of the fundamental ways of thinking that underlie environmentally wrong-headed behaviour? And second, how are these habits of mind acquired by members of culture-sharing groups – particularly in North America, where, if commonly reported statistics are to be believed, 5 per cent of the world's population consumes nearly 25 per cent of the world's energy resources and generates 25 per cent of its waste (for example Fridleifsson, 2000). That is, how are *un*sustainable ways of thinking taught, learned, and reinforced? By directing attention to these questions, it may be possible to gain insight into why dangerous patterns of ecological irresponsibility are as intractable as they apparently are.

The purpose of this chapter is to bring into high relief how schooling in the United States subtly teaches these unsustainable habits of mind. This is not, of course, to assign exclusive blame to the school for environmental problems, since it is embedded in the wider society and is but one institution of many that reflect and transmit much of what the surrounding social order values. But because the school plays a significant role in the induction of young people into their cultural milieu, inquiry into the relationship between formal education and environmental sensibility is warranted.

Gregory Bateson (1972) notes that 'there is an ecology of bad ideas, just as there is an ecology of weeds, and it is characteristic of the system that basic error propagates itself. It branches out like a rooted parasite through the tissues of life, everything gets into a rather peculiar mess' (p. 484). By examining common and easily recognizable features of schooling in the United States, my purpose is to show what some of these basic errors are with regard to human-Earth relationships and how they are acquired by young people. As Daniel Quinn's character Ishmael puts it, 'We are captives of a civilizational system that compels [us] to go on destroying the world in order to live' (1992, p. 25). My purpose here is to show how the school subtly teaches and reinforces in young people habits of mind that are fundamentally incompatible with the long-term health of the natural world.

Estrangement and the Modern Mind

Theodore Roszak uses the term 'master ideas' as a way of explaining foundational and unifying characteristics of culture-sharing groups. Such ideas 'are always there in some form at the foundation of the mind, molding our thoughts below the level of awareness' (1986, p. 91). Master ideas form 'an interlocking set of beliefs and assumptions that make up the background or horizon against which the members of a society make sense of their daily experience' (Bowers, 1977, p. 35). We tend not to be aware of these because as transparent and taken-for-granted assumptions about reality, they are simply, to use the words of Mary Douglas, 'too true to warrant discussion' (1975, p. 4), and too true to warrant much attention in the first place. 'This kind of information', says Douglas, is 'never made explicit [and] furnishes the stable background on which more coherent meanings are based ... It provides the necessary unexamined assumptions upon which ordinary discourse takes place' (pp. 3–4). Such is the case with some of the more deeply embedded, and thus more influential, characteristics of modernistic thinking – alternatively, 'modernity' (Toulmin, 1991; Uberoi, 2002)), the 'modern/industrial worldview' (Smith, 1992) or the 'Western mind' (Tarnas, 1991).

One important master idea that undergirds modern thought is that because the universe is impersonal and mechanistic – as opposed, principally, to something more organic and divine – it can and should be mastered and controlled for human purposes. Descartes, for example, viewed the cosmos as 'a vast machine, wound up by God to tick forever' (cited in Berman, 1981, p. 21). And Kepler stated in 1605, 'my aim is to show that the celestial machine is to be likened not to a divine organism, but to a clockwork' (cited in Merchant, 1980, pp. 128–129). As a consequence of this increasingly secular orientation toward nature, God came to be less an active participant in the world and more of a disinterested observer. For Richard Tarnas (1991):

> God was now distantly removed from the physical universe, as creator and architect, and was not less of a God of love, miracle, redemption, or historical intervention than a supreme intelligence and first cause, who established the material universe and its immutable laws and then withdrew from further direct activity (p. 285).

As the two tools of scientific inquiry, rationalism and empiricism, became increasingly accepted as legitimate avenues for understanding and interpreting natural phenomena, the intellectual authority of religion was reduced. Modern, secular science increasingly encroached on matters that formerly had been sacred, set aside, or otherwise made special. As Kilpatrick Sale (1990) notes:

> The task of rationalism, through science, was to show–no, better, to *prove*–that there was no sanctity about ... nature, that [nature was] not animate or purposeful or sensate, but rather nothing more than measurable combinations of chemical and mechanical properties, subject to scientific analysis, prediction and manipulation. Being de-godded, they could thereby be capable of human use and control according to human whim and desire, and Europeans ... could assume, in Descartes' words, that humans were the 'masters and possessors of nature' (1990, p. 40.)

Prior to the scientific revolution, Morris Berman asserts, 'the view of nature ... was that of an enchanted world. Rocks, trees, rivers, and clouds were all seen as wondrous, alive, and human beings felt at home in this environment' (1981, p. 2). Perhaps he waxes overly romantic, but his thinking is nonetheless relevant in that he presents an image of human-Earth interconnectedness that modern thought has put out of focus. As humans come to see themselves as separate from the world, estranged from an experience of its sacredness, mystery, and intimacy, it becomes possible for them to subordinate the natural world to their will. For Francis Bacon, as Carolyn Merchant puts it: 'The new man of science must not think that the 'inquisition of nature is in any part interdicted or forbidden'. Nature must be 'bound into service' and made a 'slave', put 'in constraint' and 'moulded' by the mechanical arts' (1980, p. 169).

In 1637 Descartes argued: '[By] knowing the nature and behaviour of fire, water, air stars, the heavens, and all the other bodies which surround us ... we can employ these entities for all the purposes for which they are suited, and so make ourselves *masters and possessors* [emphasis added] of nature.' (Cited in Berman, 1981, p. 13.) And three hundred years later, John Dewey continued this way of thinking:

> Scientific principles and laws do not lie on the surface of nature. They are hidden, and must be wrested from nature by an active and elaborate technique of inquiry ... Active experimentation must ... make [facts of nature] tell the truth about themselves, as torture may compel an unwilling witness to reveal what he has been concealing. (1948, p. 32.)

It should go without saying that this sort of separation and subordination of nature, never mind the metaphors that inform this perspective (torture, inquisition, bind into service, etc), continues to wreak havoc with the natural world today – clear cutting of old-growth forest, hydroelectric projects that disrupt fish migration, shipping canals that introduce competing plants and animals into the ecosystems of the Great Lakes, and animal testing for shampoo, soap, and other cosmetic conveniences, for example.

The evolution of this central feature of modernity can be summarized in this way: As humans come to see themselves as apart from the natural world, they assume the position of the detached and objective observer. And as they increasingly rely on methods of secular science for understanding and controlling natural phenomena, humans see themselves hierarchically situated above the natural world in ways that legitimate their subordination of it for their own purposes. In other words, the modern/industrial worldview emphasizes persons' separation from other members of the biotic community, reduces their sense of interconnectedness with them, and lessens a sense of moral obligation to them.

One way of thinking about moral sensibility is that it is easier to do what is right when two conditions obtain. One of these is when right behaviour is less a matter of choice than something that *must* happen – that is, when a moral act is more necessary than arbitrary, thus compelling a person to act in a particular way. Understood this way, right behaviour is more likely when the moral actor is moored within a community whose ethos implicitly requires that behaviour and whose traditions teach and reinforce that ethos. A second condition has to do with a sense of connection between the moral actor and the Other. For Nel Noddings:

> Apprehending the other's reality, feeling what he feels as nearly as possible, is the essential part of the one-caring. For if I take on the other's reality as possibility and begin to feel its reality, I feel, also, that I must act accordingly; that is, I am impelled to act as though in my own behalf, but in behalf of the other. (1984, p. 16.)

In other words, the closer I am to the object of my moral obligation – or, more accurately, the more intimately connected that I sense I am to the Other – the more likely I am to engage in right behaviour toward it.

Modernistic thinking places limits on both conditions for moral relationship. First, as individuals become increasingly inclined toward and confident of rational methods for solving their problems, they come to see themselves, not their community, as the source of moral authority; it is an expectation of 'modern' individuals to discover truth, including moral truth, through rational inquiry and personal investigation, instead of relying on received wisdom of community traditions. And second, by adopting rational observation and inquiry as the more appropriate means of apprehending reality, individuals separate themselves from the world. In the first instance, community traditions that encode norms for moral relationships erode. In the second, a sense of intimate connection with the natural world is diminished. Turning now to schooling, it is possible to see how both tendencies toward estrangement and environmentally deleterious behaviour are reinforced.

Implicit Curricula, Modernity and Alienation

Not all of what young people learn in school is planned; arguably, the majority of what they learn under the aegis of the school is *not* part of the school's formal and explicit curricula. Schooling's implicit or hidden curriculum:

> is what is taught outside of the prescribed curriculum; it goes beyond the specific content of the subject matter and can be expressed in the school environment, in the classroom climate and its furniture arrangement, in pedagogical methods, in teacher-student interactions, in the student-student interactions, and in many other 'invisible' dynamics.
>
> (Schugurenski, 2002, p. 5.)

Similarly, Eliot Eisner observes:

> Schools teach far more than they advertise. Function follows form ... . It is important to realize that what schools teach is not simply a function of covert intentions; it is largely unintentional. What schools teach they teach in the fashion that the culture itself teaches, because schools are the kinds of places they are. (1994, pp. 92–93.)

Teachers and students are consciously aware of some of this implicit learning – 'Teasing boys and pinching girls, advancing oneself inconsiderately in the cafeteria line ... resisting pressure to smoke marijuana' (Doll, 1986, p. 7), and knowing which restrooms tend to be unsupervised and offer the best opportunities for illicit tobacco use, for example. But others are less obvious. For example, what does a particular configuration of desks in a classroom implicitly teach about interpersonal and power relationships? What does the scheduling of reading and math in the morning five days a week and art in the afternoon one or two days tell an elementary student about what is important in life? What ways of thinking about social relationships involving class and ethnicity are subtly reinforced when most of the people eating lunch in a school cafeteria are Caucasian and most of those serving and cleaning up after them are not? These are commonplace examples of schooling's hidden or implicit curriculum and illustrate how students' thinking can be subtly influenced by learning experiences that they and their teachers tend not to be fully conscious of. For Philip Jackson and his colleagues, it is 'the unintended outcomes of schooling, the ones teachers and administrators seldom plan in advance, [that] are of greater moral significance – that is, more likely to have enduring effects – than those that are intended and consciously sought' (Jackson, Boostrom, and Hansen, 1993, p. 44).

One aspect of schools' implicit curriculum involves how students come to understand the natural world and their relationship to it. Much of what they learn about this is of course part of a school's formal curriculum – cell division, recycling, plate tectonics, the nitrogen cycle, renewable and non-renewable energy sources, and such. But David Orr argues that 'all education is environmental education. By what is included or excluded, emphasized or ignored, students learn that they are a part of or apart from the natural world' (1992, p. 90). In other words, *all* school experiences implicitly involve ways of thinking about humans' relationship with nature. And as is the case with hidden curricula, these habits of mind are taught and learned below the level of consciousness.

Over three-quarters of a century ago, John Dewey noted that 'even the most important among all the consequences of an act is not necessarily its aim' (cited in Kliebard, 1975, p. 79). Certainly it has never been the aim of Western schooling to teach students to destroy the world. Nonetheless, turning now to the intersection of schooling and modernistic thinking, we can see how this is happening.

Gregory Smith critically observes that 'the able and mature are expected to construct independent rather than interdependent lives for themselves'. Those who do not 'are seen to be spiritually, morally, or intellectually deficient' (1991, p. 31). This expectation of personal independence is a significant feature of our cultural landscape, and it is clearly in evidence in the school. Although cooperative learning has re-emerged over the last twenty or so years to an enthusiastic reception among teachers and university professors, schooling nonetheless assesses the performance of individuals and dispenses awards and recognition for individual merit and achievement. Particularly with the recent advent of high-stakes testing, student achievement is regularly measured, their work evaluated, their learning 'checked for understanding' – all on an individual basis. When this is a significant feature of classrooms, during the course of twelve or more years of formal education young people acquire the habit of mind that they are individually and personally responsible for their own achievement and well being. This in turn reduces their sense of interconnectedness with others.

Along this line, schooling places an emphasis on print literacy as a principal means of acquiring and expressing knowledge. This, too, reinforces in students a sense of individual separation from others. What we read, in school and elsewhere, is most often written by authors who are unknown to us. Partly for this reason, readers are separated from a writer's experiences except in abstract ways. Further, both reading and writing tend to be activities that persons engage in alone. Although in most classrooms one will find numerous formal and informal opportunities for direct communication among people, schools nonetheless implicitly teach that what is important to know about is acquired through reading. In this way, the school reinforces the idea that learning is an independent process and that the successful learner is one who learns independently.

What Bowers (2001) calls high-status knowledge involves 'encoding knowledge in print, which makes it appear objective', and it is distinct from low-status forms of knowledge, which includes 'face-to-face intergenerational communication and patterns of mutual support and solidarity' (p. 155). The school – its instructional materials, teachers, libraries, and other sources of expertise – is a principal custodian of high-status knowledge, and it is in this direction that young persons' attention is focussed. What is excluded, and thus delegitimated, are forms of knowledge that are situated in family and community traditions – intergenerational knowledge, folk wisdom, mythopoetic narrative, and the like. What happens as a result is that students gradually learn that the high-status knowledge provided by school-related authority is a superior and more effective basis for negotiating the world than are the quaint hand-me-down traditions of the elders of their primary community.

There are two consequences of this. One, the more obvious, is that culture-sharing communities deteriorate as their stocks of memories, traditions, and knowledge become devalued. When young persons fail to learn to respect and value the low-status elder wisdom of their community, they are less likely to participate in community traditions. And when the younger generation fails to acquire their community's store of memory, that community loses its cohesion and gradually fragments.

A second less obvious effect has to do with the decontextualized nature of high-status knowledge. Whereas low-status knowledge is anchored to a discrete community of memory, high-status knowledge gives the appearance of being a-historical and pan-cultural, and thus provides an impression of universality – that is, of representing reality that is true for all people, in all places, at all points in history. Contemporary educational psychology, for example, although replete with competing theories of how, why, and under what circumstances the human organism learns, conveys an assumption, one that is not without considerable modernistic hubris, that there are 'best practices' for schooling and that once these are determined all children will learn and none will be left behind. Social theory – Mead's symbolic interactionism or Skinner's operant learning, for example – provides a variety of explanations for how groups of people come together, maintain their cohesion, and evolve, and each gives the impression that they are equally explanatory for all groups. Moral philosophy, despite efforts to accommodate pluralistic value frameworks without foundering in moral relativism, also has tended toward universal moral verities – Lawrence Kohlberg's sixth stage, for example, which has to do with 'self-chosen *ethical principles* appealing to logical comprehensiveness, universality, and consistency' (1973, p. 632).

Most of us recognize the fact of cultural diversity and agree that difference must be acknowledged and accommodated in school and elsewhere in order to realize the moral desiderata of democracy. But what this typically means, particularly in the school, is that 'universal' theories must be refined so as to include these differences within a single and best set of theoretical perspectives. In Western classrooms, we seldom seek to teach young people what they need to know for competent participation in their primary culture group and bioregion. What we do instead is attempt to increase the effectiveness of our 'best practices' so as to make schools' high-status knowledge more accessible to all, and particularly for those targets of well-intended diversity agendas whose learning styles, background knowledge, and cultural schema make 'learning' more difficult.

The results of this are clear enough – people whose school experiences disconnect them from community and tradition; and people who have learned to regard precisely this sort of disconnection as virtuous, as a goal to be achieved, as the most effective avenue to personal well being, and as the way all right-minded modern persons should think and act so as to progress globally and advance the aims of civilization.

In his historical afterword to *Pig Earth*, John Berger (1979) accounts for the conservatism of culture groups whose economies reinforce, or perhaps compel, reenactment of traditions and time-tested ways of doing things. Because peasants are relatively less insulated from the dangers of the natural world than are groups whose economies are more cash-based and surplus than barter and subsistence, their 'experience of change is more intense' than that of modern city dwellers (p. 207):

> When a peasant resists the introduction of a new technique or method of working, it is not because he cannot see its possible advantage – his conservatism is neither blind nor lazy – but because he believes that these advantages cannot, by the nature of things, be guaranteed, and that, should they fail, he will then be cut off alone and isolated from the routine of survival. (1979, p. 208.)

Thus understood, in a subsistence economy modern initiative and innovation are dangerous at best, lethal at worst. But when modern technologies gradually intrude and insulate people from the dangers and unpredictability of the natural world, the individual's dependence on others is lessened because the protections provided by the community seem less necessary for protection and survival. And when community membership appears to have little effect on the individual's survival in the world, it becomes less necessary to conform to group norms, particularly when there appears to be no reason for them other than long-standing tradition. Whatever errors persons might commit in their autonomy, innovation, and experiment in making their way in the world – experimentation and innovativeness that might not be tolerated by a group whose safety depends on caution and conservatism – these errors appear to be potentially less lethal.

Much of what goes on in classrooms would seem to reinforce this sort of conservatism. Some of the earliest lessons children learn in school have to do with obedience to institutional norms, subordination of personal desires and impulses, respect for authority figures, and need to 'tolerate ambiguity and discomfort in the classroom and to accept a considerable degree of arbitrariness in ... school activities' (Apple and King, 1977, p. 119). And in classrooms today, particularly because of the intrusion of high-stakes achievement testing, there may be even a greater level of deference to authority than when Apple and King observed classrooms over twenty-five years ago. Thus, it would seem that the school tends not at all to reinforce personal autonomy.

But community authority is personal. That is, authority is vested in persons who are known and whose authority is largely accepted, understood, and established over time. In the school, however, much authority resides with the institution and is therefore impersonal. Teachers represent a more personal form of authority, but students' relationships with them are brief and transitory. In elementary schools, usually the first five or six years of schooling in the United States, these authority figures typically change each year. And at the middle and high school levels, students frequently move among teachers on an hourly basis. Thus, the school does not provide a long-term encounter with elder/authority figures in the way a traditional community does.

Under these circumstances, what is learned are not the sorts of dispositions that bind one to community and tradition. Rather, what young persons learn is that '"abstract and impersonal rule" ... should command human deference [and should] be linked to social institutions rather than the individuals who occupy positions within them' (Smith, 1992, p. 64).

The increasingly high profile of technology in schools further reinforces modern habits of mind. C. A. Bowers has written extensively on this topic, and two of his key ideas are worth summarizing here. First, he observes that 'computers can process only explicit and decontextualized thoughts, forms of expressions, and cultural patterns' (2001, p. 140). Culturally grounded ways of knowing that are tacit, implicit, or otherwise taken for granted can be processed digitally, but only when 'they are taken out of the context of shared meanings and tacit understandings of traditional relationships and moral norms' (p. 140). When information is acquired this way, it is 'information' that is learned, but not the experiences of participating in community life. That is, what one learns through digital media is decontextualized from concrete experience of tradition. When people learn this way and learn to place a higher value on this way of acquiring knowledge, their experiences of the world become less concrete and more abstract, less connected and more separated, and less intimate and more alienated. As a consequence, persons see themselves as autonomous, distant and disconnected – from nature, their culture-sharing communities, and other people.

Second, he observes that computers also bring into high relief an assumption that language is a neutral conduit that transmits ideas from person to person. This view of language ignores how metaphors encode culturally specific ways of thinking, historically sedimented ideas that have been carried forward over generations. Like all forms of communication, digital language contains culturally encoded metaphors.

But they tend to be obscured by the literal messages of digital media and the impression of objectivity that they convey, as well as by the speed and visual images of this sort of language. Because computer-mediated communication carries an impression of neutrality, it further reinforces a tendency toward individual separation and decontextualization, much the same as high-status knowledge does. And given the ubiquitousness of educational computing and the high-profile emphasis on technological competence in schooling at all levels, a view of the individual as autonomous, rational, and self directing is increasingly becoming the gold standard for assessing human worth.

Hannah Arendt's distinction between authoritarianism and authority is instructive here. The former has to do with explicit sorts of injunction and overt coercion, while the latter tends to involve implicit norms that are situated in the moral ethos of a culture-sharing group (1968, pp. 92–95). For purposes here, the important point is that moral norms are less easily relativized, and are thus more permanent and enduring, when as noted earlier they are fixed within the habits of mind of the group and adhered to as a matter of taken-for-granted routine. What this requires is a relatively lengthy process of enculturation that inducts young persons into the group, one that does not simply teach them the group's rules (which educational technologies could do quite well), but inculcates in them the ethos of the group – binds them to the group so that certain behaviours are not negotiable and not a matter of personal choice. But when critical thinking becomes a significant basis of formal education, when high status knowledge and ways of thinking displace local knowledge, and when digitally-based language becomes the more prestigious indicator of communicative competence, it becomes more easy for individuals to call into question traditions and normative behaviours that are maintained by their culture-sharing group and through which the group maintains itself and its survival.

It would be reasonable ask at this point whether digital language, print media, critical thinking, personal autonomy and such are necessarily bad things. Certainly they are not. Few of the plethora of medical, agricultural, social, or artistic achievements during the lifetime of anyone reading these words would have been possible without them. The issue here is not that modern habits of mind are in themselves problematic, but that their problematic effects go unnoticed. This is particularly the case with schools, where critical thinking is uncritically celebrated, competence with print media is a principal index of educational development, and technological literacy is an ubiquitous goal at all levels of formal education. What is of concern here is not that these often worthwhile features of school exist, but that their socially and environmentally dangerous effects are ignored by teachers, students, educational policy makers, and professors of teacher education.

Moral Sensibility and Environmental Sustainability

'Every social order', Ward Goodenough observes, 'necessarily contains within it a moral order' (1981, p. 81), and one function of moral order is restraint. Here, the critical connection between young persons' experience of modernistic schooling and the condition of the natural world is most apparent. As a result of technologies that increase our ability to control and manipulate nature, we have brought the world perilously close to the limits of human survival. An obvious response is for us to rationally review our behaviours and restrain them in environmentally responsible ways. But John Livingstone argues that 'conventional moral philosophy and ethics are ... prosthetic devices'. What is needed instead is an 'extended consciousness which transcends mere self' (cited in Fox, 1990, p. 228). When we think about right and wrong behaviour, we tend to deal with it in conscious context, one in which the moral actor is to objectively assess a situation, review social expectations regarding it, and consciously decide how to act. In school, this is readily apparent in the classroom management strategies of William Glasser, Lee Canter, and others. Right behaviour, when situated in individual consciousness as tends to be the case in classrooms, pushes into low relief how moral sensibility, when situated in community ethos, transcends the individual.

For at least five hundred years, we humans have learned to see ourselves as hierarchically situated above other members of the biotic community and to manipulate them for our own well being, and only recently have we begun to recognize the lethal consequences of this way of thinking. But if rational, autonomous, individualistic thinking is a principal contributor to this situation, it is unlikely that an ethical system based on that same set of assumptions will generate sufficiently mitigating results. For this reason, a rational moral approach is merely a superficial and ineffective 'prosthetic'.

Joanna Macy (1990) writes, 'It would not occur to me to exhort you to refrain from sawing off your leg. It would not occur to me or to you because your leg is part of you' (p. 46). But because of our disconnected experience of the Earth, such an exhortation with regard to our treatment of the natural world is indeed warranted. 'The trees in the Amazon Basin [are part of us]; they are our external lungs. We are just beginning to wake up to that, gradually discovering that the world *is* our body' (Macy, 1990, p. 46). Macy's observation makes sense. But simply making sense is insufficient for the deep systemic changes in humans' habits of mind to occur. Livingstone's extended consciousness, by contrast, situates moral sensibility in the taken-for-granted ethos of the group, not in explicit authoritarianism or individual judgment. It is the latter that schools teach and the former that they put out of focus. When a land ethic is located in the symbols, rituals, narratives, and other 'low-status' traditions of a culture group, human responsiveness to the Earth, its rhythms, and its life-sustaining qualities becomes not simply more likely – it becomes more mandatory, something that must be done simply because it *must* be done.

But when the lessons of environmental responsibility are situated in low-context language, authenticated by experts as scientific, logical, high status knowledge, and removed from the every-day experience of persons close to the Earth – and when the persons learning those lessons have come to see themselves as autonomous individuals whose moral judgments are based on their own reason and authority – the moral force of those lessons is diluted and environmentally sustainable behaviour becomes merely another choice that autonomous individuals are free to make – or not. This becomes even more significant when such habits of mind are acquired by young people as part of schooling's taken-for-granted assumptions.

Wendel Berry (1986) argues that the environmental crisis is a crisis of character. In this view, ecological imbalance is a consequence of habits of mind that, as I noted earlier, are contradictory to how we consciously think and talk about human-Earth relationships. We do not profess to exploit the Earth, but we nonetheless do because we have been habituated to do so. The school is responsible to one extent or another for reinforcing cultural and social norms. But with regard to environmental disarray, the school's culpability is considerable, for it is there that for thirteen or more years children acquire habits of mind that lead them to destroy the world.

References

Apple, M. and King, N. (1977), 'What do Schools Teach?' in A. Molnar and J. Zahoric (eds.), *Curriculum Theory*, Washington, DC: Association for Supervision and Curriculum Development, pp. 108–126.

Arendt, H. (1969), *Between Past and Future* (enlarged ed.), New York: Penguin.

Bateson, G. (1972), *Steps to an Ecology of Mind*, New York: Ballantine.

Berger, J. (1979), *Pig Earth*, New York: Pantheon.

Berman, M. (1981), *The Reenchantment of the World*, New York: Bantam.

Berry, W. (1986), *The Unsettling of America* (2nd ed.), San Francisco: Sierra Club.

Bowers, C. A. (1977), 'Emergent ideological characteristics of education,' *Teachers College Record*, 79, 33–54.

Bowers, C. A. (2001), *Educating for Eco-justice and Community*, Athens, GA: University of Georgia Press.

Dewey, J. (1948), *Reconstruction in Philosophy* (enlarged ed.), Boston: Beacon.

Doll, R. (1987), *Curriculum Development* (6th ed), Boston: Allyn and Bacon.

Douglas, M. (1975), *Implicit Meaning*, London: Routledge and Kegan Paul.

Eisner, E. (1994), *The Educational Imagination* (3rd ed.). New York: Macmillan.

Fox, W. (1990), *Toward a Transpersonal Ecology*, Boston: Shambhala.

Fridleifsson, I. B. (2000), Energy 2000, *United Nations Chronicle*, 37 (2), 76–77.

Goodenough, W. (1981), *Culture, Language, and Society* (2nd ed.), Menlo Park, CA: Benjamin/Cummings.

Jackson, P., Boostrom, R. and Hansen, D. (1993), *The Moral Life of Schools*, San Francisco: Jossey-Bass.

Kliebard, H. (1975), 'Reappraisal: The Tyler rationale.' in W. Pinar (ed.), *Curriculum Theorizing: The Reconceptualists*, Berkeley, CA: McCutchan, pp. 70–83.

Kohlberg, L. (1973), 'The claim to moral adequacy of a highest stage of moral judgement,' *The Journal of Philosophy*, 70, 630–646.

Macy, J. (1990), 'The ecological self,' in D. Griffen (ed.), *Sacred Interconnections*, Albany, NY: State University of New York Press, pp. 35–48.

Merchant, C. (1980), *The Death of Nature*, San Francisco: Harper and Row.

Noddings, N. (1984), *Caring*. Berkeley, CA: University of California Press.

Orr, D. (1992), *Ecological Literacy*, Albany, NY: State University of New York Press.

Quinn, D. (1992), *Ishmael*, New York: Bantam/Turner.

Roszak, T. (1986), *The Cult of Information*, New York: Pantheon.

Sale, K. (1990), *The Conquest of Paradise*, New Kork: Knopf.

Schugurenski, D. (2002), 'The eight curricula of multicultural citizenship education', *Multicultural Education*, **10** (1), 2–6.

Smith, G. (1992), *Education and the Environment*, Albany, NY: State University of New York.

Tarnas, R. (1991), *The Passion of the Western Mind*, New York: Ballantine.

Toulmin, S. (1990), *Cosmopolis: The Hidden Agenda of Modernity*, New York: The Free Press.

Uberoi, J. P. S. (2002), *The European Modernity*, New York: Oxford.

Topic Area 3:
Culture and Identity in a Culturally Diverse and Global World

Chapter 16

'Remaking Citizens': Perspectives From the Lived Temporalities of Four Singaporean Youths

Yen Yen Joyceln Woo

Background

Lauded by the West in the early 1990s as one of 'the Asian tigers' (see Jacques, 1996; Prowse, 1996), Singapore rocketed from a poor, small and newly independent state to become a modern industrialized country within a mere 30 years, garnering top rankings in many measures of development, including international educational comparisons such as the Third International Maths and Science Study (National Center for Education Statistics, n.d.). However, Singapore's economic and social miracle seems to be unravelling in the face of an uncertain international geopolitical environment and increasing competition from Southeast Asia and China. While the country's growth index recorded a sluggish 2.2 per cent in 2002, unemployment increased from 3.3 per cent in 2001 to 4.4 per cent in 2002 (Singapore Department of Statistics, n.d.) and appears likely to increase further, judging by the many layoffs announced in both the public and private sectors within the first two months of 2003. Concerns about national security and domestic racial tensions were also heightened with the uncovering of an Al Qaeda-linked terrorist plot to bomb Singapore, a staunch supporter of America.

These are challenges precipitated by a post-industrial landscape where national borders are obscured (Castells, 2000) by accelerated flows of technologies, people, knowledge, and, as evidenced by the uncovering of the terrorist plot, of ideologies. At the governmental level, many prognoses and pronouncements have been made (see Goh, 2001; Goh, 2002), many committees formed (e.g., Singapore 21 Committee, Economic Restructuring Committee, Remaking Singapore Committee), and many reform plans set in motion (e.g., reform of secondary education, changing of the policies for taxation and compulsory savings) to return Singapore to the trajectory of economic progress within a socially stable context.

A recurring theme of governmental responses to the challenges of the post-industrial landscape has been how Singaporean citizens have to be 'remade' for post-industrial, global conditions. First, the new ideal citizen should be creative and entrepreneurial. This is evident in education reform where the primary focus has been to produce more students who can think creatively, in the mold of entrepreneurs, in order to capitalize on the new 'knowledge economy' (Low, 2001; Nirmala, 2001; Davie, 2000). 'Thinking classes' have been introduced in schools (Dolven, 1998), special programs at the secondary and university levels have been implemented to train people to be flexible, adaptable to change, and to encourage entrepreneurship (Low, 2001; Davie, 2000; Davie, 2002).

Not only should ideal citizens be creative and entrepreneurial, they should be engaged, loyal, and committed to Singapore (see Goh, 2002). In line with this concern, the Ministry of Education in Singapore launched the National Education initiative in schools in 1997 that, according to Deputy Prime Minister Lee Hsien Loong, would be a curriculum that teaches students to be 'proud of our country ... proud of what we have achieved together – our economic progress, our clean and green environment, our open and clean system of government, our way of life' (Chua, 1997).

The ideal citizen should also be 'realistic' and 'self-reliant' (Goh, 2002). This emphasis constructs the present populace as being too demanding of the state, and suggests that citizens should not complain about the economic downturn nor rely on 'public assistance'. Instead, they should take whatever jobs are available under any condition because 'it will earn you some income, put food on the table, and buy clothes for your children' (Goh, 2002).

To summarize the government discourse, in order to face the challenges of a post-industrial landscape, the Singaporean citizen must be 'remade' to be:

1. creative and entrepreneurial;
2. engaged, loyal and committed to Singapore; and
3. realistic and self-reliant.

This chapter explores this discourse of 'remaking Singaporeans' by examining the lived temporalities of four Singaporean youths. In doing so, what emerges is the paradox of how young Singaporeans are in fact set up to fail the new citizenship requirements, and how the discourse strategically exonerates the state's past from the social and economic troubles precipitated by post industrialization.

Lived Temporalities as Problematic

States regularly construct what constitutes 'citizenship' through strategic management of representations of its collective past, present, and future (Shapiro, 2000). In order to understand how individuals are negotiating this process of management, especially in a post-industrial global context, one has to examine their lived temporalities, meaning how they themselves frame their pasts, presents, and futures, and everyday experiences of time. My attention to lived temporalities resonates with the feminist epistemology articulated by Dorothy Smith (1987), who advocates considering 'the everyday world as problematic,' in opposition to abstracted forms of knowing that pave over local, particular and lived experiences. Problematizing lived temporalities thus provides a theoretical frame that privileges participants' own meaning-making, in order to critique and contest the dominant discourse of 'remaking citizens'.

The Study

The data in this chapter were collected primarily through four in-depth interviews (mostly individual, but also occasionally in pairs or groups) with each of the four youths. The first three interviews in the series took place between July, 2001 to January, 2002, and the final interviews were conducted between December to January, 2003. The interviews with these four youths are part of my larger dissertation research study conducted with six Singaporean and five New York City youths.

The participants in this study were recruited to form a purposeful sample in line with my own intuitive feelings about the variety of temporal experience. The subjects were recruited by circulating advertisements for someone between the ages of 17 and 20 who might have different temporal experiences such as, being actively involved in a school-sponsored activity (Yin Mei); engaging in a serious non-school sponsored hobby (Melissa); 'hanging out' a lot (Razak); and spending a lot of time at home (John). These were simply tentative categories I started with in order to access a wider variety of temporal experience. In the youths' stories, these categories are neither permanent nor always distinct.

Amongst the eventual participants were the two young men and two young women that I highlight in this chapter. Yin Mei, Melissa, and John are ethnically Chinese, and Razak is Malay.[1] They come from varying socio-economic backgrounds and academically, they are relatively successful in that they are all full-time students in post-secondary institutions. However, the institutions they attend have different degrees of prestige within the Singaporean context.

The questions in the interview series were loosely structured, although they were directed to explore the following themes:

1. Participants' life history, i.e. what they remember of places they have lived in, schools they went to, and friends they had;
2. What their everyday lives were like in the various stages of their lives in terms of schedules, experiences of busy and free time, play and work time;
3. Their dreams and plans for the future through the different phases in their lives, and how they think they came to have those dreams and plans;
4. Cultural products in the form of books, movies, TV, and music that the participants enjoy, their associations with these products and why they enjoy them.

For reasons of confidentiality, information that can identify the youths has been altered and only pseudonyms are used. Also, in order that the youths' words can be easily understood by an international audience, I have edited the quotations in accordance with the grammatical rules of Standard English.

Yin Mei: Structured Academic Temporality

Yin Mei is an 18 year-old Chinese woman who lives with her parents and elder brother in private housing. In terms of everyday time, Yin Mei's experience illustrates the contradiction between different desires in the life of a busy, successful, and productive young person.

For instance, she has two calendars: one, a 'schoolwork calendar' and another in which she records only the 'social events,' because she does not 'want to ... look at all the tests and stuff.' (Dec 14, 2001, pp. 43–51). Tellingly, the 'schoolwork calendar' that she does not want to look at comprises activities that occupy a significant amount of time and energy in her life: she had to work 'pretty hard for Primary 4 streaming ... because [she] wanted to get into EM1',[2] and had after-school tutoring 'three times a week starting Primary 5 (Dec 9, 2001, pp. 17–19). In the first two years of secondary school, Yin Mei 'was just so uptight about going home right after school to finish up all my homework' and was 'stressed out' about not 'seeing the results [she] used to see'. She 'learned to enjoy [herself] more' in Secondary 3 and by Secondary 4, there were the O level examinations, and 'so [she] worked hard again' (Dec 9, 2001, p. 31). The most enjoyable time she recalls was a very brief period during her secondary school phase.

There is a recurrent theme of life getting increasingly busy with each new institution she gains admittance to. For instance, though she says life was 'pretty hectic' for her in secondary school, 'it can't be compared to junior college'. (Dec 9, 2001, p. 35). The second year of junior college was 'very stressful' for her as she 'took [her] SAT[3] in June', then after that, an athletics competition in August, 'prelims'[4] in September, 'then after that [she] did [her] SAT2s, then after SAT2s, [her] A levels.' Her anxiety about time in junior college was exacerbated by her spending 'a lot of time on athletics, which took up about four days of [her] week.' She was also very stressed about all the 'smart people around' from the top schools in Singapore because she 'wasn't used to so many people being smarter than [her]' (Dec 9, 2001, p. 39). The busyness and the competition from her peers keep increasing in intensity. Recently, Yin Mei won a scholarship to medical school and she says, 'I don't have free time. Basically you spend every free time you have studying.' Even weekends have become 'the most condensed study periods' (Jan 11, 2003, pp. 58–62).

At the same time that Yin Mei recounts her well-planned path to occupying coveted positions either in the private sector or in government (she will be contractually bound to work within the Public Service Commission for six years if she takes up a scholarship), she also reveals an awareness of the paradoxical narrowing of her possibilities. Far from the perceptions of optimism one usually associates with academic achievement, Yin Mei says, 'I strike off all other options and I'm left with this.' She understands herself as having no other choice but to get a scholarship in 'engineering' or 'medicine,' an area of study for which 'there is quite a good future' and not coincidentally, a career option which the Singapore government is actively promoting (see Goh, 2001; T. Tan, 2002; Davie, 2003a). However, she experiences this socially approbated future as 'all pretty monotonous' (Dec 9, 2001, pp. 109–123).

Razak: The Temporality of 'Hanging Out'

Razak is an 18 year-old Malay man who lives with his mother and brother in a 3-room Housing and Development Board (HDB)[5] flat located in one of the older public housing estates in Singapore. Razak describes himself as coming from a 'low-income family' (Dec 8, 2001, p. 63). His everyday life is marked by sporadic periods of participation in spontaneous and unplanned activity.

Razak feels his everyday life was relatively free in primary school, which he attributes to his 'bad discipline in schoolwork' (Dec, 13, 2001, p. 171). Further, after school, there would be nothing to do except to 'sit at home, watch cartoons' (Jan 5, 2003, p. 49). The only time he felt busier was when it was near major exams like the Primary School Leaving Examination (Dec 13, 2001, p. 181).

In Primary 4, he met Zainal and Imran at school, and the three of them started spending most evenings at Zainal's home, which they called 'Zainal's playground' (Dec 8, 2001, p. 146). Hanging out at Zainal's apartment led to the three boys starting their own band. During the school semester, they would 'jam during the weekends or during the weekdays, at night, try[ing] to squeeze in at least one hour of jamming time' (Dec 8, 2001, p. 40). Their 'hanging out with each other' led to unforeseen periods of busyness, such as when they starred in a local movie together, and recorded a track in a CD anthology of Singaporean musicians. Razak recalls that when they were told they were selected to star in the movie, they were 'very happy, excited'. He adds, 'the more we think about it, I'm like, oh my god, I'm going to be a star. I'm going to be in a movie, even if it's local' (Dec 8, 2001, p. 294).

This sense of unexpectedness is echoed in Razak's school experience as well. Of all the participants, he exhibits the greatest enthusiasm for school, calling it his 'favourite hang-out place,' where he goes to whenever he has a chance. On Saturdays, he likes 'to go to school and play soccer,' or 'just go there' because it is 'like a meeting place for me and my schoolmates' (Dec 8, 2001, p. 146).

When Razak talks about how he sees his future, he reiterates the spontaneous quality of his everyday life, yet with an underlying awareness of how such a temporality might be evaluated under prevailing social expectations which value a more 'planned' future. He says,

> I don't really have an ambition. I usually don't think far. I think … step-by-step. Then when people ask I'll just say, sometimes I think about being a policeman, another one will be, doctor. Those high profession[s]… It's quite common, my answer, policeman, doctor, teacher. Eventually I know I'll want to be in the education area. (Dec 8, 2001, pp. 165–169.)

Later, Razak asks me why I chose him for this study, because he does not have a lot of goals, compared to his friends, and his life is 'very common' (Jan 5, 2003, p. 109). Despite describing a 'step-by-step' temporality, Razak also feels he has to articulate his future plans in a way that is more palatable to a Singaporean audience. In his thinking, this audience wants to hear that he is goal-oriented, and that he desires one of 'those high professions.' He now wants to be a teacher, while the other part of him wants to 'pursue music, maybe as a back-up plan' (Dec 8, 2001, p. 121).

Melissa: The Temporality of Being 'Realistic'

Melissa is an 18 year-old Chinese woman who lives with her parents in a HDB flat. She is a single child and her family has experienced a downward shift economically. She is now enrolled in a business course in a polytechnic, after having successfully re-taken her O level English examinations, which she failed during her first attempt.

Melissa speaks of a childhood where 'play,' rather than schoolwork, occupied her time (Sept 5, 2001, p. 50). She has fond memories of finding a group of multi-aged and multi-racial playmates on the open floor of a shopping complex. The group roller-bladed, played soccer and badminton, and basically spent their 'daily life together' (Sept 5, 2001, pp. 98, 114). The group has since separated, as members moved out of the apartments above the complex.

Her memories of the fun days when she chose her own activities and played with her friends contrasts starkly with her description of her time-experience in the polytechnic she now attends. She describes her existence as being 'quite stressed', as she has to go to the polytechnic to study everyday, a feeling compounded by the fact that she does not like the course she is enrolled in. She adds,

> I have nothing to look forward to in school. I feel like, as far as school is concerned, it's taking up a lot of my life, [my] time. So that part is very dull, ... very boring ... I am going to endure these three years of studying ... I need to endure these three years so I can get a diploma and get to work. (Sept 5, 2001, p. 136.)

Melissa would prefer to be an animator, but feels she had 'no choice' but to enter the polytechnic's business program. Tellingly, she refers to her closed animation ambitions as 'Plan A,' and her pursuit of a polytechnic diploma and subsequent entry into the workforce as 'Plan B.' (Jan 8, 2003, p. 225) She narrates the closed possibilities of Plan A with much greater enthusiasm and detail than the Plan B she is in fact pursuing:

> Like the Slam Dunk [cartoonist] right, I want to see how he draws, how he works. I want to see, ... how he thinks of the concept of the story, how he draws it, what kind of pen he uses, ... what's his choice of pens .... All the while I've been thinking of it. (Dec 4, 2001, p. 136.)

The Plan A of being an animator is 'far from what [she is] now'. Instead, she is being 'realistic' by accumulating 'stepping stones' through her business course, towards a future she neither sees nor desires (Jan 8, 2003, p. 225).

John: Waiting to Return to the Path of Success

John is a 20-year old man who lives with his family in a private terrace house. He is currently studying architecture in a polytechnic, after which he will be conscripted into the Singapore army. John hopes he to enrol in an Australian university after completing his National Service. He says he has 'never had any stress' (Jan 4, 2003, p. 24) because he is 'quite heck care' (Jan 4, 2003, p. 26), a colloquial term which connotes a cavalier or easy-going attitude.

John initially went to Elite High School, one of the top secondary schools in the country. However, he fell in with a gang, which he says led to poor grades and his eventual leaving of Elite High to complete his secondary education in a much less prestigious private school. He talks of having 'woke[n] up' (Aug 30, 2001, p. 166) and now spends most of his non-school hours at home, his 'only place of belonging' (Nov, 2001, p. 210). Like Melissa, John experiences his everyday life in a bifurcated way. There are the rare periods of enthusiastic engagement, times when he worked hard and was successful in his activities, and the more common times of disengagement, when he displays scant enthusiasm for his everyday activities and emanates a sense of withdrawal. John leaves a strong impression of someone with abilities and capacities, who is waiting to be recognized as successful again.

There was a period of time when John worked very hard, when he was involved with Elite High School's orchestra. John remembers being invited to perform with the 'National Orchestra in a big scale one-time performance at the Expo.' He worked with 'determination', training extra hours with the orchestra and on his own, and looked forward to the night of the performance with 'anticipation.' He describes the night itself as 'an achievement like none other in his life,' as he performed alongside master musicians, and recalled feeling the 'honour of having the Brigadier-General grace the performance', and 'pride' that the audience 'clap[ped] and whistle[d] and call[ed] for an encore'.[6]

This expression of 'determination,' 'anticipation' and 'pride,' culminating with the symbolic prize of state ('the Brigadier-General') and collective (the audience's call 'for an encore') has eluded John ever since he fell from his perch in a highly-ranked secondary school. Now, he 'can't say that he is from Elite High School because [he] didn't graduate from there' (Aug 30, 2001, p. 110).

In contrast to his euphoric orchestra experience, John expresses disengagement from the institutions he has traversed since Elite High School. In the marginal space of the private school for students outside the mainstream education system, John says he could only learn 'half' of what he might have at Elite High. He did not really 'like the people there,' and his only aim was 'to use the school to sit for the O levels, that's all' (Aug 30, 2001, p. 120).

John envisions his future quite differently from his current polytechnic classmates, because most of them are being trained to be draughtsmen. He emphasizes that he 'will never be in this line' and will never 'stop here' (p. 16), 'it doesn't pay and there's no job satisfaction' (Jan 4, 2003, p. 292). However, 'this line' is the future for his classmates who, unlike him, cannot afford to go overseas for further studies. John has 'mapped out this path pretty well' (Dec 9, 2001, p. 112), the path to a 'recognized overseas university' (p. 38) in Australia since it is unlikely he would qualify for the Singaporean university. Symbolically, Australia holds the promise of John's return to Singapore's mainstream.

John would like his future to be replete with the '5 C's' that constitute the Singaporean dream: car, condominium, credit card, cash, and country club. He says: 'I like to live a very yuppie lifestyle. I want a condominium. It may not have to be big, just small and comfortable, but modern .... I love a BMW, sports car, something like that. That's my dream.' (Jan 4, 2003, pp. 232–240.)

The Ideal Citizen within the Context of Singapore's Cultural Story

In Singapore's educational policy discourse, young people are described as the nation's 'precious assets, ... the builders of tomorrow' (Chen, 2000), whose futures must be 'moulded' towards fulfilling 'the future of the nation' (Ministry of Education, n.d.). The participants' narratives, however, resist the notion that young people's lives are mere clay to be 'moulded' according to policymakers' desires. While policy discourses construct the citizen for the post-industrial landscape as (a) creative and entrepreneurial; (b) loyal and committed; and (c) tough and realistic, the youths' narratives resonate with the 'written or unwritten laws of the community' that make fulfilling these citizenship requirements an impossibility.

For instance, the figure of the creative and entrepreneurial citizen is undermined by the dominance of the 'institutionalized identit[y]' (Buchmann, 1989, p. 29) of educational credentials in the form of university degrees and their promise of material wealth. Although having garnered all the right credentials, Yin Mei recounts a stressful, busy, and competitive life spent on grades-oriented activities, virtually devoid of creative experience. Meanwhile, although Melissa has plentiful engagement with creative activities, she intuits that in 'reality', these are distractions from the chase for academic credentials and their path to the 5C's. Thus, despite the rhetoric about creative and entrepreneurial citizens, the present education system still associates dogged credential chasers like Yin Mei with success, while the Melissas or Razaks are made to feel their creative ambitions are inferior.

The narratives illustrate how the power of the cultural story does not work in a simplistic, oppressive manner. It is not merely that every young person in Singapore is busy and stressed about schoolwork, it is also how any recognition of alternative stories and pathways is systematically screened out. The narratives also show little contestation of this filtered 'reality'. There is identification (such as when John says that his aim is to achieve the 5C's); there is reluctant compliance (such as Melissa's endurance of school); and there is cynicism (such as Yin Mei's expectation that her future will be 'pretty monotonous'). There is, however, little contestation. The closest to it might come from Razak and Melissa, whose continued engagement in some level of creative activity does not fit the temporality of time-for-credentials or money's sake. Yet, attributable to their less affluent backgrounds or not, they seem unable to envision a future in which their creative pursuits form a viable or sustainable pathway to success, even though they express the greatest amount of engagement with it.[7]

Meanwhile, the second requirement that Singaporeans be engaged, loyal, and committed to Singapore is in fact in tension with the third requirement that they be 'realistic'. The participants' narratives demonstrate that disengagement and a willingness to leave the country are in fact essential strategies for being 'realistic,' insofar as being realistic means attaining certain socially acceptable benchmarks. Yin Mei's story, for example, tells us that it is in trying to be 'realistic' and the scholar that will yield her status and income, she has to maintain a 'cynical distance' (Zizek, 1999, p. 33) towards her 'pretty monotonous' future, and not consider things she might be engaged by. In Melissa's case, she feels compelled to disengage herself from her dreams of being an animator, as 'enduring' three years of business school is a more 'realistic' move. Meanwhile, although Razak is deeply engaged in his passion for music most of the time, he still feels the need to say he is considering a 'high profession', as to do otherwise would be 'unrealistic' in Singapore's cultural story.

Leaving Singapore and going 'elsewhere' is very attractive to these youths. First, it has become a 'realistic' way of achieving valued social identities. John plans to go to an Australian University as his way of getting back on the university-track so valued by Singaporeans, and Yin Mei plans to get a scholarship either in the UK or the US, the two most prestigious academic destinations for Singaporeans. Second, going 'elsewhere' also holds the promise of fulfilling desires unfulfilled in Singapore. Melissa sees going overseas as the only way she might pursue her interest of being an animator, but dismisses it because her family cannot afford to help her do so (Sept 5, 2001, p. 141). And when she is very stressed, Yin Mei imagines being 'a farmer in Yorkshire' (Dec 9, 2001, p. 121).

Finally, the individualizing experience emphasized in Singapore's materialist and credentialist cultural story undermines its call for Singaporeans to be committed and loyal to the people and the land. Yin Mei, who is socially regarded as the most successful student, due to her focused pursuit of grades, shows signs of rationalizing her relationships with her friends; for instance, she calls her closest friend in primary school her keenest 'competitor' (Dec 9, 2001, p. 49). Melissa, who used to enjoy playing with her friends, now spends most of her time studying in order to create opportunities for her to go to university. Razak has been able to continue 'hanging out' and making music with his (mainly Malay) good friends in his HDB neighbourhood, as they have all lived there for many years. However, living in the same small HDB apartment in Singapore occupies a low status in the social hierarchy as 'upgrading,' constant moving, building and rebuilding, is socially valued(see Patke, 2002; Kwok, Ho, and Tan, 2000). For instance, Yin Mei's economically mobile family 'upgraded' from public housing where her family knew her neighbours, to a private housing estate where each household has a garden and where the neighbours rarely speak to each other (Dec 9, 2001, p. 103). In other words, in the youths' lived cultural stories, connections to people and place are regularly sacrificed in favour of the individual advancement that is socially valued. However, even though the Singapore government is now saying how important it is to feel and reinstate such connections, largely due to the fact that the country's economy is in crisis and Singaporeans are increasingly going 'elsewhere' (see Goh, 2002), the participants see no corresponding change in the criteria for success imposed on them, whereby they might carve for themselves a future in which they feel engaged.

Re-making Citizenship

When reading leadership statements in Singapore, development is invariably constructed within a modernistic temporality as something happening in distinct stages in a singular direction, like 'climbing Mount Everest' (Goh, 2001). The success of transforming a small, poor, and newly independent country into an affluent, highly industrialized nation within a mere 30 years is seen as the result of extraordinary leadership, hard work, and an unwavering focus on the future, an account which is rarely contested. Disturbingly, there is an implication that citizens have to be in some ways malleable and controllable towards predictable outcomes. This orientation towards engineering predictability is especially clear in Singapore's education policy, where students undergo a rigid, complex and mainly uni-directional streaming process that differentiates students at Primary 4 (age 10), Primary 6 (age 12), Secondary 2 (age 14) and Secondary 4 (age 14). In order to ensure school accountability, secondary schools have been publicly ranked since 1992 based on students' scores in the General Certificate of Education (Ordinary) Level examinations and the Physical Fitness Index, which is a composite score of how students perform in the annually-administered National Physical Fitness test and the proportion of the school's 'overweight' students (Tan, 2002).[8]

The lived temporalities of young people in Singapore, however, disrupt and contest the official narrative's suggestion that development happens in distinct stages, and that the minds and bodies of citizens should be steered towards the developmental goals set by the state. This examination of the youths' accounts of growing up in affluent, successful Singapore shows how they have imbibed the official narrative's institutionalized identities too well, creating significant barriers to the formation of engaged, committed citizenship: Yin Mei considers her future as socially successful, but personally monotonous; Melissa's abandonment of her dream of being an animator in order to 'endure' business school is seen as 'realistic'; and John's anticipation of returning to the embrace of the Singapore dream leads him to distance himself from his classmates and present experiences. Although Razak continues his creative pursuits, he does not see them as having a place in his citizenship-formation, because these are not socially approbated activities.

Although exhorted to become more entrepreneurial, creative and engaged, it seems this must be done in line with maintaining the old materialist and credentialist narrative. To pursue one's real interests, as a truly risk-taking culture might suggest, is still lived and painted as 'unrealistic'. However, to simply do what is 'realistic' would be to fail the new citizenship requirements. Significantly, in the same speech that Prime Minister Goh asks citizens to be more creative and entrepreneurial, he also reinscribes the familiar materialist story by admonishing Singaporeans who engage in 'idle pursuits', instead of 'apply[ing] [their] creative energy' to making revenue-churning, and therefore, successful products (Goh, 2002).[9]

Underlying the youths' lived realities are nuanced and differentiated ways of 'becoming' Singaporean which have few opportunities to enter the discourse of citizenship.[10] At the same time, the onus for the state's further development is rhetorically placed on the shoulders of the young, while presuming that past policies and structures must have been good. Prime Minister Goh asserts, it is 'the turn of our young to be tested,' after 'our elders fought their way up, and built the life we now have' (Goh, 2001). Lived realities must be given opportunities to enter the discourse so that young people will not be convenient scapegoats for failing new state-defined citizenship requirements, but can be agents in re-configuring, re-interpreting, and actually re-making what it means to be citizens.[11] John Dewey warns that in preparing citizens for a 'suppositious future', we risk subsuming the 'potentialities of the present' (1938/1997, p. 49). This chapter has shown how old citizenship requirements are now presenting barriers for how young people are supposed to 'be' in a post industrialized world. If the potentialities of their present are not recognized through attending to their lived realities, then, the state, with its new citizenship requirements for yet another 'suppositious future', risks failing its citizens.

Acknowledgements

I am very grateful to the Spencer Foundation Research and Training Grant for supporting this work. I am also very grateful to Professor Nancy Lesko and Colin Goh for their insightful suggestions on drafts of this chapter. I am especially indebted to the young people from Singapore who volunteered for this study.

Notes

1   Singapore is 14% Malay, 76.9% Chinese, 7.7% Indian, and 1.4% 'other races' (Foo, Ali, and Goh, 2000, p. 41).

2   In Primary 4, at 10 years of age, students are separated into three different academic streams: EM1, EM2 or EM3. 'EM' stands for English and Mother Tongue, and reflects the level at which these languages are taught. EM1 is the highest and most desirable stream.

3   In Yin Mei's cohort, only the students who are intending to apply to universities would take the American SATs in addition to the school preliminary examinations and the A level examinations. By 2003, the two main universities in Singapore, National University of Singapore and Nanyang Technological University will be admitting candidates based on their SAT scores in addition to their A level scores.

4   Junior college students have to take the school's preliminary examinations which are supposed to rehearse students for the A level examinations.

5   86 per cent of Singaporeans live in HDB flats, housing supplied by Singapore's public housing authority (Foo et al., 2000, p. 185).

6   This part of the data was written by John and sent to me in an email in November, 2001 (pp. 88–146).

7   Razak now supports his family through his income from his National Service sting in the army, where he is serving out his conscription (personal communication, Sept 27, 2003). Melissa says that her most important concern now is to earn money and pay the bills as her family is having difficulties doing so (Sept 5, 2001, p. 141)

8   In Singapore schools, even the bodies of children are subject to state regulation, under special 'Trim And Fit' programs.

9   Specifically, he says, 'Why not be like Jack Neo,' who has made 'highly successful' movies (Goh, 2002). And he goes on to name the two movies that have yielded millions of dollars at the box-office.

10   For example, research on youths in Singapore have mainly emanated from positivistic epistemologies which pay scant attention to lived realities (see Chang, Gopinathan, and Ho, 1999).

11   For example, Razak and Melissa's stories articulate an alternative form of citizenship which emphasizes engagement and creativity. Razak dances and makes songs, and Melissa has started a web site that allows other cartoonists to post their drawings. However, these ways of becoming seem to be interrupted by the materialist and credentialist story.

References

Buchmann, M. (1989), *The Script of Life in Modern Society,* Chicago: The University of Chicago Press.

Castells, M. (2000), 'Information Technology and Global Capitalism', in P. Hutton and A. Giddens (eds.), *On the Edge: Living with Global Capitalism,* London: Jonathan Cape, pp. 52–74.

Chang, A., Gopinathan, S., and Ho, W. H. (1999), *Growing up in Singapore: Research Perspectives on Adolescents,* Singapore: Prentice Hall.

Chen, P. (2000, July 15). 'Speech by Mr Peter Chen, Senior Minister of State for Education, at the National Youth Achievement Bronze and Silver Award Presentation'. Retrieved March 25, 2003, from www1.moe.edu.sg/speeches/2000/sp15072000.htm.

Chua, M. H. (1997, May 18), 'BG Lee: knowing the past will prepare young for future'. *The Straits Times,* p. 1.

Davie, S. (2000, October 4), 'New A levels to emphasize thinking creatively', *The Straits Times,* p. 1.

Davie, S. (2003a, March 13), 'NTU doubles intake for life sciences course' [Electronic version], *The Straits Times.*

Davie, S. (2003b, July 26), 'Pupils aren't mixing, study finds' [Electronic version], *The Straits Times.*

Davies, B. (2000), *A Body of Writing, 1990–1999,* Lanham, MD: Alta Mira Press.

Dewey, J. (1938/1997), *Experience and Education,* New York: Simon and Schuster.

Dolven, B. (1998, July 23), 'Breaking the mould', *Far Eastern Economic Review,* 161, 47–49.

Foo, S. L., Ali, Z. and Goh, C. T. (2000), *Singapore 2000* eds,. Singapore: Ministry of Information and the Arts.

Foucault, M. (1984), 'Practices and knowledge', in P. Rabinow (ed.), *The Foucault Reader,* New York: Pantheon Books, pp. 121–141.

Goh, C. T. (2001, 19 August), 'New Singapore: Prime Minister Goh Chok Tong's National Day Rally 2001 Speech', retrieved October 1, 2002, from http://www.gov.sg/singov/announce/NDR.htm.

Goh, C. T. (2002, 18 August), 'Remaking Singapore – Changing Mindsets: Prime Minister Goh Chok Tong's National Day Rally 2002 Speech', retrieved October 1, 2002, from http://www.gov.sg/singov/announce/190802pm.htm.

Jacques, M. (1996, May 20), 'Hunting down the Asian tigers', *The Independent,* p. 15.

Kwok, K. W., Ho, W. H. and Tan, K. L. (eds.) (2000), *Between Forgetting and Remembering: Memories and the National Library,* Singapore: Singapore Heritage Society.

Low, E. (2001, December 3), 'Teaching NUS students to think', *The Straits Times,* p. 6.

Ministry of Education Singapore (n.d.), 'Mission statement', retrieved October 1, 2002, from http://www.moe.gov.sg/corporate/mission.htm.

National Center for Education Statistics (n.d.), 'Trends in international mathematics and science study: TIMSS 1999 assessment results', retrieved October 6, 2003, from http://nces.ed.gov/timss/results.asp£mathscience1999.

Nirmala, M. (2001, June 25), 'Teaching kids to think', *The Straits Times,* p. H6.

Patke, R. (2002), 'To frame a city: the Singaporean poet in the postmodern city', in W. Lim (ed.), *Postmodern Singapore,* Singapore: Select Publishing, pp. 106–117.

Prowse, M. (1996, January 8), 'Confucius rules: America will enjoy an economic lead over Asia for decades, but it could learn valuable social lessons from the region', *Financial Times,* p. 18.

Remaking Singapore (n.d.), 'Remaking Singapore: Beyond 5C's', Retrieved March 28, 2003, from http://www.remakingsingapore.gov.sg/.

Shapiro, M. J. (2000), 'National times and other times: re-thinking citizenship', *Cultural Studies,* **14** (1), pp. 79–98.

Singapore 21 (n.d.), 'Singapore 21 Report', retrieved March 28, 2003, from http://www.singapore21.org.sg/chapter1.pdf.

Singapore Department of Statistics (n.d.), 'Key Stats', retrieved March 23, 2003, from http://www.singstat.gov.sg/keystats/keystats.html.

Smith, D. (1987), *The Everyday World as Problematic,* Boston: Northeastern University Press.

Tan, J. (2002), 'Education in the early 21st century: challenges and dilemmas', in D. da Cunha (ed.), *Singapore in the New Millennium: Challenges Facing the City-State,* Singapore: Institute of Southeast Asian Studies.

Tan, T. (2002, October 28), 'Opening address at the welcome dinner for Biomedical Asia 2002', retrieved March 23, 2003, from http://www.sedb.com/edbcorp/detailed.jsp?artid=3302&typeid=7.

Zizek, S. (1999), *The Sublime Object of Ideology* (8th ed.). London: Verso.

Chapter 17

Mobilizing a Lesbian Identity as a Means for Educational Achievement: Mizrachi Lesbians in Israel

Liora Gvion and Diana Luzzatto

In this study we explore the nature of interethnic romantic relationships among young lesbians as a means to promote educational ambitions. We claim that Mizrachi (North African and Asian Jews) lesbians, when entering a long-term relationship with Ashkenazi (European origin Jews) women, begin to nourish ambitions of higher education and career. Our study indicates that the combination of lesbian identity, exposure to a lesbian youth culture and involvement with a woman from the dominant group is a vehicle to higher education and higher professional ambitions. A romantic relationship as such makes it possible for Mizrachi lesbians to socialize with middle-class professional Ashkenazi women. Mizrachi lesbians attribute success to exposure to the dominant group life-style in general and to the lesbian youth culture in particular, which promotes the development of personal qualifications and investment.

Scholars emphasize that the overlapping of identities causes confusion and dilemmas among lesbians of minority groups as situations releasing tension between ethnic and sexual identities are many and unpredictable (Phillips, 1998; Takagi, 1996). However, true love enables to integrate different aspects of identity (Burstin, 1999). Our study focuses on the secondary rewards, such as educational achievements, of an inter-ethnic romantic relationship.

Love, Ethnicity and Queer Theory

Ethnicity and ethnic identities are dynamic social constructs, which are formed during interaction between groups of immigrants and a hosting dominant culture and are constantly changing and therefore need ongoing reevaluation (Hall, 2000; Smith, 1997; Eriksen, 1997). The melting pot assumption, which dominated the discourse on ethnicity and immigration throughout the 1960s, assumed that ethnicity was to disappear within 3 to 4 generations as immigrants' offspring married members of the dominant group, improved their position in the job market and got better housing and better education. The melting pot assumption gave way to the rise of a 'segmented assimilation' which pointed to different patterns of integration, characteristic of various groups of immigrants and their children, based on their own experience and conditions in the host society upon immigration (Gans, 1992; Glazer and Moynihan, 1963).

However, immigrants who occupy the lower stratum of society often do not depart from their native culture as they live in ethnic enclaves and occupy positions in the job market where members of the dominant class are rarely met (Wilson, 1990; Bonachich, 1972). Moreover, their social otherness shifts from a social construct to a set of social justifications meant to explain and reinforce gaps in educational achievements, positions in the job market and economic success (Lima and Lima, 1998; Constantino and Faltis, 1998; Eldering, 1998).

One of the expressions through which ethnicity is socially constructed and exercised, yet without challenging power relations, is gender and/or sexual orientation (Sullivan and Jackson, 1999; Burstin, 1999; Aldrich, 1996). Queer theory aims to complicate the relationship between these two elements by refusing to assign priority to any identity component as sexuality and gender are active factors in the social construction of one's ethnic identity (Samuels, 1999; Weston, 1991). It further emphasizes the lack of hierarchy of oppressions: racism, sexism and heterosexism share the same root (Lorde, 1983).

Nonetheless, empirical evidence shows that communities oppressed on the basis of sexual orientation such as gay/lesbian ones tend to reproduce existing ethnic and gender hierarchies. There is little empirical research on women whereas research on intimate relationships between gay men emphasizes exploitation and eroticization on ethnic bases (Fanon, 1967; Sullivan and Jackson, 1999; Pegues, 1998; Hagland, 1998).

Our study shows that there is no visible exploitation in the lesbian community as Mizrachi lesbians are accepted on individual bases. However, they experience subtle pressure to 'voluntarily' obliterate their distinctive cultural features in favor of acceptance. While young Mizrachi lesbians experience mobility on an individual basis, the lesbian community strengthens ethnic relations within Israeli society.

Mizrachi Jews in Israel

The major immigration of Mizrachi Jews took place from May 1948 through 1952, when 350,000 new immigrants arrived to Israel. From 1954 through 1979, another 400,000 immigrated to Israel. Mizrachi Jews failed to narrow educational and occupational gaps between themselves and their Ashkenazi peers (Cohen, 1998, p. 115; Lisak, 1996; Swirski, 1990; Ben-Rafael and Sharot, 1991). This resulted in further segregation in education and housing. Far from major centers of Israeli society Mizrachi Jews were unable to obtain quality education, apply to good colleges and obtain white-collar jobs (Smooha, 1992; Semionov and Kraus, 1993).

The reasons for the reproduction of educational and occupational gaps as much as differences in earnings and life-style are many. Ayalon (1994) attributes the gaps to the nature and quality of schooling in neighborhoods and towns in which Mizrachi Jews live. Moreover, although gaps in education have narrowed in the last ten years, Ashkenazi Jews still obtain higher academic degrees, at a younger age, and as a result get better jobs that reproduce gaps in earnings (Cohen, 1998; Yona and Saporta, 2002). Mizrachi women are even more disadvantaged than Mizrachi men and than Ashkenazi men and women (Semionov and Kraus, 1993).

Youth Lesbian Culture in Israel: From Invisibility to Empowerment

Our study was conducted in Tel-Aviv, which is the center of youth culture in general and gay life in particular (Shokeid, 2003). The city represents the fast changes in attitudes towards gay culture, and in institutional ties between the gay community and the heterosexual one. In the jurisdiction area rights are granted to homosexual couples and legal actions are taken against sexual discrimination on the basis of sexual orientation. In the political area representatives of gay have been elected to serve in municipalities and parliaments.

Lesbian organizations enjoy support of feminist and academic organizations. There are three major lesbian associations 'Klaf', 'Shirazi' and 'Kvisa Shchora'. Klaf's activities focus on lectures, pamphlets, conferences, publications, therapeutic activities and group support. Shirazi focuses on leisure activities. While educated Ashkenazi lesbians tend to participate in the activities conducted by Klaf, Shirazi is less intellectually oriented and appeals mostly to Mizrachi lesbians. However, educated Mizrachi lesbians tend to avoid the Shirazi parties claiming the latter to be vulgar. They visit Klaf meetings and frequent Minerva, a famous lesbian pub. Kvisa Shchora (the black laundry) is a new lesbian organization aiming to increase awareness of social and political discrimination in general.

Methodology

This chapter is based on a study of 27 life histories of Mizrachi lesbians aged 20–25, who have been in a relationship with educated professional Ashkenazi women for at least a year. Emphasis was placed on that age group for various reasons. First, military service is mandatory in Israel. Thus women would think about higher education in their early twenties only. Second, by 25 years of age educational aspirations are pretty much set. Third, coming to terms with one's lesbian identity is usually happening during that time period. Therefore, these years are critical for the crystallization of educational and professional goals. All of our informants declared their lesbian identity as a major feature of their adult life regardless of previous heterosexual relationships. All of them either studied in college or recently graduated from college and were working as professionals.

All interviews were open-ended. Informants were asked some general biographical questions referring to their personal histories as lesbians and Mizrachi. They were asked when and under what circumstances did they first realize their lesbian orientation, did they share it with significant others? Under what circumstances did they meet their Ashkenazi girlfriend? How did family members react to both their coming out of the closet and to their Ashkenazi girlfriend? Did they view their Mizrachi and/or lesbian identities as obstacles to their professional life?

Then we held an open conversation with each informant in which we asked her about her decision to come out of the closet, the implications it had on her life, the circumstances under which she met her girlfriend and the point in her life when she decided to go to college. This allowed us to trace major milestones in the use of a lesbian identity for the formation of social ties with Ashkenazi women and their impact on educational ambitions and achievements. Our findings indicate that all of our informants related their decision to engage in higher education to the relationship with the Ashkenazi woman they were involved with.

The Route to Success Travels Through Love

Results indicate that a lesbian identity provides access to social circles not accessible to heterosexual Mizrachi women. Moreover, living out of the closet, young Mizrachi lesbians gain access to a cultural capital other than their own. Our informants attribute their professional success to exposure to an urban youth culture and intimate relationships with Ashkenazi women who nurture their personal ambitions and aspirations. Ashkenazi girlfriends are role models for them and with their strong support, they are able to study full time and work part-time. Finally, coming to terms with their lesbian identity, Mizrachi lesbians feel that new doors to Israeli society have opened to them. Thus, in the context of the Israeli stratification system, a lesbian identity may become an asset that provides access to higher education, blurring barriers stemming from Mizrachi origins.

'It wasn't until I moved to Tel-Aviv'

Being both Mizrachi and lesbian proves to have secondary rewards. A lesbian identity is mobilized to establish access to social circles inaccessible to heterosexual lower class Mizrachi women. Moreover, being a lesbian enhances the need to have a career in order to be able to make a living. Hagit, the oldest among 5 children and a law student compares her life as a lesbian to that of her younger sister:

> My sister is only a year younger than me. She has a 3 years-old boy and is expecting her second child. She never experienced living as a young woman. Looking at her I know what my life would have been if I didn't admit to myself I was a lesbian. She worked at the local supermarket until her son was born. Then her husband said it did not make sense for her to work because she would have paid the same to the babysitter.

Being a lesbian provided means to move to Tel-Aviv and live a life different from that of the environment in which the women were born. It enabled access to a youth culture and a delay of decisions with regard to establishing a family. Since the dating market was rather limited, women who were new in town and new to the lesbian community were welcome at pubs, clubs and women parties.

Smadar, who grew up in a development town came out of the closet after finishing her military service and moved to Tel-Aviv. She worked as a beautician during the day and as a waitress during the night. Later on she went to college and studied physical education. Nowadays she works as a schoolteacher. Smadar attributes her success to being a lesbian:

> If I weren't a lesbian I would never have been a friend with Mayana (the owner of a successful High-Tech company). Never! I could have been her hairdresser. I would still live in my hometown and been married to David my boyfriend from high school and have had his babies. Coming here made me feel young, something you can feel only in Tel-Aviv. It was here that I went to a pub for the first time in my life.

Nurit, too, grew up in a lower class family. According to her, her father was unaware of his daughter being a lesbian while her mother did not reject her lesbian identity. Her mother, who had been beaten by her husband, believed that living with a woman could save her daughter from troubles. Not wanting her father to know, Nurit felt uncomfortable living as a lesbian in a traditional environment: 'When I moved to Tel-Aviv I worked as a cleaner and a waitress. I started going to pubs to meet women. Thank God I was a Kusit [the common word for a good looking and sexy woman] and women thought I was exotic. I knew that in the big city I could meet women like me and be myself.'

Nurit and Smadar admitted that being a lesbian both forced and enabled them to enlarge their social circles and detach themselves from what they perceived as a path typical to Mizrachi women coming from uneducated families. They, like many others, had to leave their communities of origin in order to fully realize their sexual orientation. Upon coming to Tel-Aviv, they further learned that a sexual orientation, as opposed to an ethnic identity, embedded secondary rewards.

Upon what they regard as success, our informants tend to attribute their personal and professional achievements to their deeds and personal abilities. They create a hierarchy of identity components according to which a major emphasis is placed on an individualistic assumption that one is responsible for her destiny. Only second they mention the lesbian identity, which is perceived as an asset that enables the breaking of traditional ties and tasks. Third in the hierarchy is the ethnic identity toward which there is certain ambivalence, and is often perceived as an obstacle to overcome.

The emphasis on personal attributes for the road to success focuses on the notion that a democratic society promotes individuals based on their achievements and merits. Accepting this ideological perception prevents Mizrachi young lesbians from challenging and criticizing existing opportunity structures and from developing an ethnic consciousness.

Lila, for example, was exempted from her military service for coming from a religious background. Instead, she moved to Tel-Aviv where she has been living for four years with her Ashkenazi girlfriend. She teaches at a primary school. Lila was the first in her family to have graduated from high school and gone to college. When asked to what extent did the relationship she was involved in effect her educational achievements she said: 'I always dreamt that I would go to college and live a different life than my family, but neither my parents nor my teachers encouraged me to do that. I needed that push, I guess, and it was my girlfriend who encouraged me to go for it.'

Zohar, who worked as a personal coach at a health club supported Lila's observation:

> It is through my job that I met women. They were all either studying or after college. They were the first ones that brought up the idea that I go to college. They all said I could do it, that I was a quick learner. It is I, my abilities that matter.

Lila and Zohar, attributed personal mobility to their talents, motivation and work, yet acknowledged the role of their sexual orientation and social circles in the process of getting education. The encounter with the Tel-Aviv youth culture allowed them to look up at Ashkenazi young lesbians as role models. These encounters turned their dreams of education and success into a reality that can be pursued and accomplished.

'Once we were Together I adjusted': Acquiring New Cultural Codes

Aside from encouraging their mates to study and establish a professional career, Ashkenazi girlfriends also introduced them to a new life-style. Ester, for example, was a daughter and sister of manual laborers. She was the only one in her family to have graduated from high school and pursued her academic studies. She came out of the closet in her late teens. Until then she was dating men one of whom she almost married. She worked as a telephone receptionist at a big newspaper. Meeting Rinat, a graduate student and a part-time employee in a high-tech company changed her life:

> Rinat was the one who told me I should do something with my life, and I could not keep working as a receptionist forever. She used to spend part of the evening reading and writing papers while I would watch T.V. She would discuss her papers with me and I realized that I could understand and contribute ideas. She made me realize I was capable of succeeding in college and becoming a professional. My last boyfriend, the one I almost married, would never have suggested that.

Our informants claim that successful women, unlike men, do not want to dominate a relationship. However they aim sharing their lives with mates with similar aspirations, achievements and life-styles. When asked how do intimate relationship with Ashkenazi women result in developing educational ambitions whereas relationships with men fail to achieve that, Orit, 23 years old who majors in educational psychology and dates a social worker, says:

> Men want to be in control of women and of the relationship. Women, on the other hand, want to be with someone equal to them. This is why it was important to me to go to college and I would start my master next year. I wanted my girlfriend to feel that she could talk to me, that we could share experiences and understand each other.

Orit points out what she believes to be a major difference between heterosexual relationships and lesbian relationships attributing the latter an ability to push Mizrachi women toward educational achievements. Elaborating on the matter Limor, a future theater director who has been living with Irit for two years, suggests a complementary angle:

> Men want all the other men to think their girlfriend to be the most attractive woman in the room. Women are different. They care about brains. It is not that they would do with an ugly woman but they want her to be able to engage in conversations, to be intelligent and to be a full partner. She needs to be someone you could share things with, someone who would understand the things you have been through and not only smile and nod.

It is possible to conclude, therefore, that educational achievement is an intrinsic and a long lasting reward of love relations between women who interpret them as based on equality, mutual understanding and sharing.

Our respondents' aspirations were not limited to education, but extended to dressing codes and changes in appearance, all part of a cultural capital attributed to professional middle-class women. No overt pressure was exerted on Mizrachi women to change their dressing style however they were expected to change it once establishing long-term relationships with Ashkenazi women. Gradually, Mizrachi women adopted the 'young lesbian chic', consisting of low cut pants and shoes with laces. They abandoned heavy make up and nail polish and started styling their hair, keeping it short mostly (Luzzatto and Gvion, 2003). According to Batia, her Ashkenazi friends served as role models:

> I got a job as a vendor at a men's shop on Shenkin Street (the main bohemian and youth hang out place). Coming back from work I was so depressed. It was clear to me that I didn't have the proper clothes. I started looking around, but I didn't know what to buy. Little by little I started observing the Ashkenazi women I was meeting on a regular basis and imitating their style.

Silvia too started imitating her girlfriend Shira's dressing style. She felt that once adopting a new dressing style she won acceptance by the Ashkenazi lesbian circles: 'Shira never said she wouldn't walk the streets with me the way I was dressed, but it was understood that once we were together I had to adjust'.

Inbal, a 22 years old college freshman at the school of business management, tells us about a similar experience she has been going through with her girlfriend Tamar, a 26 years old medical student:

> Tamar never asked me to change clothes or to give up my high heels. But somehow I got the message. She would look at me and say things such as 'I like it better when you wear jeans' or she would compliment me on what ever she thought I looked good with. I recall one time when I was doing my nails. I took a red nail polish. I wanted to give it to the secretary in the office I was working for. Looking at the secretary I started telling myself I no longer liked shocking nail polish. Anyway, Tamar saw me with the red nail polish and said: 'you are not going to put it on, are you?'

In summary, young Mizrachi lesbians go through an overall change mainly as a result of the wish to share a common reality, based on equality and similarities in culture, with their Ashkenazi girlfriends. Moreover, coming in touch with Tel-Aviv youth culture they absorb subtle messages about informal cultural codes of behavior and appearance tied up with aspirations and achievements.

'My Mother called her my Daughter in-Law'

The adoption of an urban youth culture and Ashkenazi life-style has a double impact on the relationship of young Mizrachi lesbians with their culture of origin. On the one hand, they maintain an isle of authenticity as a cultural tool-kit to be mobilized upon interaction with their families. Simultaneously, upon acquiring new cultural, educational and behavioral codes, they claim the latter to facilitate the acceptance of their sexual orientation by their families. Interestingly enough, Mizrachi parents often perceive having an Ashkenazi 'daughter in-law' as an indication of their daughters' social mobility, which facilitates coming to terms with her sexual orientation. Lea, 25 year-old physiotherapist, told us about her mother's reaction to her Ashkenazi girlfriend:

> My mother was so happy when I started bringing home Ashkenazi girlfriends. She would say they were much nicer than the men I used to date and the women in my neighborhood.

She was grateful to my girlfriend to have convinced me to go to college. When I first started she gave me 1000 shekels (about 200 euros) to help me with the tuition. I know how hard it was for her to have saved the money. She told me to look at my girlfriend and learn from her.

Rona described her mother's reaction to her Ashkenazi girlfriend in similar terms: 'She called her 'my daughter in-law' and she felt honored that a lawyer from a good family loved her daughter. She kept comparing her to my brother's wife who worked at a local supermarket.'

Our informants' mothers were so proud of having an Ashkenazi 'daughter in-law' that some informants actually used their girlfriends as a strategy to soften up their coming out of the closet. Take Rita, for example:

I was afraid to tell my family I was a lesbian. So I just told them I would bring a friend with me on my next visit. When they met Ilana they literally fell in love with her. She complimented my mother for her food, she asked my little sister about her friends and studies. The next time I came I felt comfortable enough to tell them I was a lesbian. They accepted it just fine.

It is possible to conclude that Mizrachi lesbians change their life-style upon meeting an Ashkenazi girlfriend. Such a change does not make them feel deprived of their culture but rather as gaining entrance into the Ashkenazi one.

'Coming Back to My Roots'

As much as Mizrachi lesbians tended to attribute their decision to take the route to education to their relationship with an Ashkenazi woman and exposure to an urban youth culture, they accredited their professional success to their personal skills. Upon success, they started emphasizing their ethnic origins, and mobilized them to form a distinctive ethnic-lesbian identity. As part of this process, they looked at their adolescence in retrospective and reinterpreted the route to success. They admitted education, romantic ties and access to new cultural stocks of knowledge to be vehicles to self-awareness.

Zizi immigrated to Israel from Turkey at the age of fourteen. Her family suffered downward mobility upon immigration, since her father didn't manage to establish a successful business like the one he had in Turkey. For a short period her mother even worked as a cook at well-off people houses. She was sent to boarding school in order to make sure she would get a full high school diploma. There she fell in love with her literature teacher, a relationship she was never able to realize. She had a single heterosexual relationship that left her frustrated and fully sure of her lesbian identity. Her first relationship with a woman was in her senior year when she and her new roommate fell in love with each other. After her military service she met Irena, a former Soviet Jew from Moscow, who never hid the fact that it would be easier for herself and her family to accept Zizi would she to get an academic education. Zizi graduated from the department of comparative literature with distinction and was about to start her masters. Irena graduated the school of engineering.

Zizi didn't bother to think about the ethnic conflict and her ethnic identity until she was a senior in college. A course on ethnic writers made her relate theoretical assumptions to her personal experience:

All of a sudden it all became clear to me. It was then that I understood all the humiliation my parents went through, I could see why my older brother and sister didn't go to school. It occurred to me that it was something within the system, not my family's fault. They are brilliant people of the world and connoisseurs of the Western culture. Do you know what they have given up? My father was a major figure in the Jewish community before he came here. And my brother! He hesitated whether to come to Israel with us or to go to England to study.

Personal success then is embedded with a reinterpretation of one's origins and life story. Zizi understands the connection between belonging to a minority and the possibility of educational achievement. Access to members of the dominant class as well as professional success enables her to look at her family as a case study of a larger cultural phenomenon.

As part of the process Zizi underwent, she joined a feminist reading group and an active Mizrachi Jews social group. She started attending conferences and seminars and became a Mizrachi lesbian activist herself. This is where she met other successful Mizrachi women who came back to their roots. In the course of a lesbian feminist conference during which hetero-centric oppression was discussed, Orly, a Mizrachi lawyer, stated: 'By repressing our ethnic origins we collaborated with the oppressors of our families and friends. It is only recently, after I got recognition as a lawyer that I was able to admit my origins and apply my knowledge to assist in political action.'

Many of our informants believe that, once introduced into the lesbian community, ethnicity is no longer a variable that affects one's possibility to succeed in schooling and career. Orly who relates to the Mizrachi – Ashkenazi conflict points to the illusionary aspect of success i.e. Mizrachi are admitted to Ashkenazi circles, as individuals, to be modeled by their Ashkenazi girlfriends according to the standards of the latter.

Educated Mizrachi lesbians were aware of rejection patterns but tended to claim they never experienced it personally. Moreover they believed that only lower class Mizrachi lesbians suffered from racism. Dalia, a PhD candidate in comparative literature claimed that women were likely to see the person rather than his/her origin and value education more than men did: 'Education, for me was a major vehicle to improve my professional and social status. It was education, I believe, that made it possible for me to date well-educated and professional women.'

Radical feminists, regardless of their ethnic origins, were the ones who raised issues of subtle oppression. Take Hannah, an Ashkenazi lesbian activist and a historian:

When I was younger I used to think that if all women were lesbians the world would have been a better place since women would not discriminate each other. I know I was wrong. Mizrachi lesbians could be accepted as individuals, but never as a social category in itself, the way I would consider Palestinians, gays or even women.

Upon success a number of Mizrachi lesbians develop a critical stand in relation to the lesbian community. Events and interactions, in which subtle prejudice is implied, are no longer denied. They admit that the lesbian community might be as biased against the Mizrachi Jews as the heterosexual one. It is then that ethnic origins are mobilized to form a distinctive ethnic-lesbian identity. They also realize that as successful as they are, oppression is still part of their daily experience. Orna, who is about to finish her doctorate dissertation in sociology, claims: 'I joined Klaf (feminist lesbian organization). There I felt at ease with my lesbian identity but there was no room for ethnicity. Although all are welcome it is mostly Ashkenazi women who make the important decisions.'

In summary, parallel to their acceptance into the lesbian culture in Tel-Aviv, Mizrachi lesbians develop a measure of ambivalence toward their Ashkenazi peers and become critical toward some attitudes perceived as patronizing. Simultaneously, they come to accept the ethnic component of their identity feeling that the latter would not undermine professional and social achievements. This is when they allow themselves to re-experience and redefine their ethnic origin as a cultural identity to be mobilized for social empowerment and recognition.

Conclusion

A romantic relationship between Mizrachi and Ashkenazi lesbians in Israel makes it possible for the former to socialize with middle-class professional Ashkenazi women in the frame of urban youth culture in Israel. This in turn, enhances educational aspirations as the Ashkenazi girlfriend is seen as a role model, encourages her Mizrachi lover and gives her support. Upon success, Mizrachi lesbians come to terms with the ethnic component of their identity and adopt a critical view of Mizrachi–Ashkenazi relationships in Israel. In addition, they develop ambivalence toward the Ashkenazi cultural superiority feelings and attitudes.

We believe our study to be a potential contribution to application of queer theory to specific communities. By showing that in the lesbian community love and subtle oppression of the loved one can co-exist, it calls to differentiate between ethnic oppression on the one-to-one basis and oppression toward a social group at large. Ashkenazi lesbians are not much different from the larger community in that they grasp their cultural traits as preferable. However, they seem ready, due to both ideological stand and limited dating market, to share their life with the same individuals who are willing to accept a measure of molding.

The study further stresses that hierarchies of oppression are flexible in the sense that they are contextually specific. Although Mizrachi lesbians as rewarding in the sense that it allowed educational and professional mobility, once reached success, interpreted giving priority to a lesbian identity they reinterpreted it. Our results also point to the need for Queer theory to incorporate more empirical studies centered on changing perceptions of oppression in dynamic processes, drawing connections between life-stories and social experience.

References

Aldrich, R. (1996), 'Homosexuality and Colonialism', *Thamyris: Mythmaking from Past to Present*, 3 (1), 175–191.

Ayalon, H. (1994), 'The Effects of Community Characteristics on Differential Educational Opportunity', *Megamot*, **34** (4), 382–401. (In Hebrew).

Ben Refael, E. and Sharot, S. (1991), *Ethnicity Religion and Class in Israeli Society*, Cambridge. Cambridge University Press.

Bonacich, E. (1972), 'A Theory of Ethnic Antagonism', *American Sociological Review*, 37, 547–559.

Brant, B. (2000), 'Writing Life, Wor(l)ds: Communicating Acts', *Journal of Lesbian Studies*, 4 (4), 21–34.

Burstin, H. E. (1999), 'Looking Out, Looking In: Anti Semitism and Racism in Lesbian Communities', *Journal of Homosexuality*, 36 (3/4), 143–158.

Cohen, Y. and Haberfeld, Y. (1998), 'Second Generation Jewish Immigrants in Israel: Have the Ethnic Gaps in Schooling and Earnings Declined?', *Ethnic and Racial Studies*, 21, 507–528.

Constantino, R. and Faltis, C. (1998), 'Teaching Against the Grain In Bilingual Education', in Y. Zou and T. Trueba (eds.), *Ethnic Identity and Power*, New York: State University of New York Press, pp. 113–131.

Eldering, L. (1998), 'Mixed Messages: Moroccan Children in the Netherlands Living in Two Worlds', in Y. Zou and T. Trueba (eds.), *Ethnic Identity and Power*, New-York: State University of New-York Press, pp. 259–282.

Eriksen, T. H. (1997), 'Ethnicity, Race and Nation', in M. Guibernau and J. Rex (eds.), *The Ethnicity Reader*, USA: Polity Press, pp. 33–42.

Fanon, F. (1967), *Black Skins, White Masks*, New York: Grove Press.

Gans, H. (1992), 'Second Generation Decline: Scenarios for the Economic and Ethnic Future of the Post 1965 American Immigrants', *Ethnic and Racial Studies* 15 (2): 173–192.

Glazer, N. and Moynihan, D. (1963), *Beyond the Melting Pot*, Cambridge, MIT Press.

Hagland, P. E. P. (1998), 'Undressing the Oriental Boy', in D. Atkins (ed.), *Looking Queer. Body Image and Identity in Lesbian, Bisexual, Gay, and Transgender Communities*. New York: Harrington Park Press, pp. 277–293.

Hall, S. (2000), 'Old and New Identities, Old and New Ethnicities', in Les Black and Solomons (eds.), *Theories of Race and Racism*, London: Routledge, pp. 144–153.

Lisak, M. (1996), 'Ethnic Groups and Ethnicity in a Historical Perspective', in M. Lisak (ed.), *Israel Toward the Year 2000*, Jerusalem: Magnes, pp. 74–89. (In Hebrew).

Lorde, A. (1983), 'There is no hierarchy of oppressions', *Interracial Books for Children Bulletin*, 14 (3/4).

Pegues, C. (1998), 'Piece of Man', in D. Atkins (ed.), *Looking Queer*, New York: Harrington Park Press, pp. 259–275.

Phillips, L. (1998), "'I' is for Intersection: At the Crux of black and White and Gay and Straight', in D. Atkins (ed.), *Looking Queer*, New York: Harrington Park Press, pp. 251–257.

Samuels, J. (1999), 'Dangerous Liaisons: Queer Subjectivity, Liberalism and Race', *Cultural Studies*, 13(1), 91–109.

Semionov, M. and Kraus, V. (1993), 'Gender, Ethnicity and Income Inequality: The Israeli Experience' in Y. Azmon and D. Izraeli (eds.), *Women in Israel*, New Brunswick: Transaction Publishers, pp. 97–111.

Shokeid, M. (2003), 'Closeted Cosmopolitans: Israeli Gays between Center and Periphery', *Global Network*, 3(3), 387–399.

Smith, A. (1997), 'Structure and Persistence of Ethnie', in M. Guiberneau and J. Rex (eds.), *The Ethnicity Reader: Nationalism, Multiculturalism and Migration*, USA: Polity Press, pp. 27–33.

Smooha, S. (1992), *Arabs and Jews in Israel: Change and Continuity in Mutual Intolerance*, San Francisco: San Francisco University Press.

Sullivan, G. and Jackson, P. (1999), 'Ethnic Minorities and the Lesbian and Gay Community', *Journal of Homosexuality*. 36 (3/4), 1–28.

Swirski, S. (1990), *Education in Israel: Schooling for Inequality,* Tel-Aviv: Brerot. (In Hebrew).

Takagi, D. (1996), 'Maiden Voyage: Excursion into Sexuality and Identity Politics in Asian America', in S. Seidman (ed.), *Queer Theory/Sociology*, Cambridge: Blackwell Publishers, pp. 243–258.

Weston, K. (1991), *Families We Choose: Lesbians, Gay, Kinship*, New York: Columbia University Press.

Wilson, W. J. (1990), *The Declining Significance of Race: Blacks and Changing American Institutions*, Chicago: University of Chicago Press.

Yona, Y. and Saporta, Y. (2002), 'Vocational Schools and the Formation of the Israeli Working Class'. In H. Hever and Y. Shenhav (eds.), *Mizrachim in Israel: A Critical Observation into Israeli Society*, Jerusalem: Van Leer, pp. 68–104. (In Hebrew).

Chapter 18

Cool Nostalgia: Indian American Youth Culture and the Politics of Authenticity

Sunaina Maira

The massive beats of a new sound reverberated in New York City nightlife in the mid-1990s, product of a subculture created by second-generation Indian Americans that centres on music and dance, specifically a mix of Hindi film music and bhangra, a North Indian and Pakistani dance and music, with American rap, techno, jungle, and reggae.[1] This youth subculture has become a recognized part of New York City popular culture, and also constitutes a transnational subculture of the Indian/South Asian diaspora. Bhangra remix was popularized by British-born South Asian youth in the mid-1980s and since then has flowed between New York, Delhi, Bombay, Toronto, and Port-of-Spain, and other nodes of the South Asian diaspora (Gopinath, 1995). This essay explores the tension between the production of cultural nostalgia and the performance of 'cool' in this subculture, and shows how the dialectic between these structures of feeling (Williams, 1977) reveals the contradictory cultural politics of authenticity for Indian American youth.

The remix youth subculture in New York includes participants whose families originate from other countries of the sub-continent, such as Bangladesh and Pakistan, yet these events are often coded by insiders as the 'Indian party scene' or 'desi scene'; the word 'desi' signifies a pan-South Asian rubric that is increasingly emphasized in the second generation and which literally means 'of South Asia,' especially in the context of the diaspora. The creation of this Indian American, and South Asian American, youth culture in Manhattan has, in part, been made possible by the presence of the largest local Indian immigrant community in the US. The initial wave of Indian professionals and graduate students who migrated to the US has been followed by a second cohort of working- and lower-middle class Indian immigrants in the 1980s and 1990s, many of whom migrated through family reunification visas (Lessinger, 1995).

The 'scene' is a differentiated one: there are Indian American youth who are not in college and who attend these parties at clubs, restaurants, and college campuses, and there is a mix of first- and second-generation partygoers. Manhattan provides a particular context for desi parties because of the presence of city clubs, such as the Madison, the China Club, or S.O.B.'s (Sounds of Brazil) that draw droves of desi youth. S.O.B.'s, a world music club in downtown Manhattan, became home to one of the most well-known regular 'bhangra parties' in March, 1997 when DJ Rekha launched Basement Bhangra, the first Indian remix music night to be featured monthly at a Manhattan club – and the first to be hosted by a woman deejay. The phenomenon of desi parties fits in with the larger structure of clubbing in New York and other cities, where clubs host different 'parties' that are ethnically, racially, and sexually segregated, and that feature deejays who spin distinctive mixes for their target audience.

The music is remixed by deejays, generally young Indian American men and women, some of whom are college students who do this is as a source of part-time income and have helped create an urban South Asian American youth subculture. Every weekend, remix parties in Manhattan attract desi youth from New York, New Jersey, Connecticut, and even Pennsylvania, areas that have large concentrations of Indian, and South Asian, immigrant families as well desi student populations. Cover charges are steep but not atypical for New York parties, ranging from ten to twenty dollars, yet the parties draw hordes of youth from a range of class backgrounds who are willing to fork out money for leisure activities.

In conjunction with the fusion of musical genres, this subculture displays the construction of a culturally hybrid style, such as mixing Indian-style nose rings and bindis[2] with hip hop fashion and performing ethnic identity through dance, as in the borrowing of folk dance gestures from bhangra while gyrating to club remixes. Indian American women were sporting bindis long before Madonna did, but they now do so in the context of commodified ethno-chic, with mehndi kits – 'Indian body art' – and bindi packets – 'body jewels' – having sprouted in clothing stores, street fairs, and fashion magazines (Durham, 1999). The mainstreaming of Indo-chic in the late 1990s has been a hotly debated issue, especially for young desi women, and demonstrates the ways in which consumption is used to negotiate issues of ethnic authenticity, cultural ownership, and racialization, even as it is made possible by the globalization of American capital and cheap South Asian labor (see Maira, 2000).

My analysis of this youth subculture focuses more on the meanings that remix music, dance, and style have in the lives of the participants, rather than an ethnomusicological treatment of the sounds and lyrics, or a focus on the deejays themselves. What is being produced in this subculture is not just forms of music or dance, but ways of being an Indian American, female or male, 'subject' (McRobbie 1999, p. 145). Popular culture expresses what Juan Flores calls 'the problem of contemporaneity,' the simultaneous 'coexistence of tradition and modernity' (2000, p. 21), a temporal dialectic that is deeply embedded in second-generation youth cultures that are always wrestling with notions of presumably vanishing 'traditions' and derivative or threatening practices of the present. This popular culture is a critical site for understanding the ways in which second-generation youth are positioning themselves in the landscape of ethnic and racial politics, because it showcases performances of ethnic authenticity, cultural hybridization, racialized gender ideologies, and class contradictions. I argue that in remix youth culture, the politics of nostalgia is infused into the production of 'cool,' a dialectic that has revealing implications for understanding processes of ethnicization and racialization for second-generation youth in the US.

Subcultural Theory and the Politics of Youth Culture

Viewing this Indian American youth music and youth style as products of a subculture draws on the particular tradition of youth culture studies associated with neo-Marxist theorists in the UK, particularly the early emphasis on a materialist ethnography (Kirschner, 1998; Turner, 1990). According to Stuart Hall and other theorists of the Birmingham school (Clarke et al., 1976, p. 47), individuals belong to a shared subculture when there is 'a set of social rituals which underpin their collective identity and define them as a 'group' instead of a mere collection of individuals. They adopt and adapt material objects–goods and possessions–and reorganize them into distinctive 'styles' which express the collectivity ... [and] become embodied in rituals of relationship and occasion and movement.' The term youth subculture refers to a social group that is distinguished by age or generation, but the Birmingham school theorists also note that the category of 'youth' is one that is socially and culturally constructed, and has often been the focus of debates over social control as well as a marketing principle for the music and fashion industries (Clarke et al., 1976).

Understanding a subculture, such as this one, and its rituals helps explain why a popular culture based on music in particular has such strong appeal for youth. Simon Frith (1992, p. 177) writes that 'for young people ... music probably has the most important role in the mapping of social networks, determining how and where they meet and court and party.' Frith argues that by providing a subtle and complex means of individual and collective expression, '[music] is in many respects the model for their involvement in culture, for their ability to see beyond the immediate requirements of work and family and dole' (1992, p. 177). This provides the basis for the Birmingham school's central argument, which has had a significant influence on youth cutlture studies, that youth subcultures are based on rituals that resist the values inherent in the dominant culture. The creation of a subculture is understood as a response to the personal, political, and economic contradictions or crises that youth confront on the brink of adulthood (Clarke et al., 1976). Early subcultural theorists were particularly interested in decoding the political implications of youth style and socialization and drew heavily on structuralist and semiotic approaches (Cohen, 1997, p. 157). Dick Hebdige (1979, pp. 2–3) writes that 'the tensions between dominant and subordinate groups can be found reflected in the surfaces of subculture–in the styles made up of mundane objects which have a double meaning.' He suggests that, on the one hand, these signs act as markers of difference for the dominant culture, but 'on the other hand, for those who erect them into icons ... these objects become signs of forbidden identity, sources of value' (1979, pp. 2–3).

The Birmingham school's approach to subcultures has met with criticism from cultural studies theorists and sociologists who point out that this school of subcultural theory often over-interpreted social action in terms of resistance and symbolic resolution, glossing over the contradictions and conflicts within these subcultures (Cohen, 1997; Epstein, 1998; Thornton, 1997a). Feminist critiques have also pointed out that this early research de-emphasized, or even mis-interpreted, the role of women and girls, focusing instead on male, working-class youth and portraying females as more passive or identified with the 'mainstream' (McRobbie, 1991; Pini, 1997; Thornton, 1997b). Contemporary subcultural theorists and researchers have a more complex vision of subcultures, but acknowledge that the basic tenets of subcultural theory, reaching back to its early Chicago school roots, are still useful (Duncombe 1989; Leblanc 1999; Sardiello 1998).

Mediating Multiplicity

The early Birmingham theorists viewed youth subcultures as attempts to symbolically resolve the tensions between the larger group culture, or 'parent culture,' to which they belong and their own generational concerns. Similarly, in the case of the desi party scene, one can read this diasporic subculture as an attempt to mediate between the expectations of immigrant parents and those of mainstream American peer culture, by trying to integrate signs of belonging to both worlds. By sampling Indian music, second-generation youth draw on the sounds from Hindi movies and Indian music that their parents introduced to them as children in order to inculcate an 'Indian' identity. By remixing this with rap and reggae and donning hip hop 'gear' or brand-name clothes, Indian Americans display the markers of ethnicity and material status used in a multi-ethnic, capitalistic society. The experiences of second-generation and immigrant youth challenge notions of a monolithic, all-embracing American culture into which they seamlessly assimilate, as do the daily realities of youth of color or teenagers struggling to support their families. Postmodernists would argue that cultural dissonance and multiple identities mark all our lives in an era of global capital, media, and migration. However, there is a certain specificity to the cultural tensions that the children of immigrant parents must juggle daily, as suggested by psychological and ethnographic research on Indian immigrant families in the US and Canada (Agarwal, 1991; Bacon, 1996; Gibson, 1988; Wakil, Siddique, and Wakil, 1981).

One of the themes running through the findings from the larger study (Maira 2002) is that the immigrant generation's desire to preserve an authentic ethnic identity lingers in the second generation, for whom being essentially Indian becomes a cultural ideology used to calibrate the authenticity, and the goodness, of self and others. Yet Indian American youth are, simultaneously, positioning themselves in the racial and class hierarchies of the US and coming of age in contexts shaped by public institutions such as schools, colleges, and the workforce. A uniquely Indian American subculture thus offers second-generation youth ritual events to socialize with ethnic peers while re-interpreting Indian musical and dance traditions using the rituals of American popular culture. As Jean Comaroff suggests, 'Syncretistic ritual ... movements are ... 'at once both expressive and pragmatic, for they aim to change the real world by inducing transformation in the world of symbol and rite,' – 'a world,' Nicholas Dirks adds, 'in which representation is itself one of the most contested resources' (cited in Dirks, 1994, p. 487). For Indian American youth who are in college and who participate in the ethnically demarcated club culture of New York, representation through campus organizations and popular culture rituals becomes a way to stake a claim in local spaces in the context of US multiculturalist politics, but it is a claim with limited potential for changing the categories that define them.

Some youth culture theorists argue that in presumably 'oppositional' subcultures, the 'resistance of the subculture is reduced to ritual' and this ritualized 'resistance itself becomes an end' (Epstein, 1998, p. 11). The 'subcultural solution' to the crises of youth, as conceptualized by the Birmingham school, is enacted only in the realm of the social and symbolic. However, using the notion of ritual as a site for reimagining the social order, Phil Cohen argues that such a subculture is seductive to youth because it helps to ideologically resolve the paradoxes between the different social spheres that they occupy, by enacting an option that may not be possible in actuality (in Clarke et al., 1976). The performances made possible by remix youth culture in New York, while not enabling wider systemic change, do, however, fulfill an immediate social and affective need for desi youth and have a pragmatic, not just symbolic, dimension. Les Back (1994), analyzing the 'intermezzo culture produced in the fusion of bhangra and reggae in Britain, 'argues that in the alternative public sphere of the dance, liminal ethnicities are produced which link together different social collectivities' (cited in S. Sharma, 1996, p. 36). Since this popular culture revolves around events that are almost exclusively attended by South Asian youth, it is often condoned by parents who would be more hesitant to allow their children to go out to regular clubs or parties with non-South Asian friends, especially while they are still in high school or living at home. Madhu, who grew up in New Jersey, and whose parents were actively involved in social networks from the region in Gujarat to which they belonged, said:

> I think for the party scene, overall, I think they like us to go because it keeps you hanging out with the Indians. I think they're realizing that ... you know, it's not like all these Indians are that good, and that the fights go on, and Indians actually do drink and they do stupid things, a lot of other stuff, but I think they probably figure that stuff goes on in all parties so we might as well have it with other Indians than with Americans.

Parental approval, at least during the initial years of this 'desi party scene,' seems to have been a largely unintended benefit for youth seeking to participate in the rituals of American youth popular culture, such as clubbing, dating, and performances of subcultural style. Ravi, who grew up in California, and was a veteran of the party scene on both East and West coasts, noted the 'two sides' that most of his second-generation peers displayed, one for 'Indian parents' and the other for public spaces outside parental scrutiny. He laughingly mused about the literal 'switching' of these situational identities symbolized by the practice of layered clothing:

> ... to the point where a couple of girls [going to parties] would change in the car afterwards, which was funny ... They would wear a nice long shirt when they went out, but the shirt would come up to the mid-riff, [a] halter, you know? Or they'd wear it underneath but a sweater over it and the sweater comes off all of a sudden ... So I mean, there's definitely that side.

However, after the party is over, youth must return to the constraints of interacting with their parents, peers, and communities (Cohen, 1997; Gelder, 1997). Sanjay Sharma points out that the 'liminal ethnicities' represented by British Asian dance culture, if created at all, may be limited to the 'transitory and contingent spaces of the dance floor' (S. Sharma, 1996, p. 36).

Hybridity, though fashionable in cultural theory and also literally in 'ethnic chic,' is not always easy to live, for social institutions and networks continue to demand loyalty to sometimes competing cultural ideals that may be difficult to manage for second-generation youth. For many, liminality is an ongoing, daily condition of being betwixt and between cultural categories (Turner, 1967; 1987, p. 101, 107) that is symbolically expressed in remix culture. However, this is only one of several spaces that Indian American youth negotiate, and other contexts—such as immigrant community events or campus 'culture shows' – elicit a more bounded, fixed notion of Indian-ness (see Maira, 2002).

The performance of a visibly hybrid ethnicity belongs to a range of identity performances in everyday life. Indian American youth still switch between multiple identities as they did when moving between high school and family, only now perhaps they change from the baggy pants and earrings that they wear among peers to conservative attire on the job, or from secret relationships at college to dutiful daughters on visits home. These transitions clearly have a gendered dimension, and the negotiation of ethnic identity and national culture is embodied differently by women than men, as is visibly enacted in this remix music subculture.

The Paradoxes of Petrification

The ways in which Indian American youth make meaning of this youth culture reveal that there are several paradoxes of identity embedded in discussions of what this popular culture signifies. Vijay, who grew up in Queens, voiced the views of several youth who participate in this subculture themselves yet remain anxious about its authenticity:

> You have a dichotomy of, sort of, two cultures, you have an Indian culture which is sort of a real Indian culture, which, you have, Bharata Natyam [classical Indian dance] and other people who are really interested, and you have another sort of culture, which is the bhangra culture, you know, where you're looking at Bally Sagoo [British Asian musician] remixes as a means to explore cultural identity, which is not exactly … I mean I enjoy listening to those songs as well, but, er, there has to be a separation between what is real, and why you're really doing something.

Timothy Taylor (1997, p. 166) cites a dismissive posting on the Internet that characterized 'bangra' music as essentially 'American,' and therefore un-Indian: 'Bangra is a music for [those who] … are willing to shame towards their own culture. I really don't like Indian music either, but I have respect for it because it is a display of Indian culture. If y'all start listening to bangra, y'all are giving up on your own culture.' For these second-generation Indian Americans, authenticity is still tied to the vision of India that is filtered through their parents' socialization, that is, a definition of culture based on classical arts, selected historical traditions, and religious orthodoxy (see Maira, 2002).

This ethnic orthodoxy has been transmitted, in part, by the parental generation whose desire to preserve an 'authentic' culture overseas has led to the selective importing of elements and agents of Indian culture, with religious specialists, classical musicians, dancers, and film stars touring the United States and performing at community events. Thus while there is a circulation of hybrid popular culture in the diaspora, such as remix music and Indian films that are often a cultural pastiche, there is also a parallel transnational circuit that has helped to reify images of Indian identity overseas (Prashad, 1997). The selective importing of culture from the sub-continent is driven by the frozen furrows of memory and the politics of nostalgia, with immigrants harking back to the India they left a few decades ago, or to a mythical land of spirituality, 'good values,' and unchanging tradition. The production of nostalgia is predicated on *absence*, a cultural anchor that is both missing and missed, and on the assumption of an earlier time of cultural wholeness that is now at risk of fragmentation, if not dissolution.

The yardstick of ethnic authenticity in this tightly-knit youth culture is finely calibrated. Those who do not socialize exclusively with other Indian Americans or South Asians, or who are part of an alternative subculture – whether based on a different style, progressive politics, non-Hindu religious groups, or alternative sexual orientations – say that they often feel marginalized. Paul Gilroy (1993, pp. 83–84) finds a similar tension in his analysis of black diasporic culture, and attributes these rigid boundaries to 'rhetorical strategies of cultural insiderism' that support an 'absolute sense of ethnic difference' and construct the nation [or national identification] as ethnically homogenous.' The regulation of ethnic authenticity is always being negotiated in youth cultural productions that challenge monolithic understandings of ethnicity or nationalism, so that the beats of 'cool' are mixed into tracks that flow into nostalgia, and vice versa. The dialectic between these cultural complexes, 'cool' and 'nostalgia,' is a response to the confluence of market forces and multiculturalist projects in education and commodity culture. Indian American youth in New York City use the rituals of popular culture to negotiate their racialized, gendered, and classed positioning in the wider social context, and sometimes to reshuffle their parents' expectations of racial identification, but the discourse of purity runs deep.

I argue that the gap, or space of contradiction, between the discourse of ethnic authenticity among second-generation youth, on the one hand, and the performance of hybridity in remix youth culture and in everyday life, on the other, suggests that what is at stake in this youth subculture is not just a struggle over definitions of Indian music and dance; rather, this disjuncture also reveals conflicts over attempts by Indian American youth to be 'authentic' in both local and diasporic spaces, the belief of immigrant parents in the American Dream, and the complicity of Indian Americans with US racial hierarchies. Race politics is deeply implicated in the question of what it means for a young woman or man to become an (Indian) American subject, and for second-generation youth, the question of what it means to participate in performances of urban 'cool' or of collective nostalgia. The adoption of black style by desi youth in this remix youth culture can be seen as a response to the black/white racial binary and the attempts of second-generation Indian Americans to position themselves in relation to the monochromatic racial boundaries of the US In some instances, as I argue in the larger study, these youth seemed to show an acceptance, or more of a passive non-rejection, of the racial status quo, but in other contexts, they explicitly identified as non-white and resisted anti-black racism (see Maira, 2000, 2001).

For women in this subculture, many noted that a 'hoody,' or streetwise hip-hop, image was not considered as appealing as it was for men, and the pervasive image of desirable femininity rested on designer-inspired New York fashion. Manisha, whose friends were mainly African American and Latino, and who often dressed in hip hop gear – with a gold 'Om' pendant dangling around her neck – reflected that:

Guys can get away with [the 'hoody' look] but girls who are considered 'cool' dress prettier. I think the guys are intimidated by that [girls with a hip hop look], it's taken as a sign of being closer to Latinos or blacks, of being outside of the Indian circle, as I am … . the guys may think we're rougher, or not as sweet.

While this demure, 'sweet' femininity is favored by most men over the hip hop look when worn by women, it is in turn passed over for women who perform a more sexualized style on the dance floor–the 'hoochy mamas.' Yet, these same women are considered 'loose,' that is, not the type of Indian American woman a man would like to marry. For Indian American men, however, there seems to a somewhat wider range of images of desirability, although these are no less racialized than for women.

For young men in the desi party subculture, a different set of norms for heterosexual appeal operate than for women and 'doing gender' is more closely tied to negotiations of material status (Leblanc, p. 141). Several youth pointed explicitly to the need for men who belong to this subculture to flaunt brand-name 'gear' to signal their buying power and thus their appeal in the heterosexual dating market. The behavior of Indian American men, however, is not read as a marker of ethnic authenticity. While men who project a sexualized, or promiscuous, image within this 'party scene' were often criticized by the women I spoke to as being unreliable and unappealing for long-term relationships, they were never described as being somehow 'less Indian' for their hyper-sexuality. However, machismo becomes linked to nationalism, and in some cases even to specific regional identifications, through practices that are common in club culture more generally, such as masculine aggression and violent brawls, but are framed in the desi party scene by a discourse of ethnic marginalization and internal differentiation.

Promiscuous Cool and Chaste Nostalgia

Reflecting on the complex contradictions emerging from an analysis of Indian American youth culture in New York, it seems that the creation of this ethnic youth subculture actually uses a very pervasive means of expressing identity in the American context, that is, the marking of ethnic boundaries, and uses common commodities and social practices, such as fashion, music, and dance, associated with American youth culture. Georges Balandier (1970) points out: 'The supreme ruse of power is to allow itself to be contested ritually in order to consolidate itself more effectively' (cited in Stallybrass and White, 1986, p. 14). This is not to dismiss the significance for many second-generation youth of a social and cultural space they can claim as their own, but to recognize the ways in which this subculture, rather than overturning established trajectories of socialization, recreates gendered sanctions or moralized judgments that reinforce a conservatizing discourse about ethnic purity. Rather than subverting the dominant tropes of cultural identities at work in the second generation, this subculture has provided a setting in which to *contain* the presumed paradoxes of second-generation experiences, by performing a hybrid identity which is still questioned by many of these youth themselves. Gopinath (1995, p. 312) also concludes that 'bhangra as performance must be understood, ... as a creative response to the demand for coherence and stability within specific racial and cultural contexts, a means by which to "work the trap that one is inevitably in."'

Critiques of this second-generation popular culture by youth themselves often portray ancestral traditions as 'pure' and 'innocent' while mainstream American cultural tropes are referred to as 'seductive' and 'polluting' influences. The language used in evaluating identities, by both first- and second-generation Indian Americans, is that of chastity and corruption. There is clearly a moralizing dimension which is tied to the debates over gender and sexual roles in the second-generation, one that has real consequences for the lives of young Indian Americans. James Brow argues that the 'moral authority' that allows tradition to become 'doxa,' or the natural order of things, stems from a process of imbuing ethnic ties with a certain sanctity, so that 'the primordiality of communal relations is preserved only by their incarceration in the doxic prison of innocence' (1990, pp. 2–3). Brow, however, does not link ethnic absolutism to the politics of gender and sexuality, the other half of the tension in this instance of ethnic orthodoxy.

Feminist and post-colonial analysis have shown how women are used to signify tradition and so must be controlled in order to maintain the boundaries of community or nation (Anthias and Yuval-Davis, 1989; Jayawardena and de Alwis, 1996; Goddard, 1987; Ortner, 1996), as evident in diasporic communities as well (Bhattarcharjee, 1992; Mani, 1993). There is a *sexualizing* of ethnic identities that imbues them with a moral force, enabling the enforcement of notions of cultural purity in the second generation. A discourse centreing on female sexuality is inserted into the rhetoric of ethnic authenticity to uphold the dichotomy of identity choices. The sexual undercurrents of this subculture express the generally shared concerns of adolescents, but are also cast in a particular way that reflects on questions of second-generation identity for this subculture, and reveal the limitations of hybridity when expressed in the realm of style alone. Desi youth construct a vision of second-generation 'coolness' by working markers of urban youth style, such as hip hop, into the nostalgia for an uncontaminated Indian culture. Clearly these performances of desi 'cool' and of collective 'nostalgia' are not in opposition to each other; one is embedded in the other, although this dialectic is often unevenly and viscerally felt, especially by young women.

Conclusion

Cultural theorists have sometimes privileged notions of fluid, fragmented identities without paying sufficient attention to the ways in which actors often negotiate *both* shifting identities and reified ideals in their everyday lives. The contradictions on the ground are sometimes more complex than theorists acknowledge, for example, in the ways Indian American youth disrupt the very fictions of authenticity they construct, using remixed dance music or hip hop to mark a style that is distinctly diasporic. Dirks points out that the performative nature of ritual events demonstrates the contingent nature of authenticity: 'Each ritual event is patterned activity, to be sure, but it is also invented anew as it happens. ... the authenticity of the event was inscribed in its performance ... in its uncertainty and contestability (499).' Authenticity, then, is not located in some authentic moment of expression. The practice and rhetoric of nostalgia in the second generation is premised on the social fiction of authenticity but, at the same time, it is a fiction that is continually retold in performance because it *does* have tangible cultural and political significance in the lives of youth who co-produce this expression of yearning for ethnic purity. It is important to integrate a critique of essentialization in studies of popular cultures with an approach that draws on lived experience and daily practice, to guard against the inclination to devise mythical interpretations in solitary engagement with cultural 'texts.' The romance of popular culture should not cloud our insights into the ways in which second-generation youth cultures still remix strains of nostalgia and beats of gendered myths.

Notes

1   Bhangra music traditionally involves three instruments: the dhol and dholki (drums), and the thumri (a stringed instrument). The lyrics traditionally celebrate the beauty of Punjab, village life, and women.
2   Traditionally, powdered dots, and more commonly today, small felt or plastic designs, worn by women between the eyebrows.

References

Agarwal, P. (1991), *Passage from India: Post-1965 Indian Immigrants and Their Children: Conflicts, Concerns, and Solutions*, Palos Verdes: Yuvati.

Anthias, F. and Yuval-Davis, N. (1989), 'Introduction', in F. Anthias and N. Yuval-Davis (eds.), *Woman, Nation, State*, New York: St. Martin's Press, pp. 1–15.

Back, L. (1994), *X amount of sat sri akal: Apache Indian, reggae music and intermezzo culture*. South Asia Seminar Series, ICCCR, Universities of Manchester and Keele, United Kingdom.

Bacon, J. (1996), *Lifelines: Community, Family, and Assimilation among Asian Indian Immigrants*. New York: Oxford University Press.

Bhattacharjee, A. (1992), 'The habit of ex-nomination: Nation, woman, and the Indian immigrant bourgeoisie', *Public Culture* **5** (1), 19–44.

Brow, J. (1990), 'Notes on community, hegemony, and the uses of the past', *Anthropology Quarterly* **63** (1), 1–6.

Clarke, J., Hall, S., Jefferson, T. and Roberts, B. (1976), 'Subcultures, cultures, and class', in S. Hall and T. Jefferson (eds.), *Resistance through Rituals: Youth Subcultures in Post-War Britain*, London: Hutchinson, in association with the Centre for Contemporary Cultural Studies, University of Birmingham, pp. 9–79.

Cohen, S. (1997), 'Symbols of trouble', in K. Gelder and S. Thornton (eds.), *The Subcultures Reader*, London: Routledge, pp. 149–62.

Das Dasgupta, S. and Dasgupta S. (1996), 'Women in exile: Gender relations in the Asian Indian community', in S. Maira and R. Srikanth (eds.), *Contours of the heart: South Asians map North America*, New York: Asian American Writers' Workshop, pp. 381–400.

Dirks, N. (1994), 'Ritual and resistance: Subversion as a social fact', in N. Dirks, G. Ely, and S. Ortner (eds.), *Culture/Power/History: A Reader in Contemporary Social Theory*, Princeton: Princeton University Press, pp. 483–503.

Duncombe, S. (1988), 'Let's all be alienated together: Zines and the making of underground community', in J. Austin and M. Willard (eds.), *Generations of Youth: Youth Cultures and History in Twentieth-Century America*, New York: New York University Press, pp. 427–51.

Durham, M. G. (1999), 'Effing the Ineffable: U.S. media and images of Asian femininity', in T. K. Nakayama (ed.), *Asian Pacific American Genders and Sexualities*, Tempe, Ariz.: Arizona State University, pp. 75–92.

Epstein, J. S. (1998), 'Introduction: Generation X, youth culture, and identity', in J. Epstein (ed.), *Youth Culture: Identity in a Postmodern World*, edited by. Malden, MA: Blackwell, pp. 1–23.

Esser, D. et al. (1999), 'Reorganizing organizing: Immigrant labor in North America-Interview with New York Taxi Workers' Alliance', in B. Mathew and V. Prashad (eds.), *Amerasia (Special Issue – Satyagraha in America: The Political Culture of South Asians in the U.S.* **25** (3), 171–181.

Flores, J. (2000), *From Bomba to Hip Hop,* New York: Columbia University Press.

Frith, S. (1992), 'The cultural study of popular music', in L. Grossberg, C. Nelson and P. A. Treichler (eds.), *Cultural Studies,* New York: Routledge, pp. 174–86.

Gelder, K. (1997), 'Introduction to part three', in K. Gelder and S. Thornton (eds.), *The Subcultures Reader,* Routledge, pp. 145–48.

Gibson, M. A. (1988), *Accommodation without assimilation: Sikh immigrants in an American high school,* Ithaca: Cornell University Press.

Gilroy, P. (1993), *The black Atlantic: Modernity and double consciousness.* Cambridge: Harvard University Press.

Goddard, V. (1987), 'Honour and shame: The control of women's sexuality and group identity in Naples', in P. Caplan (ed.), *The cultural construction of sexuality,* London: Tavistock, pp. 166–92.

Gopinath, G. (1995), '"Bombay, U.K., Yuba City": Bhangra music and the engendering of diaspora', *Diaspora,* **4** (3), 303–21.

Hebdige, D. (1979), *Subculture: The Meaning of Style,* London: Methuen.

Jayawardena, K. and Alwis, M. de (1996), 'Introduction', in K. Jayawardena and M. de Alwis (eds.), *Embodied violence: Communalising women's sexuality in South Asia,* London: Zed Books, pp. ix–xxiv.

Kirschner, T. (1998), 'Studying rock: Towards a materialist ethnography', in T. Swiss, J. Sloop, and A. Herman (eds.), *Mapping the beat: Popular music and contemporary theory,* Malden, MA: Blackwell, pp. 247–68.

Leblanc, L. (1999), *Pretty in punk: Girls' gender resistance in a boys' subculture,* New Brunswick: Rutgers University Press.

Lessinger, J. (1995), *From the Ganges to the Hudson: Indian immigrants in New York City,* Boston: Allyn and Bacon.

Maira, S. (2000), 'Henna and Hip Hop: The Politics of Cultural Production and The Work of Cultural Studies', *Journal of Asian American Studies,* **3** (3), 329–369.

Maira, S. (2001), 'B-Boys and Bass Girls: Sex, Style, and Mobility in Indian American Youth Culture', *Souls: A Journal of Black Politics, Culture, and Society',* **3** (3), 65–86.

Maira, S. (2002), *Desis in the house: Indian American youth culture in New York City,* Philadelphia: Temple University Press.

Mani, L. (1993), 'Gender, class, and cultural conflict: Indu Krishnan's *Knowing her place*', in Women of South Asia Descent Collective (eds.), *Our feet walk the sky: Women of the South Asian Diaspora,* San Francisco: Aunt Lute Books, pp. 32–36.

McRobbie, A. (1999), *In the culture society: Art, fashion, and popular music,* London: Routledge.

Mukhi, S. M. (2000), *Doing the desi thing: Performing Indianness in New York City,* New York: Garland.

Ortner, S. (1996), 'The virgin and the state', in S. B. Ortner, *Making gender: The politics and erotics of culture.* Boston: Beacon Press, pp. 43–58.

Pini, M. (1997), 'Women and the early British rave scene', in A. McRobbie (ed.), *Back to reality? Social experience and cultural studies,* Manchester: Manchester University Press, pp. 152–69.

Prashad, V. (1996), 'Desh: The contradictions of 'homeland'', in S. Maira and R. Srikanth (eds.), *Contours of the heart: South Asians map North America,*. New York: Asian American Writers' Workshop, pp. 225–36.

Sardiello, R. (1998), Identity and status stratification in Deadhead subculture, in J. Epstein (ed.), *Youth culture: Identity in a postmodern world,* Malden, MA: Blackwell, pp. 118–47.

Sengupta, S. (1996), 'To be young, Indian and hip: Hip-hop meets Hindi pop as a new generation of South Asians finds its own groove', *New York Times,* June 30, section 13: 'The City,' p. 1.

Sharma, S. (1996), 'Noisy Asians or 'Asian noise'? in S. Sharma, J. Hutnyk and A. Sharma (eds.), *Dis-Orienting rhythms: The politics of the new Asian dance music,* London: Zed Press, pp. 32–55.

Stallybrass, P. and White, A. (1986), *The politics and poetics of transgression,* Ithaca: Cornell University Press.

Taylor, T. (1997), 'Anglo-Asian self-fashioning', in T. Taylor, *Global pop: World music, world markets,* New York: Routledge, pp. 147–72.

Thornton, S. (1997a), The social logic of subcultural capital, in K. Gelder and S. Thornton (eds.), *The subcultures reader,* New York: Routledge, pp. 200–209.

Thornton, S. (1997b), 'General introduction', in K. Gelder and S. Thornton (eds.), *The subcultures reader,* New York: Routledge, pp. 1–15.

Turner, G. (1996), *British cultural studies: An introduction* (2nd ed.), London: Routledge.

Turner, V. (1967), *The forest of symbols: Aspects of Ndembu ritual,* Ithaca: Cornell University Press.

Turner, V. (1987), *The anthropology of performance.* New York: Performing Arts Journal Publications, 1987.

Wakil, S. P., Siddique, C. M. and Wakil, F. A. (1981), 'Between two cultures: A study in socialization of children of immigrants', *Journal of Marriage and the Family* **43** (4), 929–40.

Williams, R. (1977), *Marxism and literature,* Oxford: Oxford University Press.

Chapter 19

Teenage Pregnancy in Mexico:
Why the Panic?

Noemi Ehrenfeld Lenkiewicz

Introduction

The aim of this paper is to analyse adolescent pregnancy in contemporary Mexico comprehensively rather than from a one-dimensional statistic-based perspective. Age, marital status, number of pregnancies and other indicators usually taken as fixed, static references of Mexican adolescents' sexual and reproductive health, will be considered here as a part of a more flexible framework. Adolescent pregnancy became an issue of great concern for different sectors in Mexican society during the last fifteen years. Despite the continuous decrease of newborns to adolescent mothers during the last twenty years (Guzmán, Contreras and Hakkert, 2001) and a reduction in the adolescent fertility rates (CONAPO, 1996, 2000), the topic is socially and culturally constructed and represented as a 'social problem'. Considering adolescent pregnancy as a problem stems mainly from a positivist theoretical conceptualisation of the issue.

This paper focuses on adolescent pregnancy in its social and cultural context. Symbolic interactionism provides useful conceptualisations for analysing the quantitative data and relating them to the qualitative material. Following Bloomer (1969), the generic variables are not exactly generic and universal; they do have a content given in the particular circumstances of application. And following this theoretical position, it is possible to take the standpoint of the others, which in this case are the adolescents themselves.

It is relevant to discuss some of the official national data within this framework in order to establish some important points related to adolescent sexuality, reproductive health, as well as adolescent motherhood. Since health public policies address adolescent pregnancy as a problem, the media have expressed concern about the 'alarming data'. In particular, these alarming data about adolescent pregnancy are seen as related to drug use, violence, family breakdown, loss of moral values within the family and society, and so. It is also claimed that adolescent pregnancy and future poverty and marginalisation are closely related.

The Mexican Context

Mexico is undergoing a significant 'demographic transition' and it has been claimed that the population growth dropped from 3.2 per cent to 1.8 per cent per annum over the last three decades. This change is almost entirely due to a significant decrease in the fertility rates (CONAPO, 2000). Despite these apparent changes, the population group classified officially as 'young' (between 15 and 24 years old) still represents an important share of 20.3 per cent of the total, in raw numbers, 20.2 million people. The reproductive behaviour of this group has a decisive impact on the overall global fertility rate, because the average age for marriage is 21 years old, and pregnancy or childbirth are expected to take place within the first year of cohabitation.

The Mexican Institute of Youth (Instituto Mexicano de la Juventud, 2002) considers the group comprising the ages of 12 to 29 as 'adolescent and young people'.[1] The arbitrary consensus in most Latin American countries and Mexico to fix the lower limit at age 15 years restricts the possibility to better analyse sexual and reproductive health behaviors among younger girls. Including teenagers 12 to 14 years old, the total Mexican population encompassing age groups 12 to 19 years old by year 2000 are 16, 384,550 millions. Different issues like education, health status, social class, poverty, age at first sexual relation, age at first birth, marital status, employment, the presence of violence, etc., are closely connected to the living conditions for female adolescents. In Mexico there are still important differences among urban and rural adolescent women's lives, as well as among urban very poor and middle class adolescents and among young women belonging to ethnic groups.

It becomes important to analyse the official data about adolescent pregnancies and birth. The same source provides contradictory data at times. For example, the number of births by adolescent mothers (15–19 years old) is reported as 315,869 in year 2000, which represent about the 14.9 per cent of the total births in the country. For year 2003 the number of births by adolescent mothers was 271,895, which represents 13.5 per cent of the total number of births. The contradictions concerning the data depend on different factors. Some data are obtained via projections, others through the census or by demographic researchers. Births registered at hospitals are fewer than those registered at the registry offices, because women give birth at home in rural areas and small towns where the access to health services is difficult or not available. However, people often register their babies months or even years after the birth.

The social concern that is regularly expressed through different media has at various times been focused on the number of pregnancies, moral issues related to premarital sex, and unsafe abortions (Milenio, 2003; Excelsior, 2004). The media have called attention to this 'problem' as a serious one that endangers the whole society and its institutions. It is also claimed that the fertility rate of the adolescent group has not been declining at the same rate as in other age groups. Therefore, it is claimed that the contribution of this group to the total fertility rate has been increasing in the last 15 years, is projected to be 14.9 per cent by year 2000 (see Figure 19.1).

In Figure 19.1 it is clear that the fertility rate of the 15–19 age groups is decreasing, but the contribution of this age group to the number of births is still significant due to the absolute number of adolescent women, a population of about 10.5 million. To get a better understanding of the social contexts of adolescent pregnancy, it is necessary to take an in-depth look at the views of adolescents themselves.

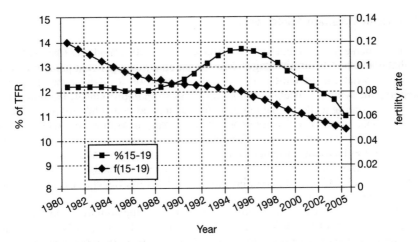

Figure 19.1   Fertility rate women 15–19 years old and percentage of total fertility rate

Source: CONAPO, La situacion demografica de Mexico 1999 (CONAPO, 1999)

Methodology

In this study in addition to the quantitative demographic data, semi-structured interviews and focus groups were used to elicit an understanding of the complexities surrounding adolescent pregnancy in different social and cultural contexts.

Altogether 150 semi-structured interviews and two focus groups were conducted. The number of participants in focus groups ranged from 7-9 adolescents. Whilst the average age of the interviewees was 17 years, 43 per cent of the girls were 16 years or younger (65 adolescents), and 20 per cent (30 women) were 15 years old or younger. The interviewees were urban marginal pregnant adolescents who were contacted at a public hospital providing care for low-income patients in southern Mexico City. The adolescents requested health services related to their pregnancies at the obstetric out patient service.

Individual and focus group interviews focused on questions such as: How do the adolescents experience their pregnancy? How do they perceive it? Is there an individual decision behind this pregnancy? The interviews consisted partially of questions designed to obtain information about the socio-economic situation and reproductive health indicators, e.g., use of contraceptives, number of pregnancies, etc. Most of the questions on gender perceptions, sexual roles, motherhood, sexual life, future expectancies, and other issues were open-ended questions. At the first contact, all young women were informed about the objectives of the study. If they decided to participate, their interviews would be completely confidential, meaning that their participation either in interviews or in focus groups would not be recorded in the hospital files. Interviews and focus group interviews took place in a small building apart from main building of the hospital.

Who are the Pregnant Adolescents?

Young women expressed that to live in 'free union' has its advantages over marriage, but that it also has its disadvantages. Most of the interviewees declare themselves to be part of what can be called 'free union'. In addition to being a marital status category,[2] the symbolic meaning is important. For some highly educated women, free union is becoming a choice that marks individuality and independence. In the urban marginal population as well as for people living in rural areas, free union is the easiest way to start living together with no bureaucratic formalities. In a free union there are responsibilities based on a mutual commitment. To be in 'free union' means that 'it is easier for men to leave the girls and their children' (Focus group). Marriage means that 'it is more difficult to leave the girls'. But both marriage and free union are preferred over being alone.

Low education levels and poor educational achievement are considered contributing factors to adolescent pregnancy. In most cases, in Latin America adolescent mothers have already quit school before they become pregnant (UNFPA, 2001). In Mexico it is often argued that pregnancy in adolescents is one of the main reasons for the dropping out. However, among the interviewees at the time of the interviews, only 15.3 per cent of the 150 adolescents were still in school. A few weeks ago, when they realized that they were pregnant, only 36 per cent were attending school. Forty per cent of the interviewees have not completed the basic years of education, which is a higher figure than expected, considering they are living in Mexico City. Attending school seems to be one of the most efficient ways to prevent pregnancy, because adolescent women get another perception of the world and themselves. When considering the living context, it is important to discuss the meaning of the concept that adolescent have of 'living with his family' or 'alone'. The economic dependence is the main issue that compels young women to live with their in-laws. Less than one out of five adolescents considers that living in a separate room, or in the backyard of the parents' house is to live alone. About 60 per cent of the adolescents who have a partner, move from their parental home to live with the boy and his parents; most of these adolescents adhere to a cultural, traditional and paternalistic mandate. About 20 per cent of girls with partners continue to live with their mothers, maintaining their position as daughters in their family of origin, as the 35 per cent of those without partner do.

A move to the male partner's home has several implications. These adolescents do not have enough social, emotional and cultural resources to oppose to their boyfriends' request to follow them. To leave their mothers' home and move to an unknown family is difficult. Mothers-in-law have power and control over the new couple; it is still today common to hear such older women say: 'Fine, she comes to live with us but she should pay as I paid.' Girls have to work in order to be fully accepted into the new family. Quite often, this means that they have to perform designated household chores such as doing the laundry for the whole family or prepare tortillas for everyone. Most of the adolescents (82.67 per cent) declared that they were in their homes, doing housework. However, none of them considered working at home, either helping at a family business or with domestic labour as a proper work.

Adolescent mothers are not able to be independent, live alone and support their children. They will not become heads of family.[3] Researchers such as Salles and Tuirán, (1998) argue that social transformations are also reflected in profound transformations of family structures. They refer to living in a separate house as part of an individuation process that is becoming harder to achieve – if not impossible – due to the recent series of economic crises. Looking at changes in the families in different contexts Stromquist (1998) argues that the family roles have become varied and that patriarchal values are questioned. This condition is closely linked to the labour market transformations and women's participation in it, with necessary changes inside the domestic unit, gendered roles, and individual developments. Despite these claims, urban marginal adolescents seem to reproduce the traditional patterns, in which women are still not fully participating in the formal labour market.

Why do the Girls Engage in Sexual Relations?

Looking closer at sexual practices and the context in which adolescents become pregnant, some important questions emerge. Why do the girls engage in sexual relations? If they are looking for pleasure and love, why do they get pregnant? These questions have no simple answers, but the following discussion sheds some light on the issues. Adolescent women should be able to decide about their own bodies as persons with full sexual and reproductive rights. However, many factors that intervene in the decision-making chain are not in their hands but in their social context. About 88 per cent of the interviewees are compelled to start sharing their lives by living with partners because they have become pregnant. Most of the adolescents are compelled to start living with their boyfriends during the first six months of the pregnancy when the pregnancy becomes evident and can not be hidden from the girl's mother and family. The usual word adolescents associated with their first sexual relationships is love: 91 per cent of the adolescents in the sample believe that sexual relations should be experienced only when there is love between partners. These women start their sexual life under different circumstances, but almost all have been told to be very attractive to their boyfriends, and most of them report that the boys told them that they were in love with them. However, for some of them, the boyfriends' expressions included other components. For example, about 30 per cent of the adolescents had been told by their partners 'I want us to have a child' and a 6 per cent had been told 'I want you to give me a child'. To express desires about having children together instead of only sex, sends the message that could be translated into: I don't want just to take you to bed, I want something serious, steady with you.

Girls in this sample seem to be trapped in a seductive-coercion game. If they refuse to have sex, they lose their love. If they agree to have sex they change their status to another potentially higher emotional and social status, that of a mother. It is also a tempting proposition considering their poor living conditions with no opportunities for education or a good job. However, this topic was not usually discussed by the focus groups, but a couple of girls said: 'He told me that if I don't sleep with him, he would do it with the other, a girl who lives close from home … and I know he would.' (16 years old)

I got pregnant two months after I had my first relation ... and yes, I married now (I am in my fifth month of pregnancy now) ... why? ... because now I will be a mother ... I thought it would be better ... that is what they say, my sisters ... everybody. (17 years old)

Therefore sex, pregnancy and union have an intricate and complex relationship with brief periods of time between them. The average age at first sexual relation for adolescents in the sample is 15.7 years old. The average age at the onset of pregnancy is 16.3 years old. The average months elapsed between 1st sexual relation and 1st pregnancy is 6.02 months. This brief period between becoming sexually active and the onset of pregnancy reduces the opportunity to build a relationship.

The use of contraceptives by adolescents at the very first sexual relationship is linked to educational level, availability of sex education programmes that started at childhood, cultural practices, and a degree of democracy and permissiveness in relation to the sexuality mores of society. Most of the adolescents in the sample, when first asked about the use of contraceptives,[4] declared that they did not use contraceptives at their very first sexual relation with present partner or with the boy responsible for the current pregnancy. While 74 per cent of adolescents in sample did not try to prevent the pregnancy, 26 per cent did so including those who used the rhythm method.

What to do with Unexpected Pregnancies?

Adolescent girls and their partners do not have the time to let their relationship mature. Pregnant girls and their partners have to make important decisions quickly. They have to decide what to do with the unexpected pregnancy, whether to continue their schooling or get a job, whether and how to inform their families about the pregnancy. The decision about marriage and free union is sometimes taken by the adolescents, sometimes by their partners, and sometimes by their parents. The girls want the boys to stand by them but they accept, and even justify the situation, if the boys leave them pregnant. They accept pregnancy as a female responsibility, as a natural destiny. Seventy-one per cent of the girls would have postponed the pregnancy, which suggests that the current pregnancies were unintended and unexpected.

Since the girls feel that they do not decide for themselves whether to become sexually active, they are not really responsible for the consequences. This attitude might be influenced by different factors such as low education, ambivalence about the family's demands of chastity and peer pressure to be sexually active, tensions between cultural traditional views and the media messages about 'liberal' adolescents. It is claimed that knowledge about sexuality and reproductive health leads to more responsible adolescent sexual behaviour. Hence, knowledge about contraceptives should be a variable in preventing pregnancies in adolescents. However, 74 per cent of the interviewees did not use contraceptives at their first sexual relationship, while about 98 per cent of them knew about at least three modern contraceptives. Then, how to explain these pregnancies? In all the focus group discussions, the pregnancy emerged as an accident, as an unplanned event.

The social context influencing the girls about whether they want a child or not, is complex. First, in Mexican culture it is expected that women have children, no matter at what age. Pregnancies, at a first glance, are not as problematic as in other cultural contexts, because, in general, children are accepted and welcomed as part of the 'normal' life of women and men. Second, as abortion is illegal, most of the pregnancies result in newborns. Third, it is difficult for a pregnant adolescent to express that the current pregnancy is unwanted. It is not honourable to have sex just for pleasure.

Boys initiate the sexual relation. In fact, it looks like the girls have sex at the boys' 'request'. And pregnancies are too, as a consequence of unprotected sex, because boys do not use condoms and adolescent women do not say no. In both situations, there are cultural and social advantages for boys over women, becoming therefore a relationship in which boys have more power and control. Mexican culture privileges the importance of men's roles largely over women's roles. In this unequal situation it is not possible for urban marginal Mexican adolescent girls to really make a choice.

The discourse of boys is the most attractive and seductive that these adolescents could receive: boys want to have sex with them not in order to create a space of mutual knowledge, pleasure, intimacy or just for sex: they want to have sex in order to change their status as women to a better and higher stage, e.g., mothers. When adolescents in interviews were asked if they think that a pregnant woman is more important or valuable than a non-pregnant one, sample adolescents answered affirmatively in 89.33 per cent (that is 134 women). When asked if, in their opinion men considered it so, the figure dropped slightly to 84.67 per cent (127 women). The discussion within the focus group about what is a 'valuable' woman was immediately substituted by girls with the words 'motherhood', or 'maternity'. In addition, about seven out of ten pregnant adolescents think that men regard a sterile woman as 'less womanly, less feminine'.

'yes, it is not now, at our ages, but a child ... is the most important thing that can happen to a woman.'

'to be able to have a child, to give birth ... is something nice ... to feel a baby inside you ... a child makes me a woman'

'I think that to be a mother is very important ... to me it is it something incredible.'

The male partners of these pregnant adolescents seem to have found the 'key' that tears down women's resistance: boys say what girls expect to hear from them in order to accept sexual requests. It is okay to become mothers – which is socially expected and reinforced – through having sex, because 'giving in' and 'love' are the only valid reasons to lose virginity and neither minds if the girl becomes pregnant. This seductive discourse made by adolescent men promises adolescent women two treasures: to get love and to become mothers. Importantly, partners of these adolescent women, are adolescents themselves, most of them under 20 years old.

Even though becoming a mother is a highly valued status, the price that adolescents have to pay facing their pregnancies is very high, at least up to this stage: feelings and sensation of loss, fears, inadequacy, loneliness and emotional isolation are feelings regularly present.

I already lost my mother, because she was very angry ... To have the baby means to lose that many things ... now I lost my mother, my boyfriend does not even talk to me, and he doesn't love me. That's what I did not want. I didn't want to lose the love of my whole family because I will have a child'. (19 years old)

I do not mind if my father doesn't allow me to go to parties now when I am pregnant. I didn't like parties before it happened ... and well, now I would like to be single, that is I mean not pregnant ... we (my brothers and me) never had much confidence with my father ... he never was trustworthy ... and since this woman is with him, much less ... however, my father always helped me and supported me. Now I feel still worse, we don't talk since I told him I am pregnant and I still feel bad. I can't talk about all this with anybody, but at nigh when I am alone I just cry because I can't find the answers. (19 years old)

I felt bad, my parents' opinion, my reputation. But, what is done is done. I have no regrets ... Physically, I don't feel well with my pregnancy, but morally I feel good, because I will be a mother. Speaking honestly, you become fulfilled, I will be a mother and I am happy about that. Yes, well, I also feel uncomfortable, truly, because it was not planned.

Pregnant adolescents find themselves immersed in a very complex situation, were they have to make, consciously or pre-consciously, critical decisions for the long term future and the timing of the actions are disastrous. This timing is both an emotional, subjective experience and a social one. They engage in an emotional relationship with few and poor conditions to develop intimacy, they have their first sexual experiences not always really willingly, they become pregnant and thus, they have to decide if telling this to the families and – some of them who have partners – to the boys. They face a future where there is not much space for them. Their social conditions are poor, economically and culturally, and where few friends are present since they are no longer in school, with very scant social resources to improve their material conditions.

Reflections and Conclusions

What becomes relevant is that these urban marginal adolescent girls are not visible in terms of being considered as important or valuable persons in society, among friends or within the family. Female adolescents in order to get recognition as individuals or cultural beings need to attain the category of 'woman'. Pregnancy or a child is a common road to become a mother. It is mentioned that the two main pathways to transit from adolescence to adulthood are through work or by founding their own family. Adolescents in urban marginal milieus have poor educational and job opportunities. Education and jobs would give a different and better status to adolescent women. However, social and economic conditions in Mexico have become seriously impoverished and it is particularly difficult for the young and poor. If education and work are not possible alternatives for adolescent women to reach a different status, then motherhood is the most realistic option. To become a mother results in an immediate recognition of being a 'valuable woman', at least in the short term and therefore, this is a better status than any other for these adolescents. Personal aspirations of adolescents seem to be centred more on the projection of becoming mothers, than in the experience itself of really having the presence of a child. The child is still in a blurry horizon far away, where different tensions appear: where to live, with whom they will live, the presence or not of a partner, and the economic difficulties. However, for some of them, to raise a family is the expected destiny and they accept facts with less mixed feelings than others might do.

In the interviews, when adolescents were asked why it is important that a woman has a child, half of them answered to get somebody to live for and about one out of five, to get a love forever. These answers clarify the conditions in which these adolescents are living their current pregnancies – they live in emotional isolation. Their poor status within their family and community is mainly based in the ambiguous category of adolescence, and in particular, because they are not at school or working. In fact, their peers are cousins or very young aunts and the young people that are living few blocks from their homes. To get somebody to live for could be interpreted as the absence of a strong sense of who they are as individuals as well as of their future prospects. The need to conform as women through their reproductive success also indicates the lack of interest in and opportunities to have an educational career or thinking of work as a real possibility to achieve a better life. Therefore, it is an impoverished social and cultural status that is expressed as the need to get somebody other who gives sense to their own lives. They do not have the resources to construct their own self. In other words, the other becomes more a 'fundamental other' than a 'complementary other'. And following the traditional overvalued role of motherhood, a child is the most convenient, 'natural' way to get to construct a meaningful life. To get a love forever could refer to the romantic and idealistic conception of love. But it also indicates the need to have a sense of security, to have someone that does not fail to provide love all through life. They place this expectation of lifelong love onto the child; the child is expected to fulfil the emotional needs of these adolescent mothers. Meanwhile, in a world where emotional security has become rare, adolescents seem to be in great need if it. When society does not provide for other ways to enhance one's status than through a socially acceptable, even if somewhat controversial, adolescent motherhood, society will need to accept the consequences.

Notes

1 There are problems with definitions about who is an adolescent. The operational criteria of WHO (1983, 1989, 1995) is probably the most frequently used. WHO considers that adolescence is comprised of people between 10 to 19 years old. However, the upper limit of adolescence is still discussed and there is no agreement among different sources and institutions. This is due to the blurry distinction between an adult and a young person.
2 Civil law marital status of free union gives almost the same rights for women and children as marriage.
3 Head of family (jefes de familia) is a generic and statistical indicator in the official data to visualize who (he or she) provides the main economic support for the house, but it is also the person culturally recognized by the members of the family as their generic leader. Until the census of year 2000, the person was always referred to as he. This could have produced a distortion regarding the collection of the data of house holdings headed by women.

4   Contraceptives can be considered as traditional and modern. Traditional contraceptive methods are considered the following: condom, rhythm and coitus interruptus.

References

Blumer, H. (1969), *Symbolic Interactionism, Perspective and Method*, Upper Saddle River, NJ: Prentice-Hall.

CONAPO (1996), *Situación demográfica del Distrito Federal, Consejo Nacional de Población*, Mexico.

CONAPO (2000), *Situación actual de las y los jóvenes en México. Diagnóstico sociodemográfico*, Serie Documentos Técnicos, Consejo Nacional de Población, Mexico.

Denzin, Norman K, (1992), *Symbolic Interactionism and Cultural Studies*, Blackwell Publishers, USA, pp. 27–28.

Excelsior, 19 January 2004, Mexico City, México, p. 19-A.

Guzmán, J. M., Contreras, J. M. and Hakkert, R. (2001), 'La situación actual del embarazo adolescente y del aborto', in *Diagnóstico sobre Salud Sexual y Reproductiva de Adolescentes en América Latina y el Caribe*, UNFPA, DF, México, pp. 19–40.

Instituo Mexicano de la Juventud (2000), 1° Encuesta Nacional de Juventud 2000, November 2002, México.

Milenio, 26 December 2003, Mexico City, México, p. 12.

Salles, V. and Tuiran, R. (1998), 'Cambios demográficos y socioculturales: familias contemporáneas en México'. In *Familias y Relaciones de Género en Transformación*, EDAMEX – The Population Council, Mexico, pp. 83–126.

Stromquist, Nelly P. (1998), 'Familias en surgimiento y democratización en las relaciones de género', In *Familias y Relaciones de Género en Transformación*, EDAMEX – The Population Council, Mexico, pp. 127–152.

UNFPA Diagnóstico sobre Salud Sexual y Reproductiva de Adolescentes en América Latina y el CaribeDF (2001), México, pp. 159–202.

World Health Organisation (1983), *Adolescent reproductive health: an approach to planning health service research*, Geneva: WHO.

World Health Organisation (1989), *The health of youth*, A42, Technical Discussion/2, Geneva: WHO.

World Health Organisation (1995), *Adolescent health and development: The key to future*, Geneva: WHO.

Index